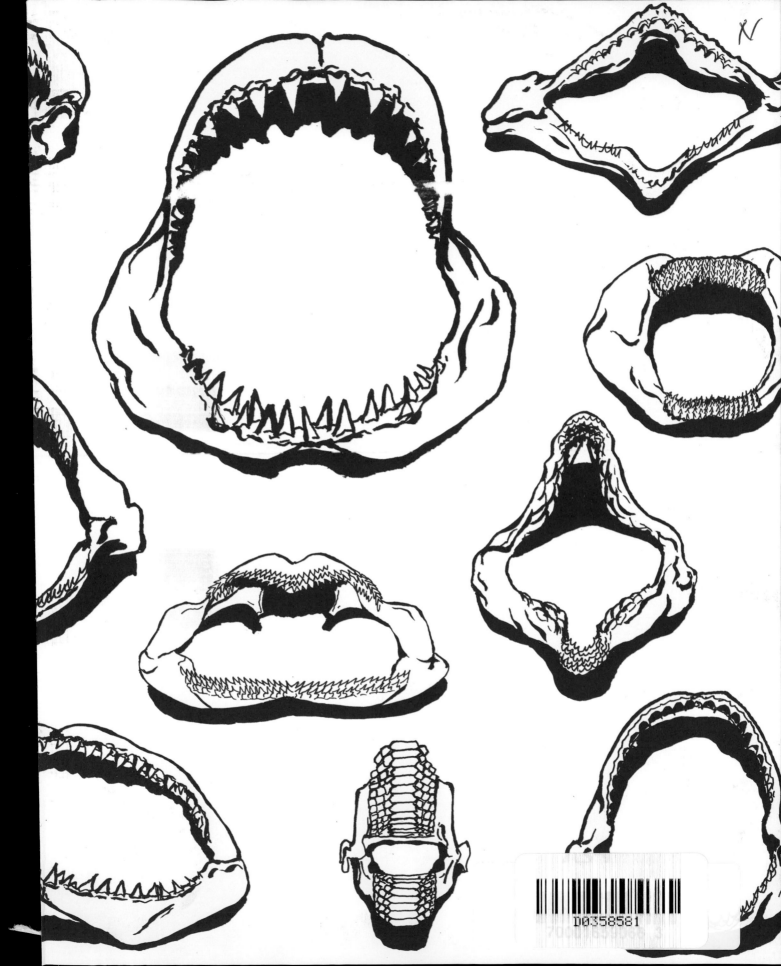

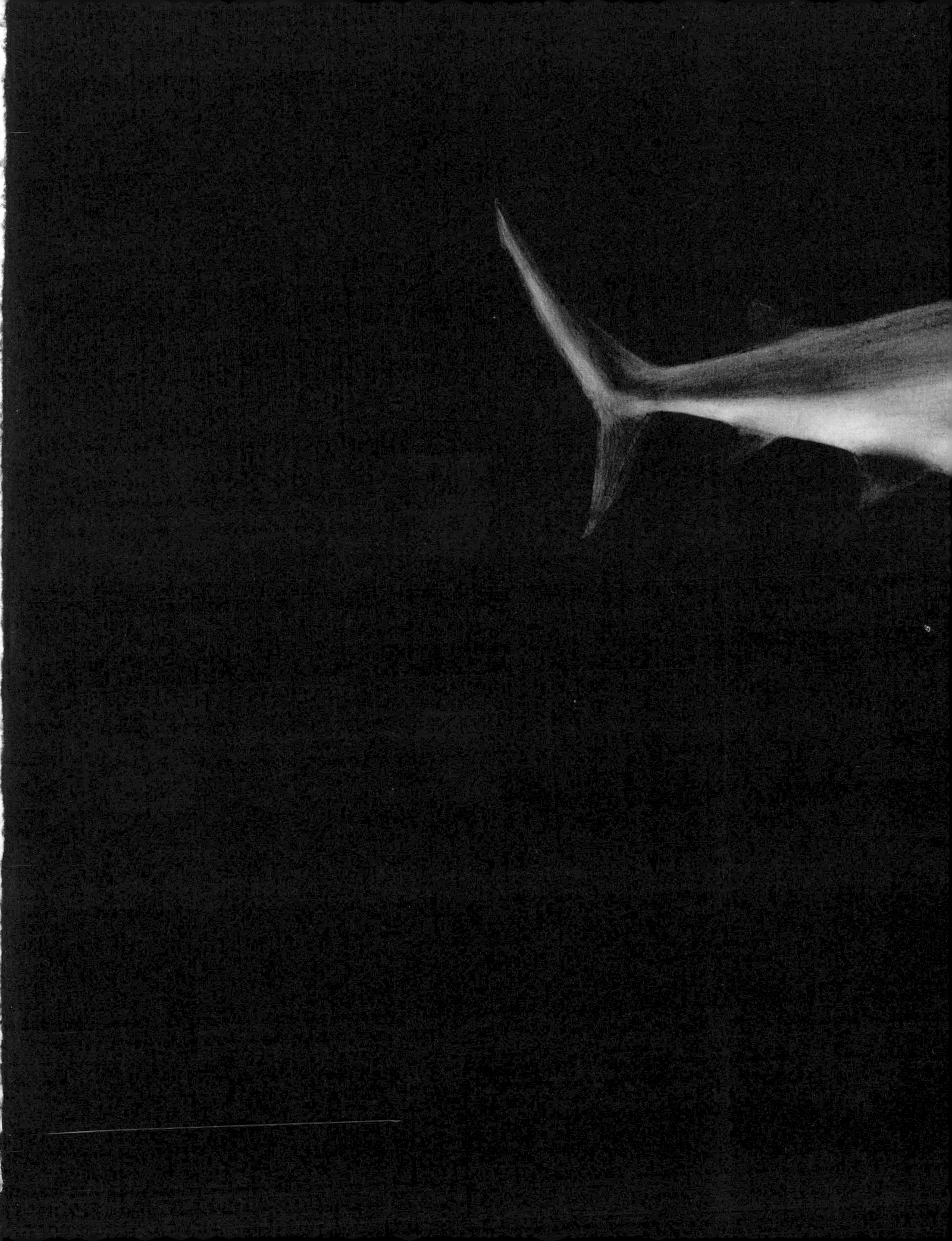

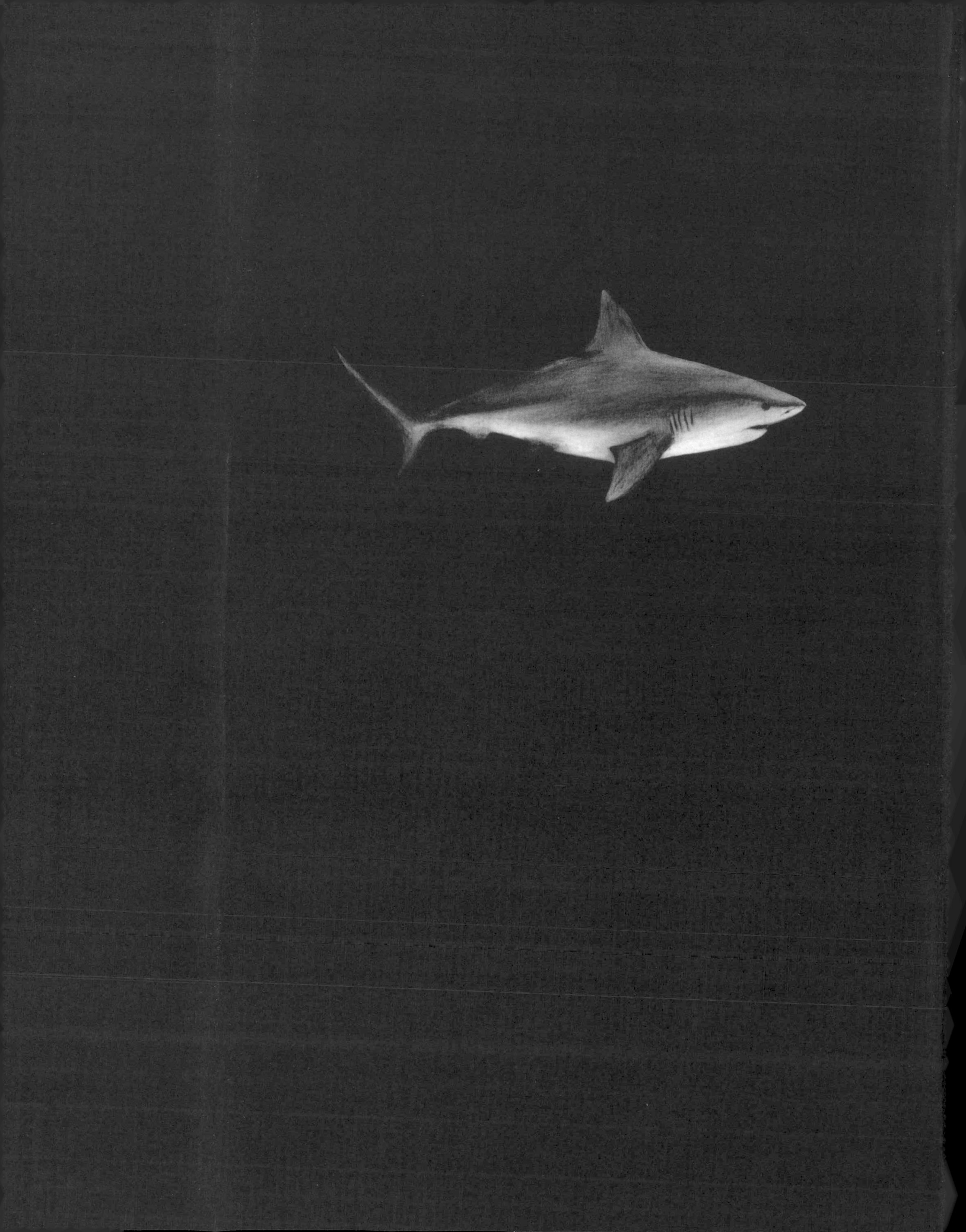

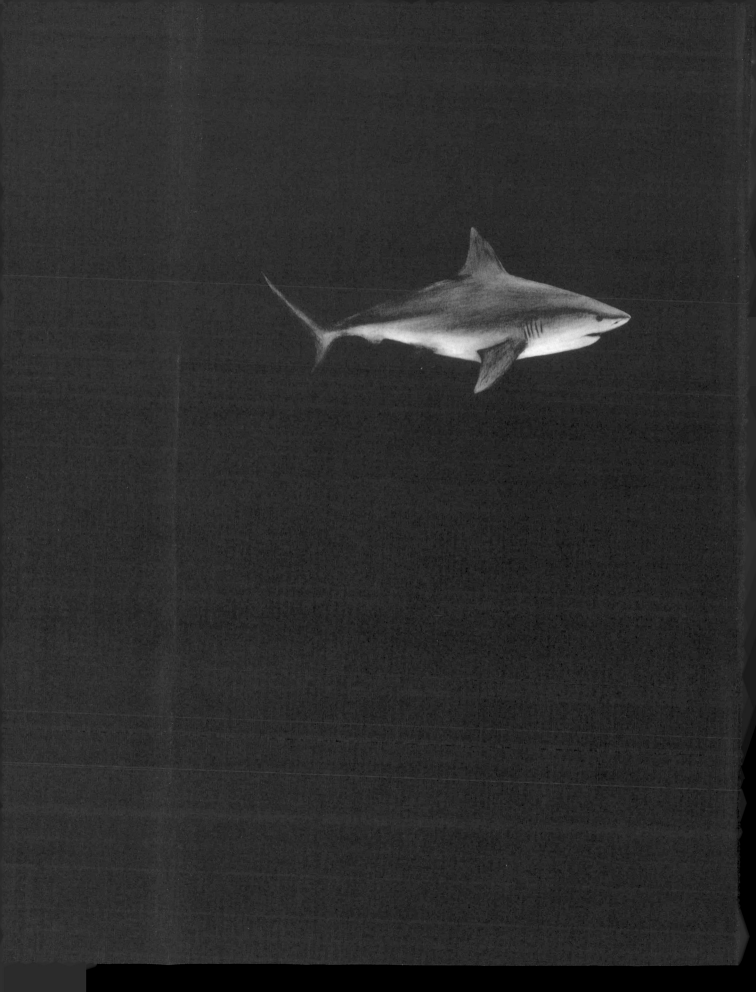

EVERYTHING IS TEETH

EVIE WYLD

JOE SUMNER

JONATHAN CAPE
LONDON

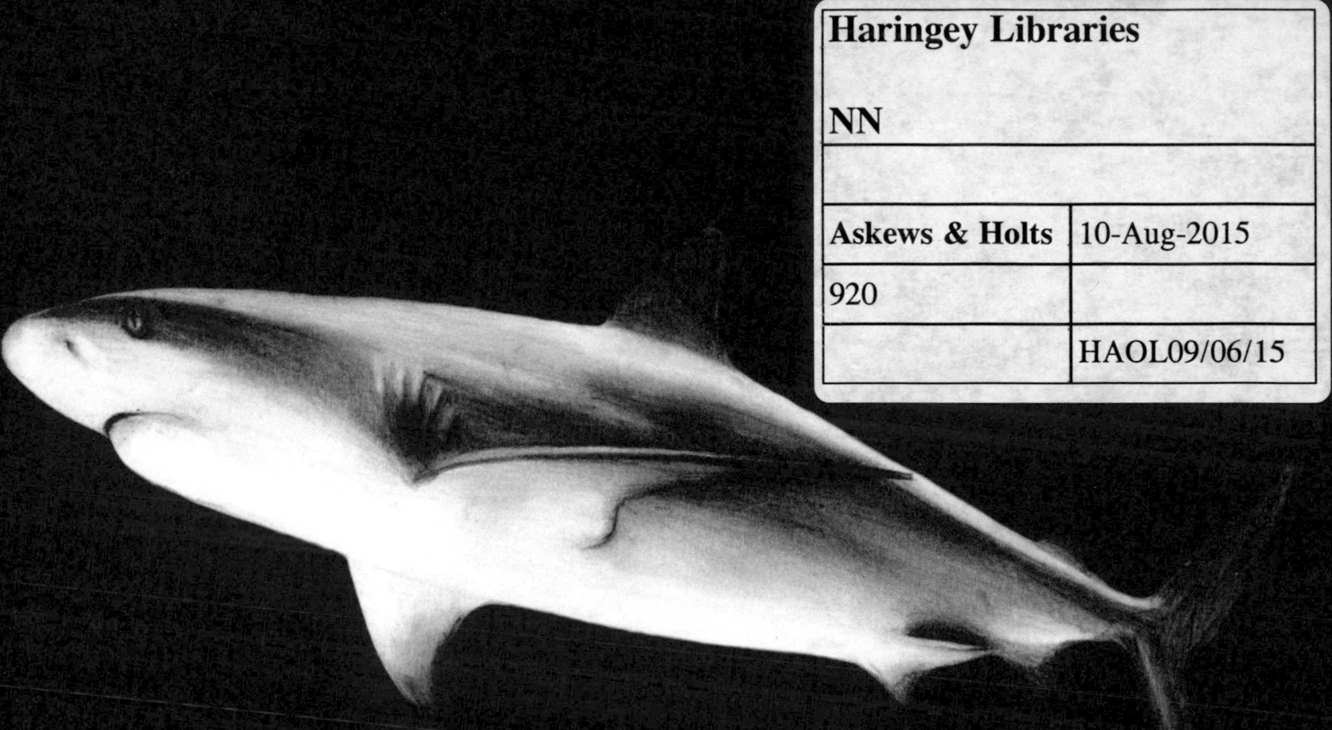

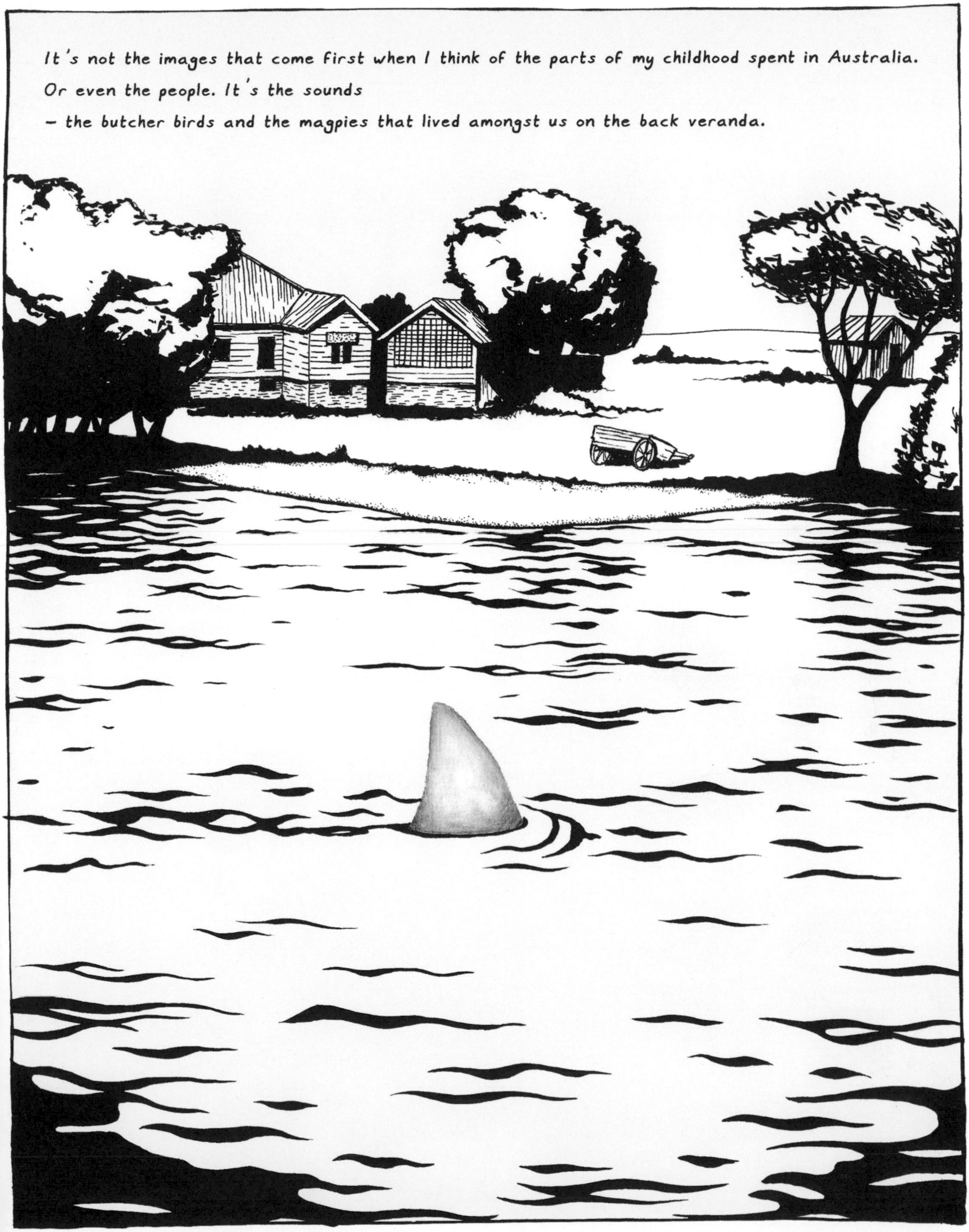
It's not the images that come first when I think of the parts of my childhood spent in Australia.
Or even the people. It's the sounds
– the butcher birds and the magpies that lived amongst us on the back veranda.

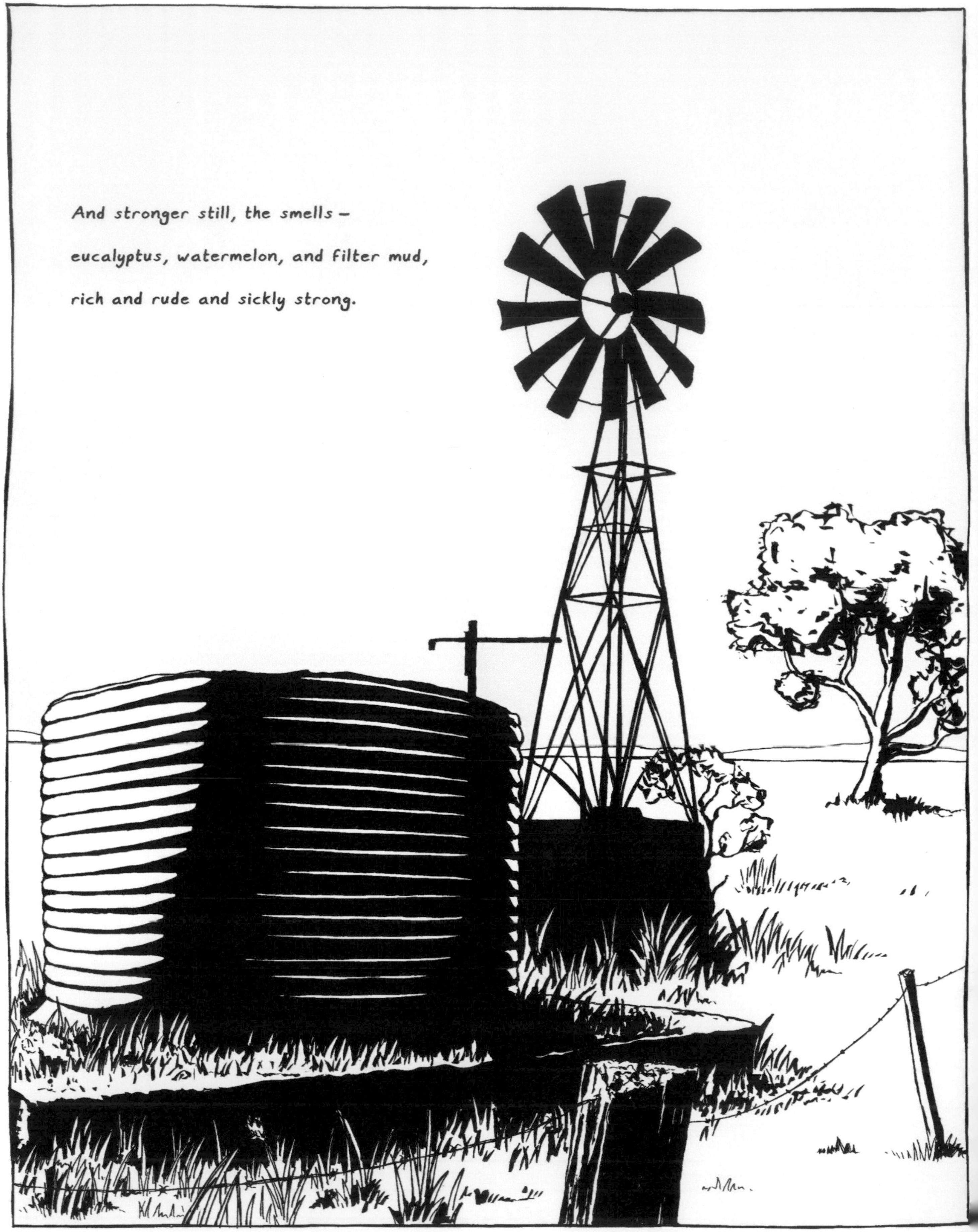
And stronger still, the smells –
eucalyptus, watermelon, and filter mud,
rich and rude and sickly strong.

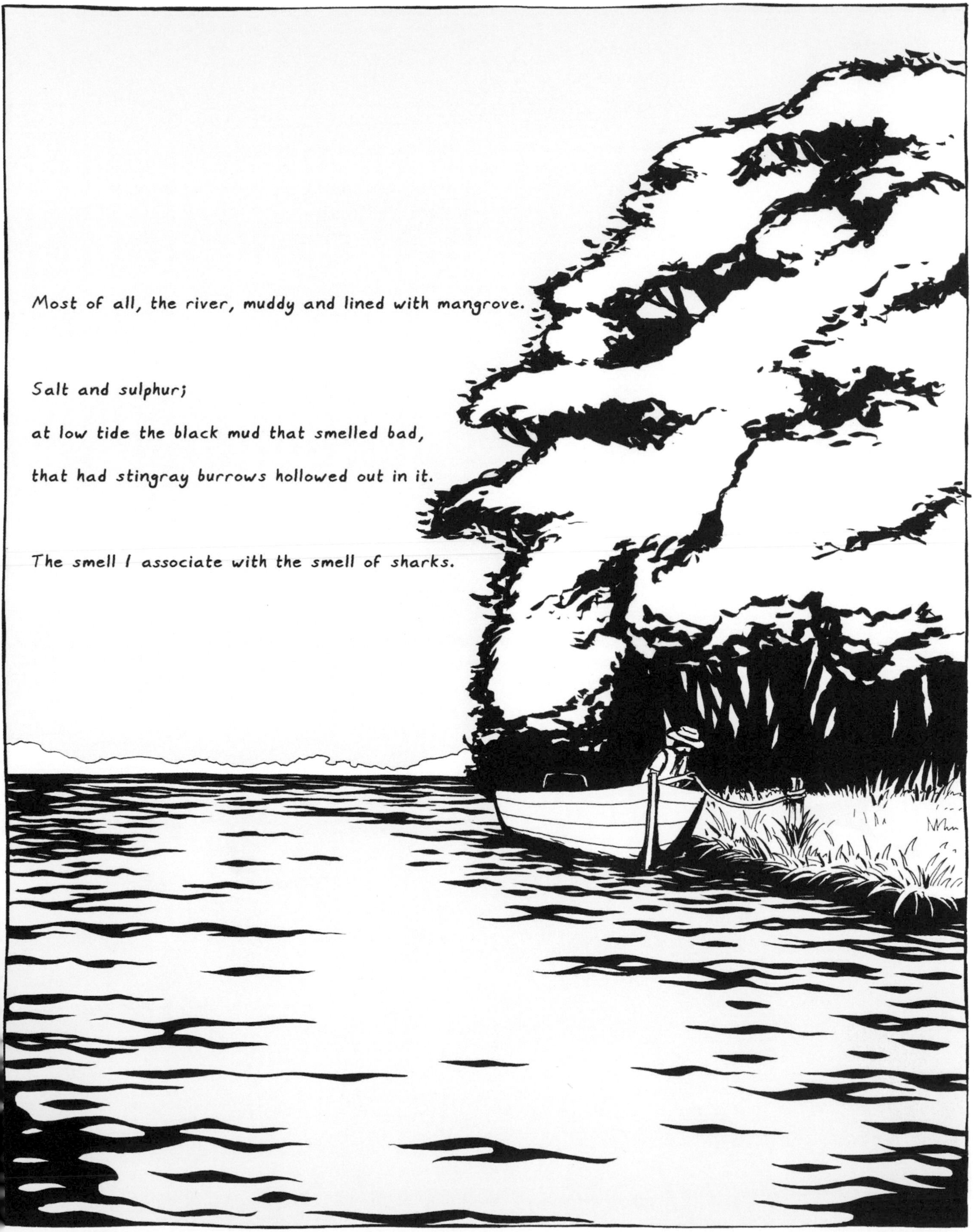
Most of all, the river, muddy and lined with mangrove.
Salt and sulphur;
at low tide the black mud that smelled bad,
that had stingray burrows hollowed out in it.
The smell I associate with the smell of sharks.

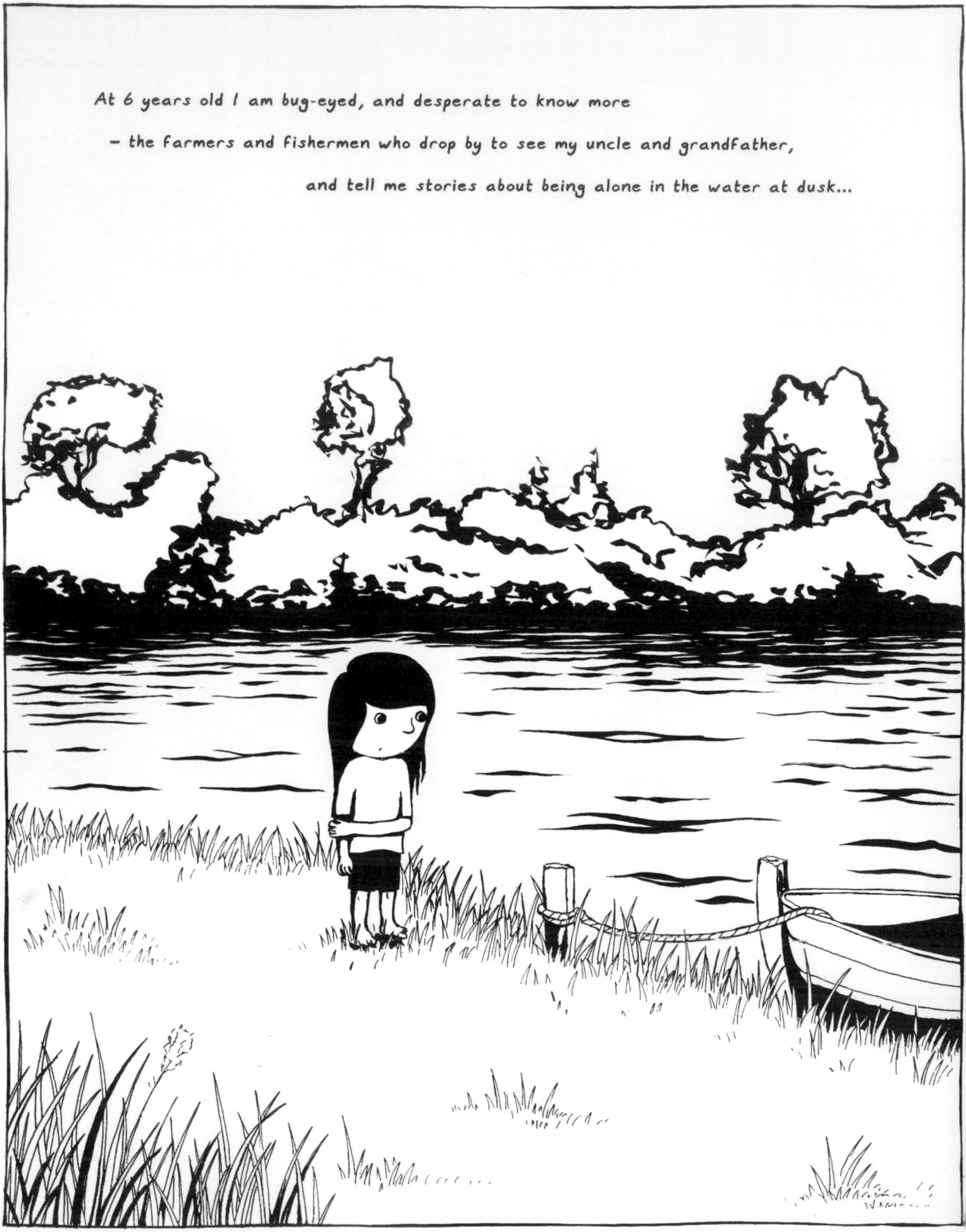
At 6 years old I am bug-eyed, and desperate to know more
– the farmers and fishermen who drop by to see my uncle and grandfather,
and tell me stories about being alone in the water at dusk...

...with something that lurks beneath the surface.

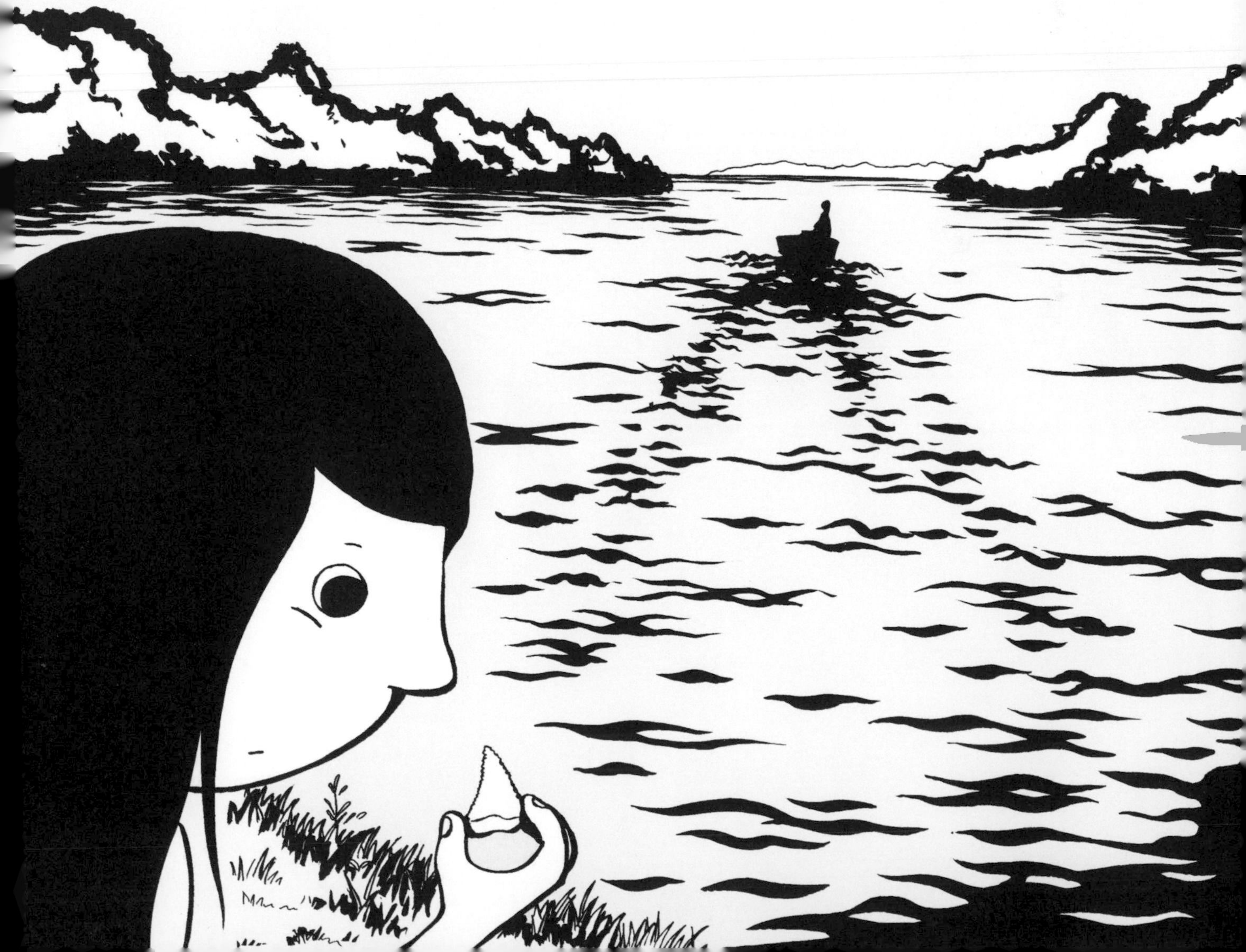

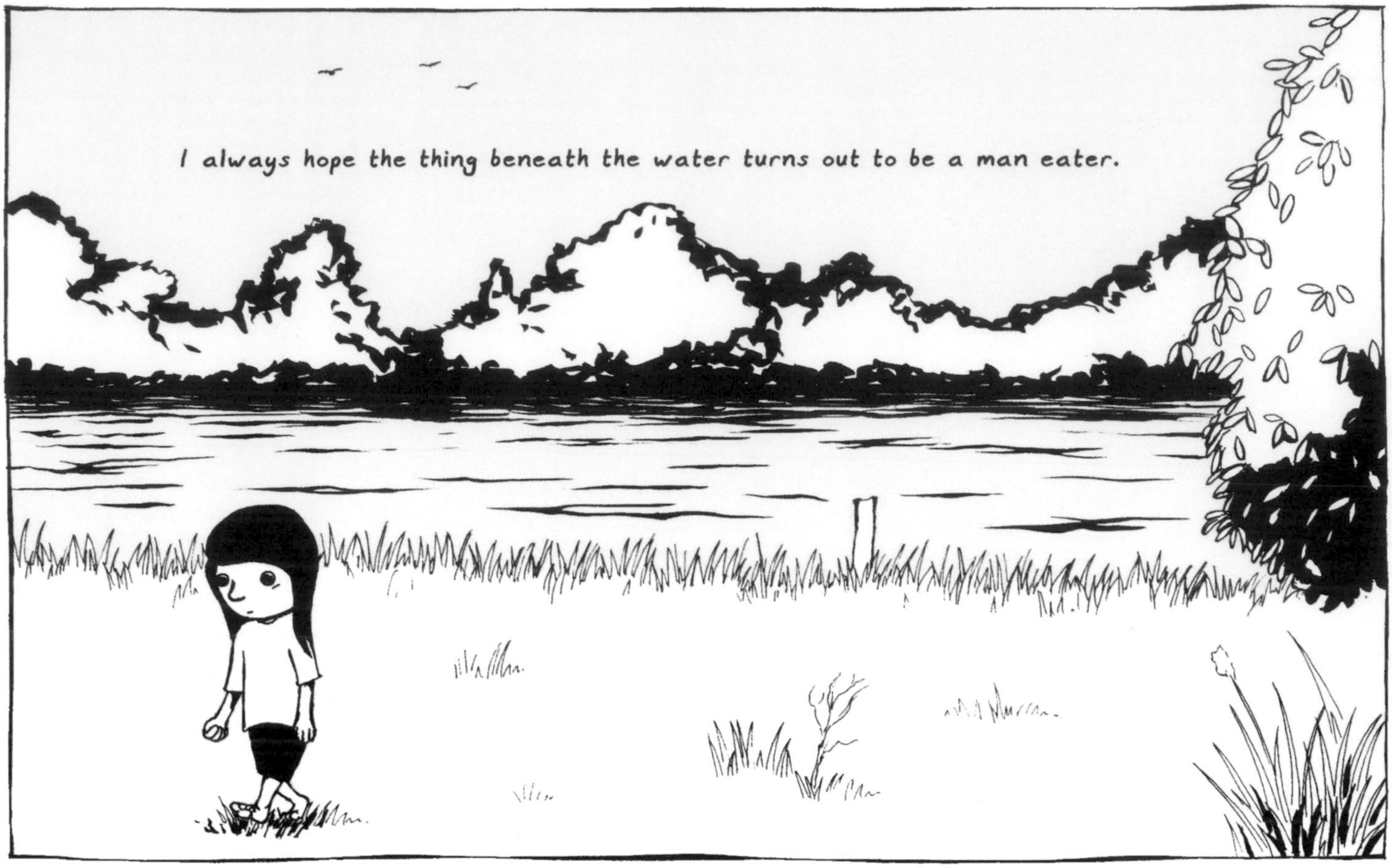
I always hope the thing beneath the water turns out to be a man eater.

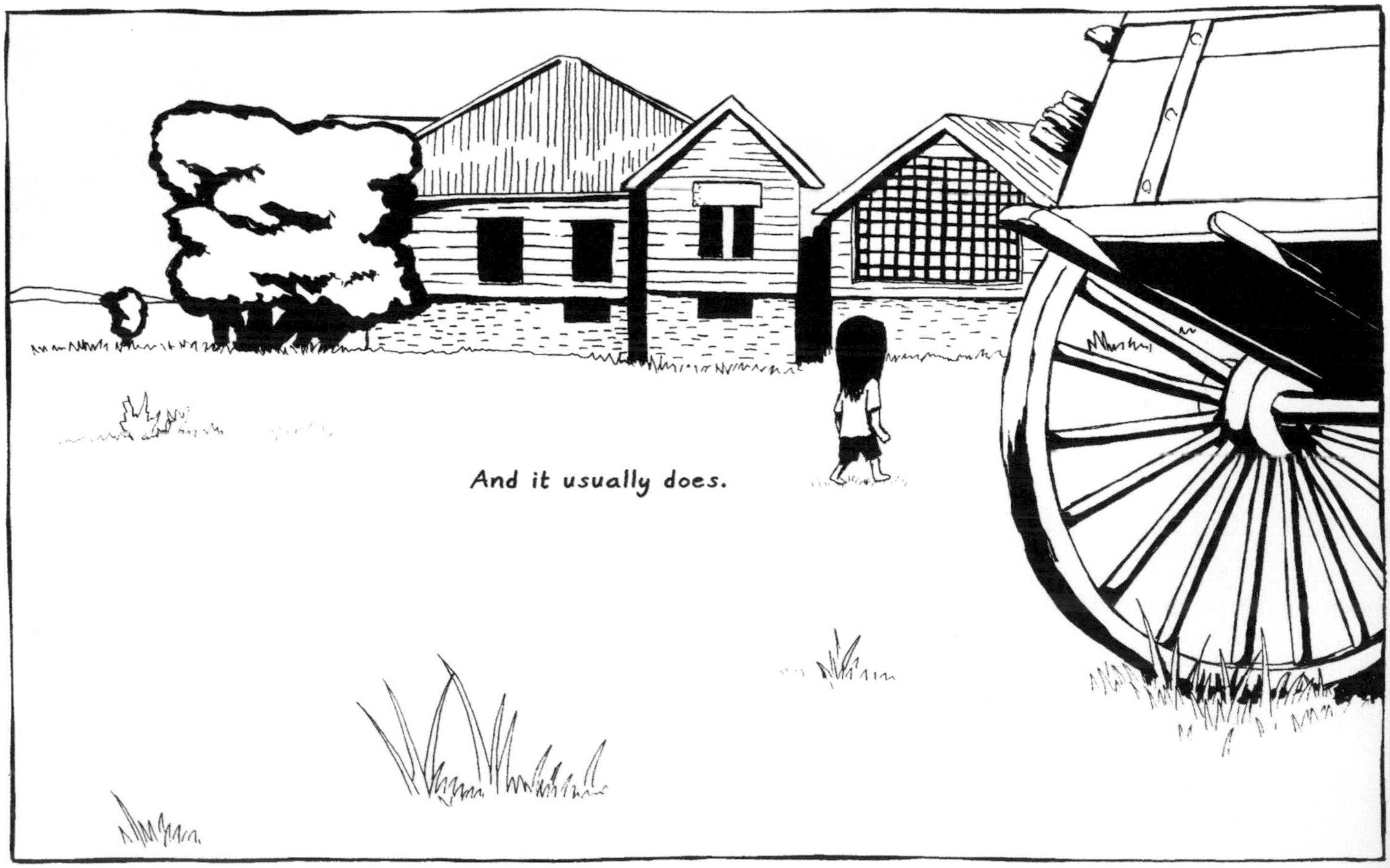
And it usually does.

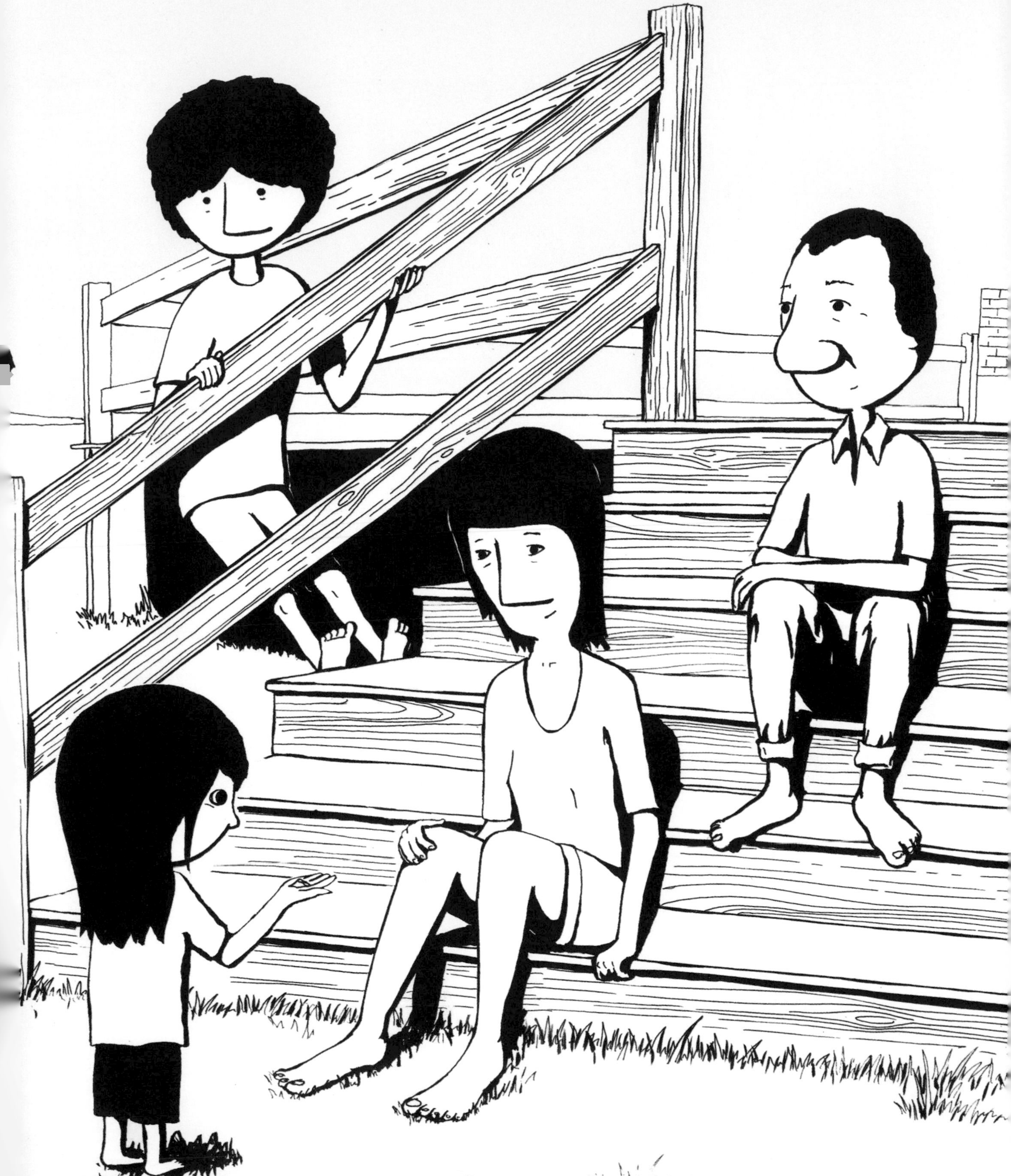

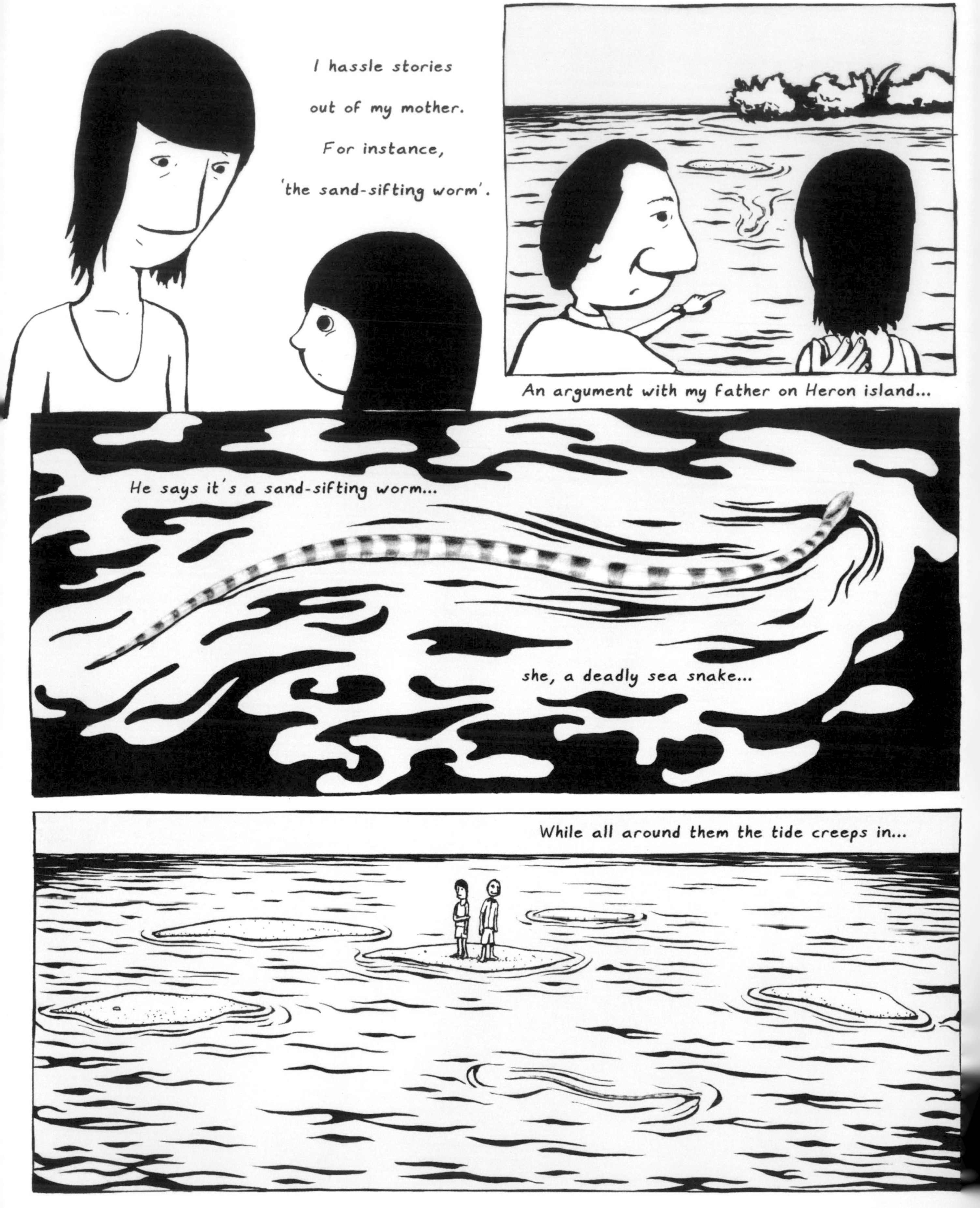
I hassle stories
out of my mother.
For instance,
'the sand-sifting worm'.
An argument with my father on Heron island...
He says it's a sand-sifting worm...
she, a deadly sea snake...
While all around them the tide creeps in...

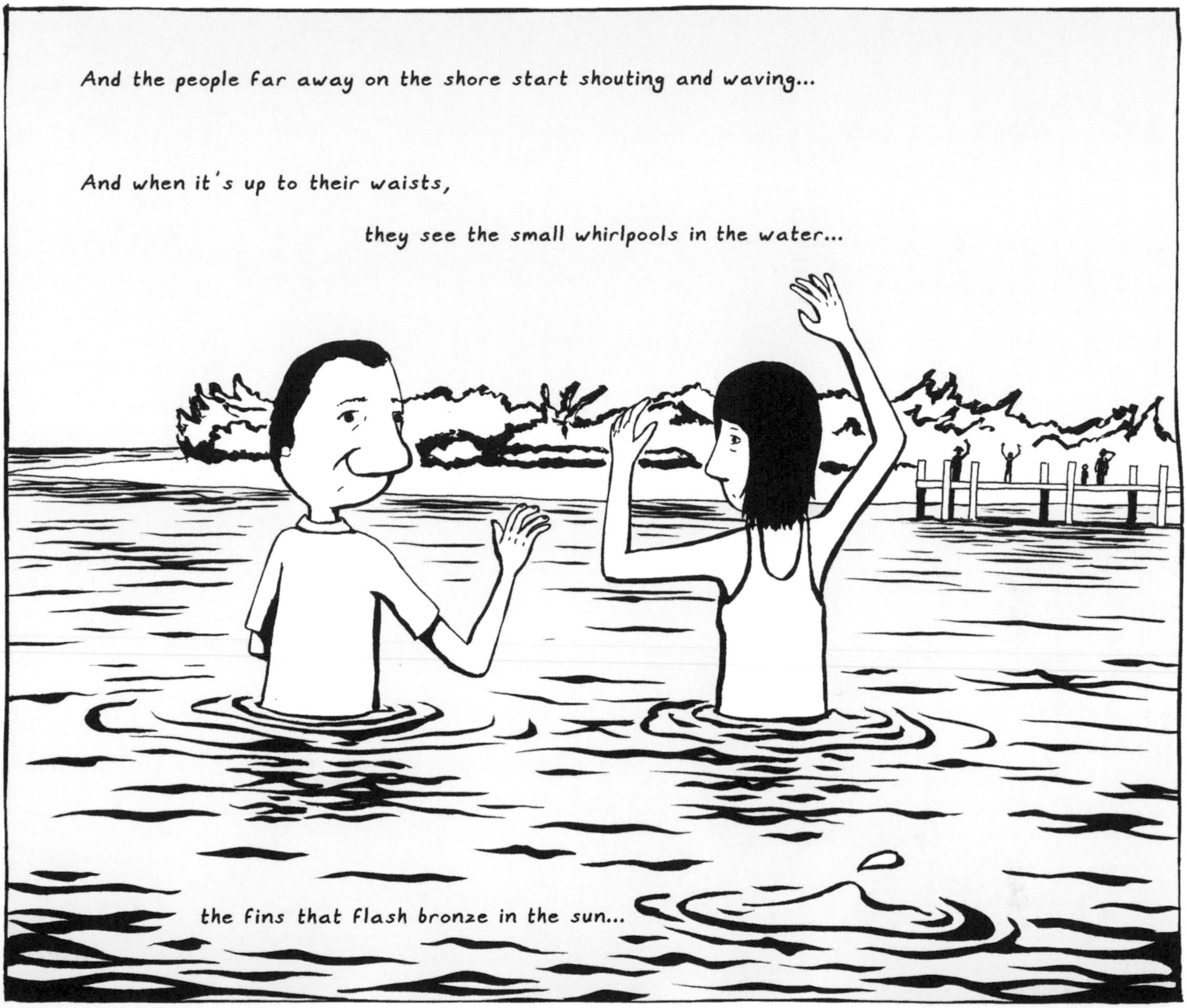
And the people far away on the shore start shouting and waving...
And when it's up to their waists,
they see the small whirlpools in the water...
the fins that flash bronze in the sun...

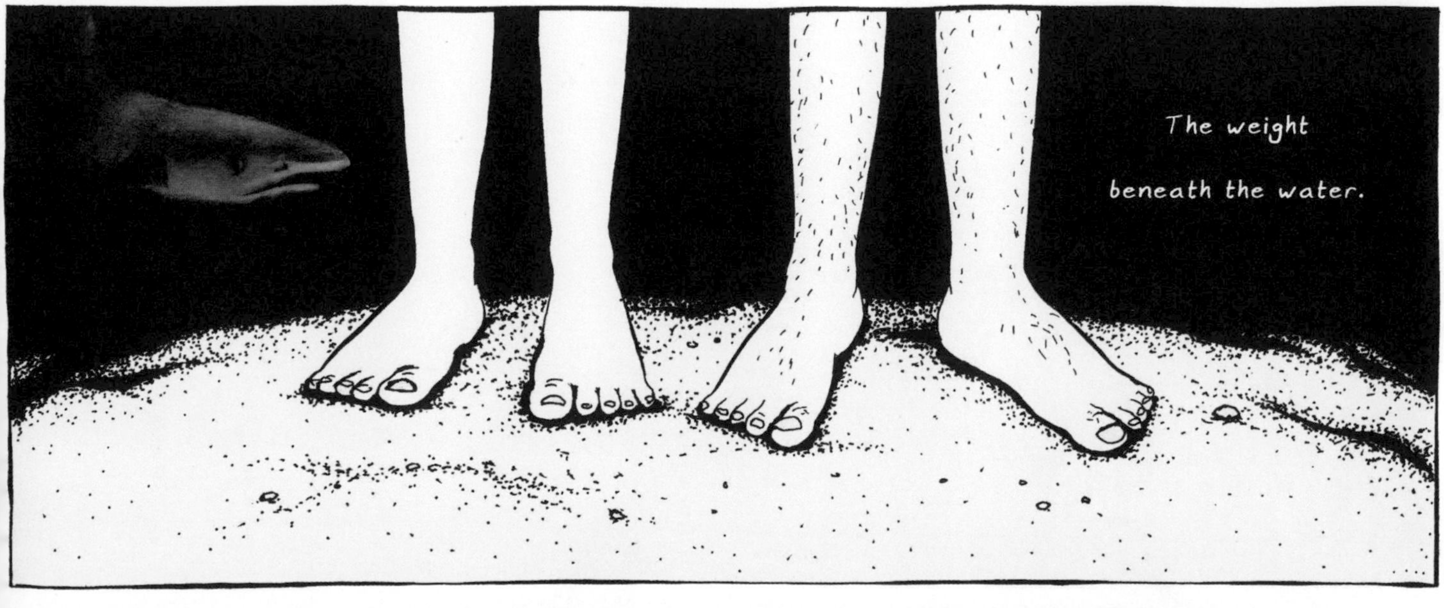
The weight
beneath the water.

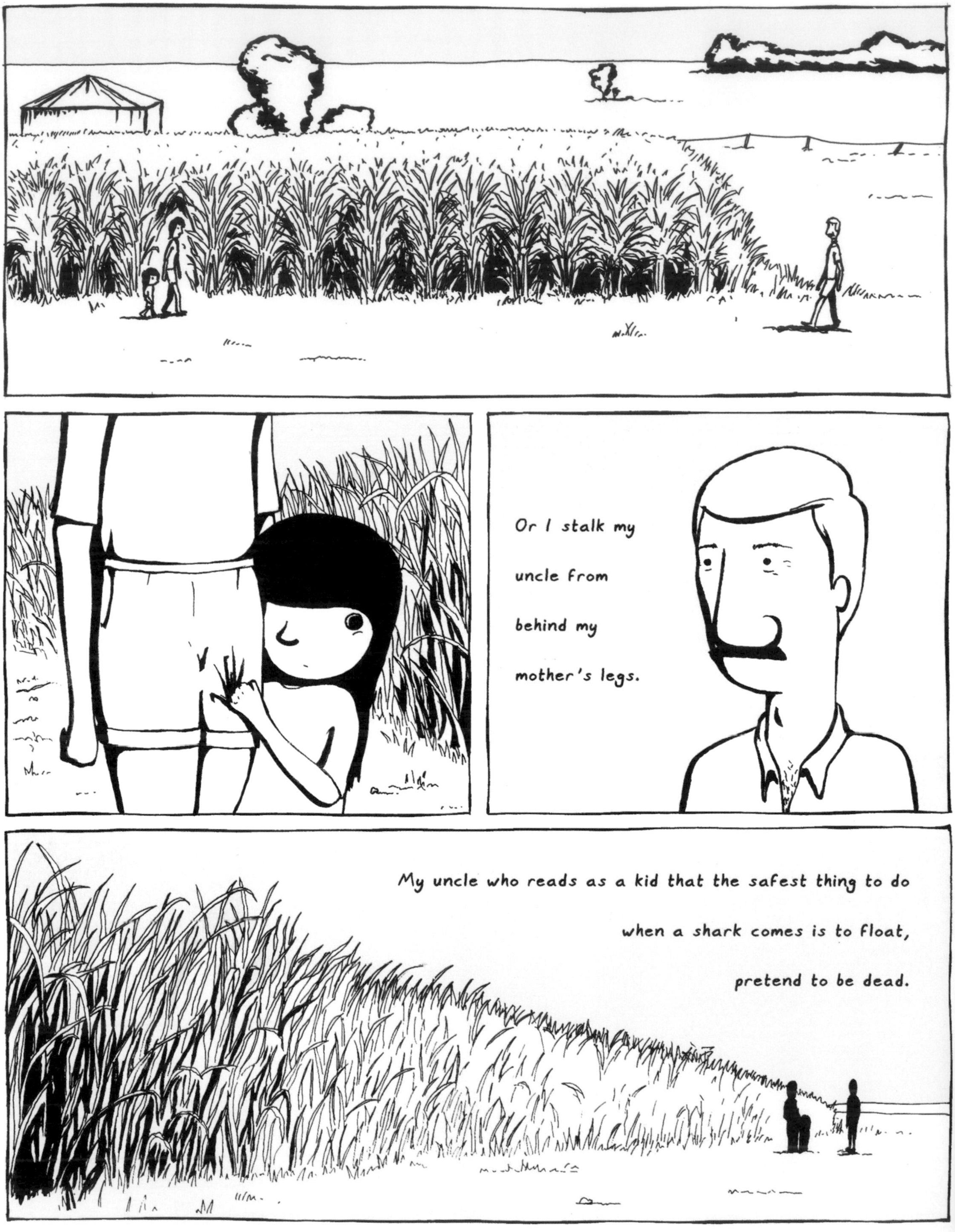
Or I stalk my uncle from behind my mother's legs.
My uncle who reads as a kid that the safest thing to do when a shark comes is to float, pretend to be dead.

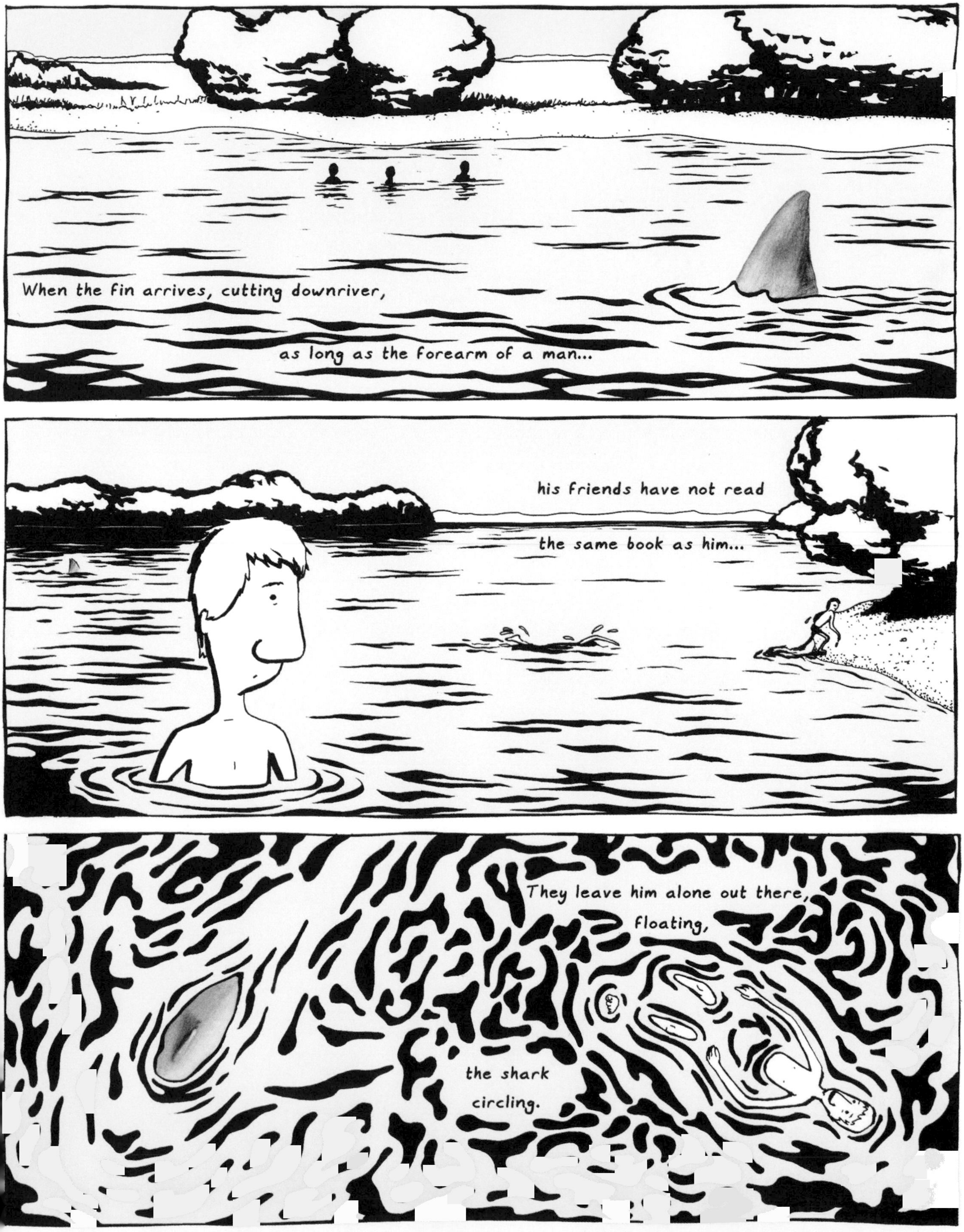
When the fin arrives, cutting downriver,
as long as the forearm of a man...
his friends have not read
the same book as him...
They leave him alone out there,
floating,
the shark
circling.

My father is not a natural on an Australian farm.

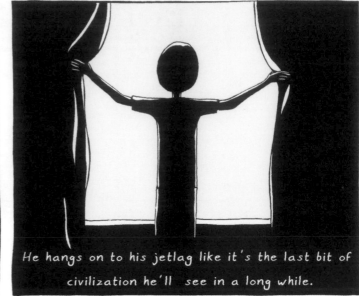

He hangs on to his jetlag like it's the last bit of civilization he'll see in a long while.

He is milk-bottle white,

something my Australian family point out to him often.

He'll burn up lovely.

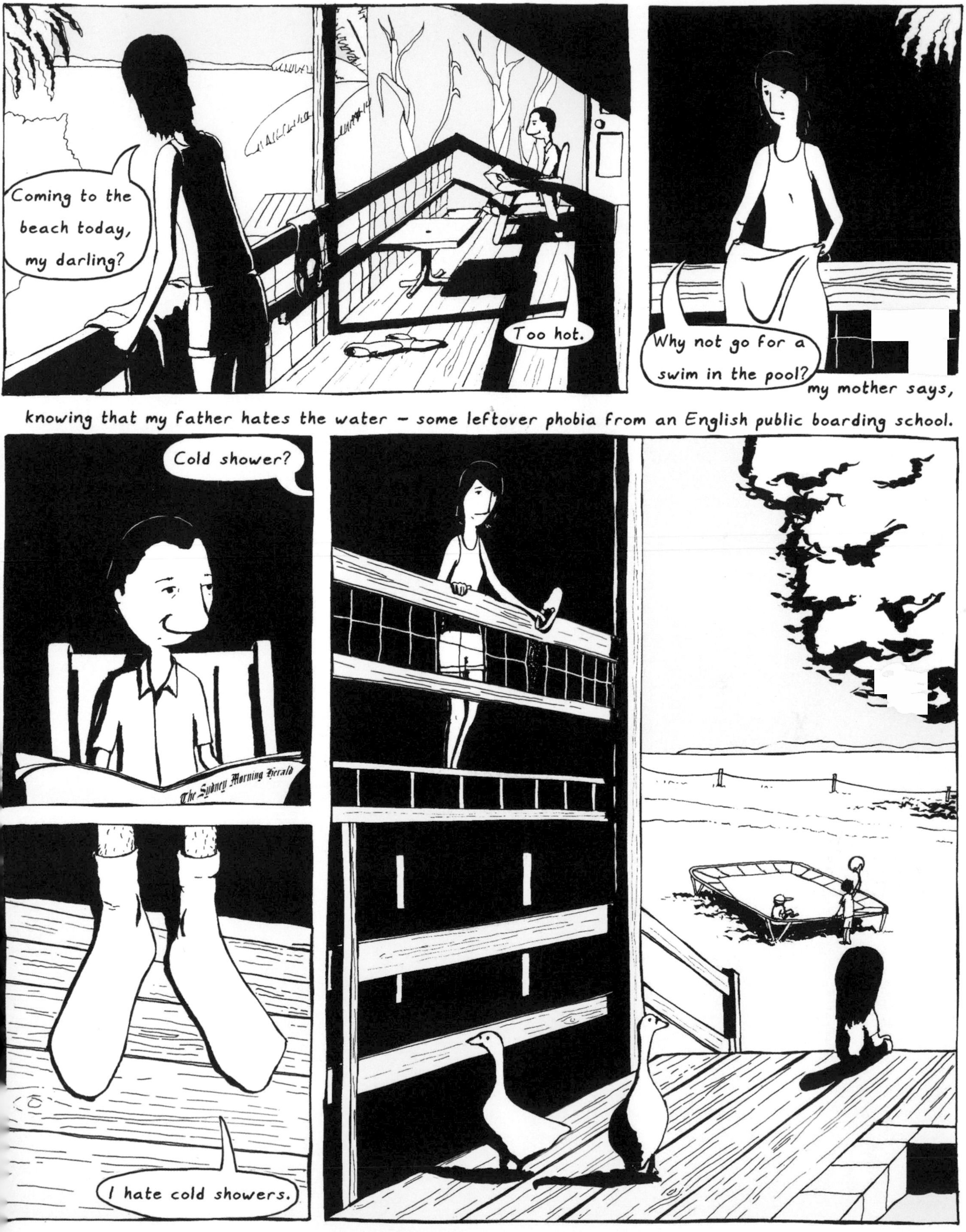
Coming to the beach today, my darling?
Too hot.
Why not go for a swim in the pool?
my mother says,
knowing that my father hates the water – some leftover phobia from an English public boarding school.
Cold shower?
The Sydney Morning Herald
I hate cold showers.

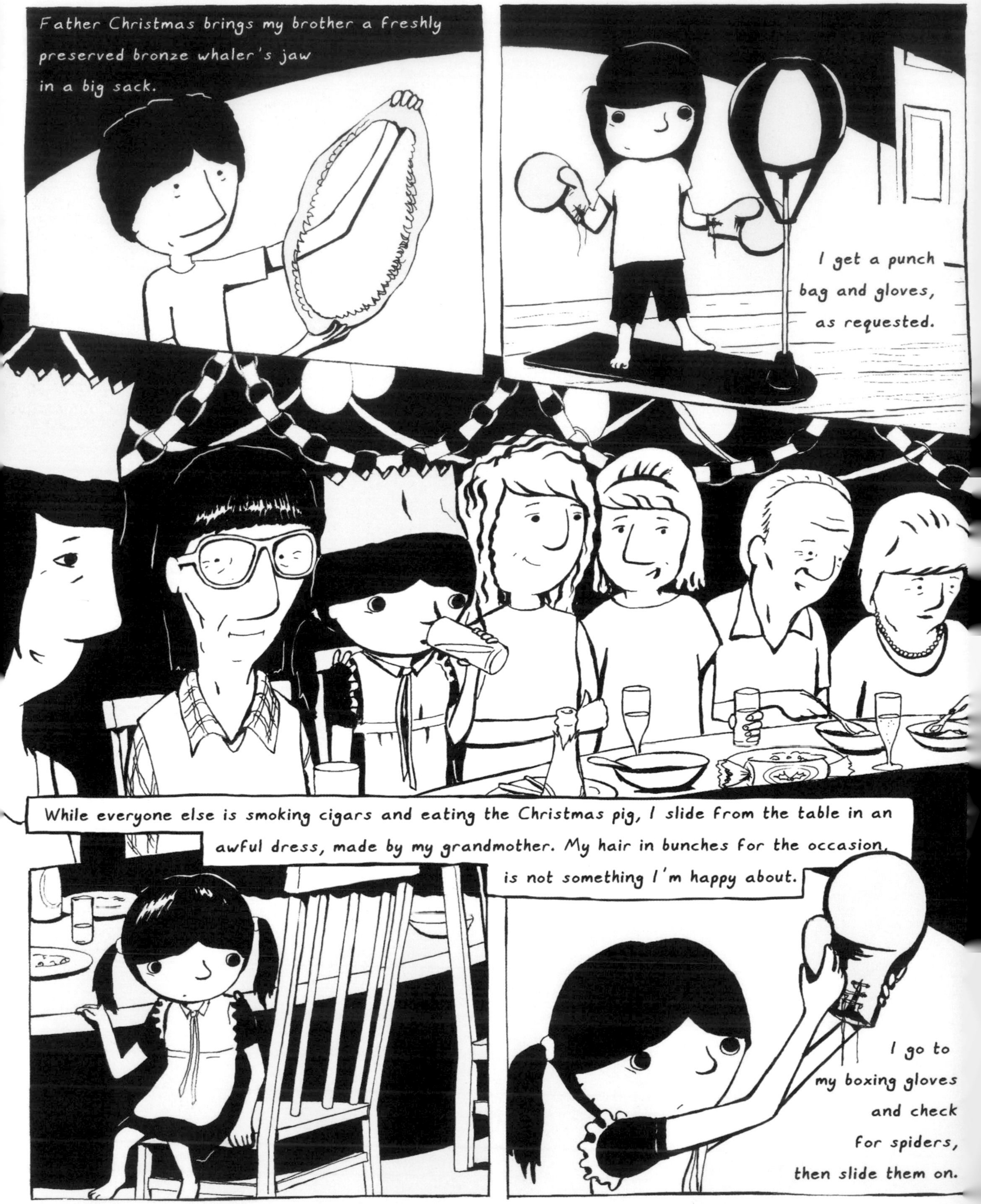
Father Christmas brings my brother a freshly preserved bronze whaler's jaw in a big sack.
I get a punch bag and gloves, as requested.
While everyone else is smoking cigars and eating the Christmas pig, I slide from the table in an awful dress, made by my grandmother. My hair in bunches for the occasion, is not something I'm happy about.
I go to my boxing gloves and check for spiders, then slide them on.

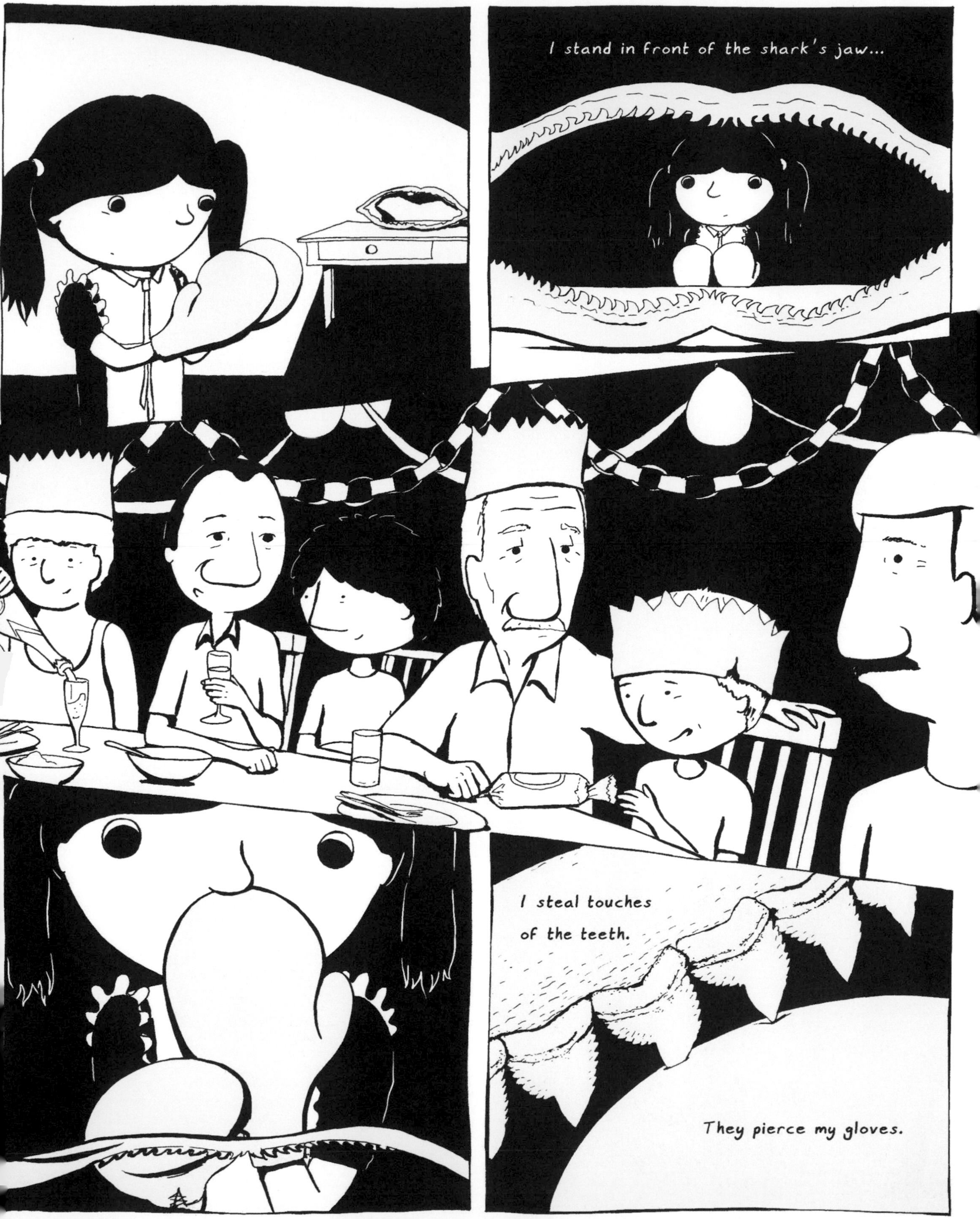
I stand in front of the shark's jaw...
I steal touches
of the teeth.
They pierce my gloves.

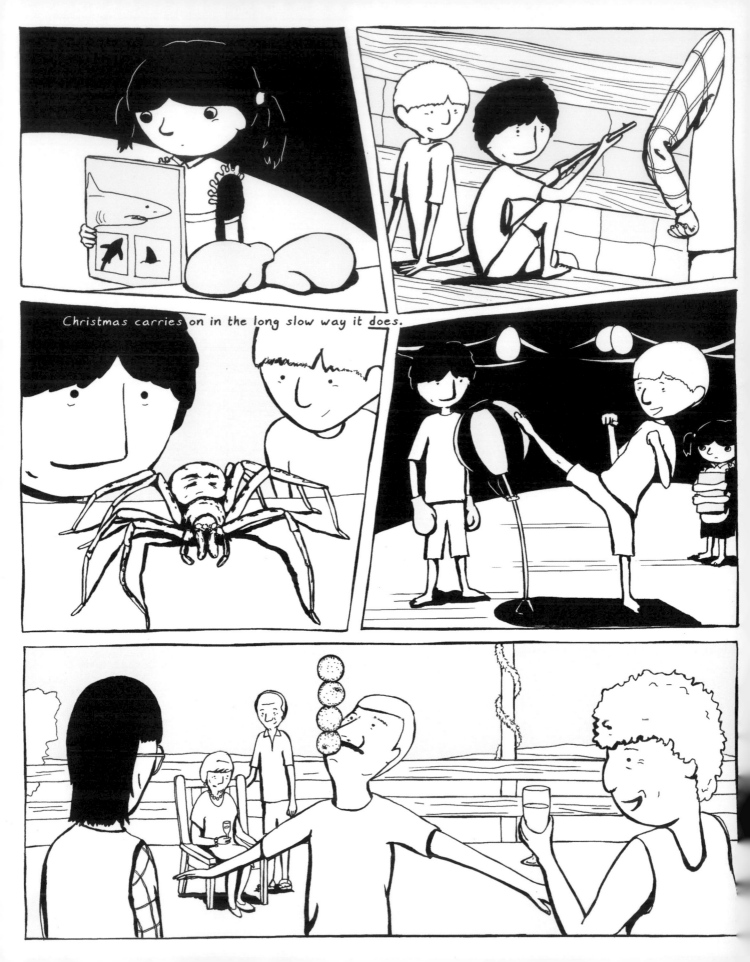

Christmas carries on in the long slow way it does.

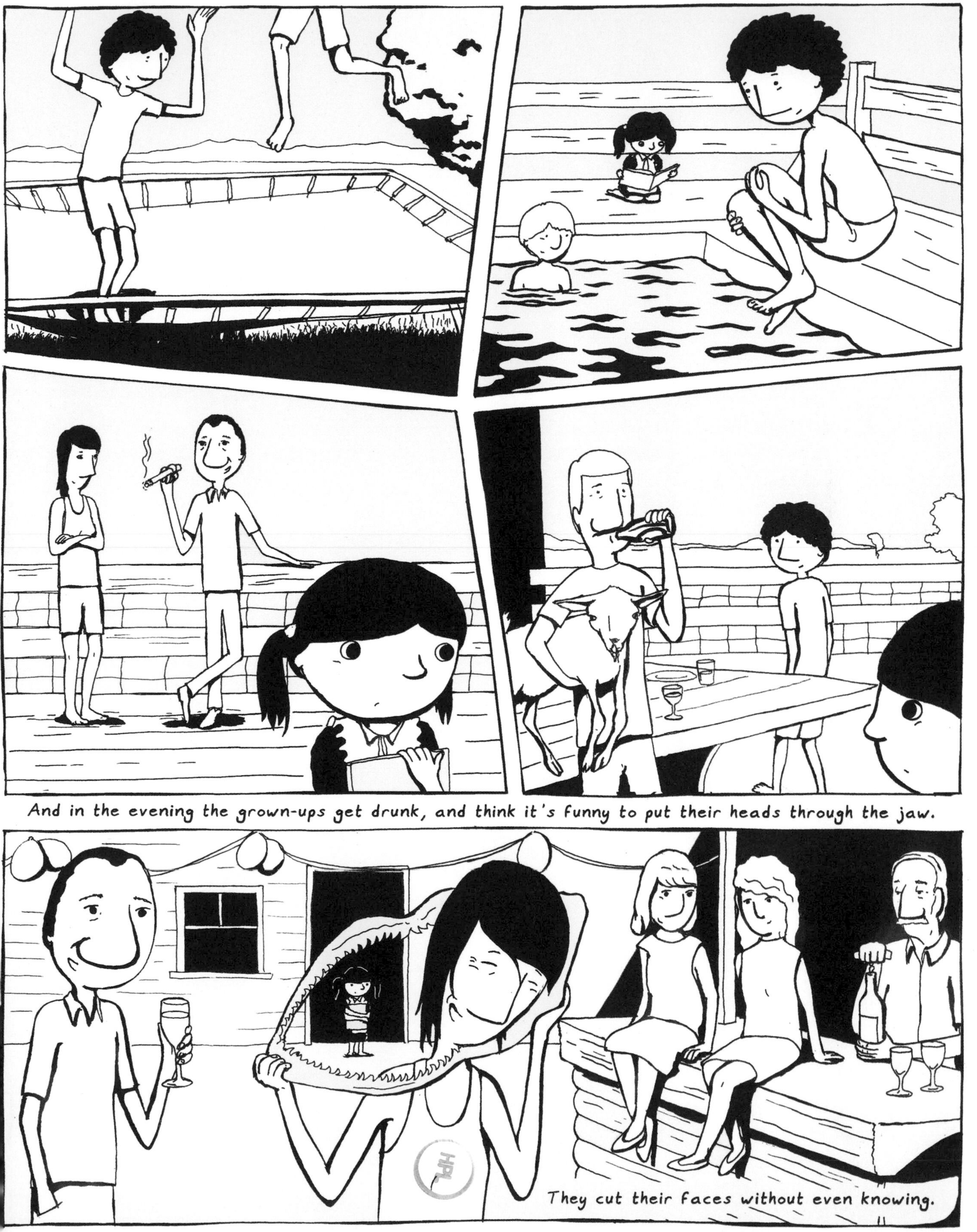
And in the evening the grown-ups get drunk, and think it's funny to put their heads through the jaw.
They cut their faces without even knowing.

I find a book...

SHARK ATTACK!

... and I fall in love.

Rodney Fox, I fall for you at 6 years old.

I see right inside your viscera and you tell me about surviving. I read about how your abdomen was opened and all your ribs broken. Your diaphragm punctured, lung ripped open, shoulder blade pierced, spleen uncovered.

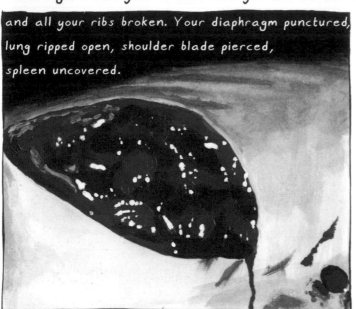

The main artery from your heart exposed.

The tendons in your hand all cut...

and how the shark left behind a tooth, still stuck in your wrist.

I see the before photograph, impossible red sausages stuffed into an empty carcass, the white skin tender, swollen and peeling away.

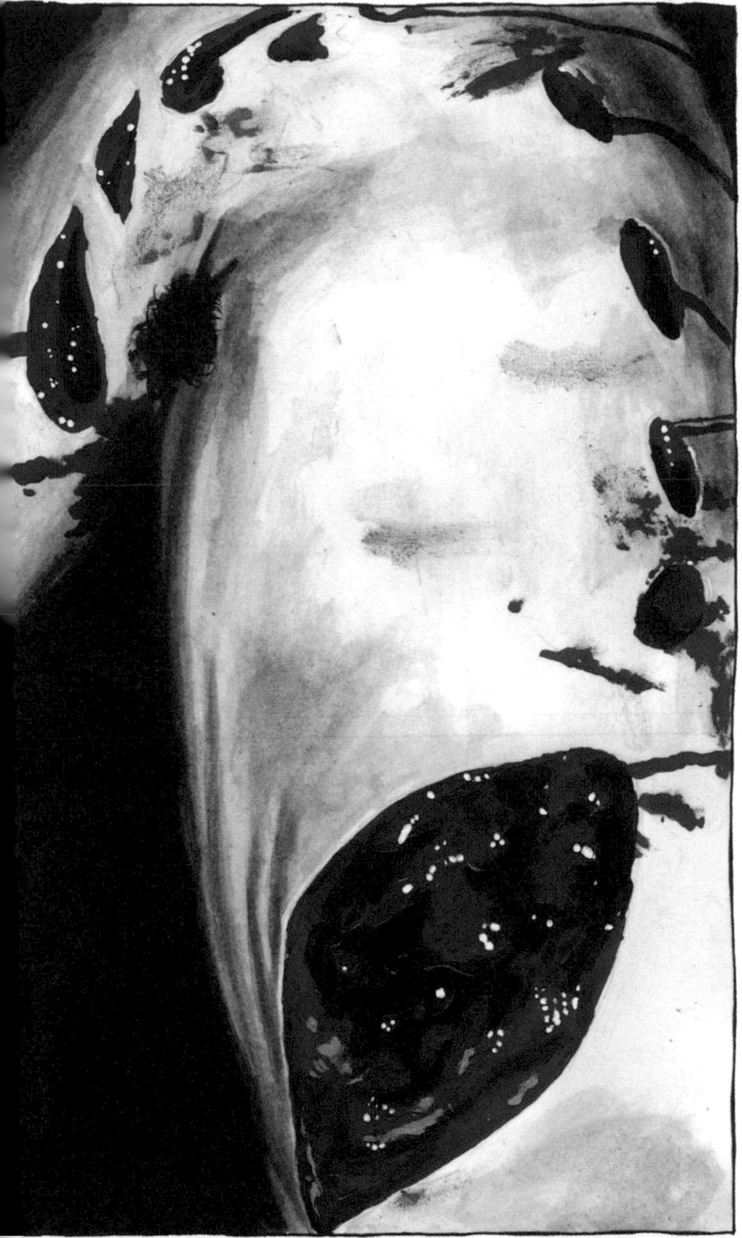

And I see the after photograph, the horsehair stitches, that make a perfect semi-circle from shoulder to ribs – a cartoon apple bite.

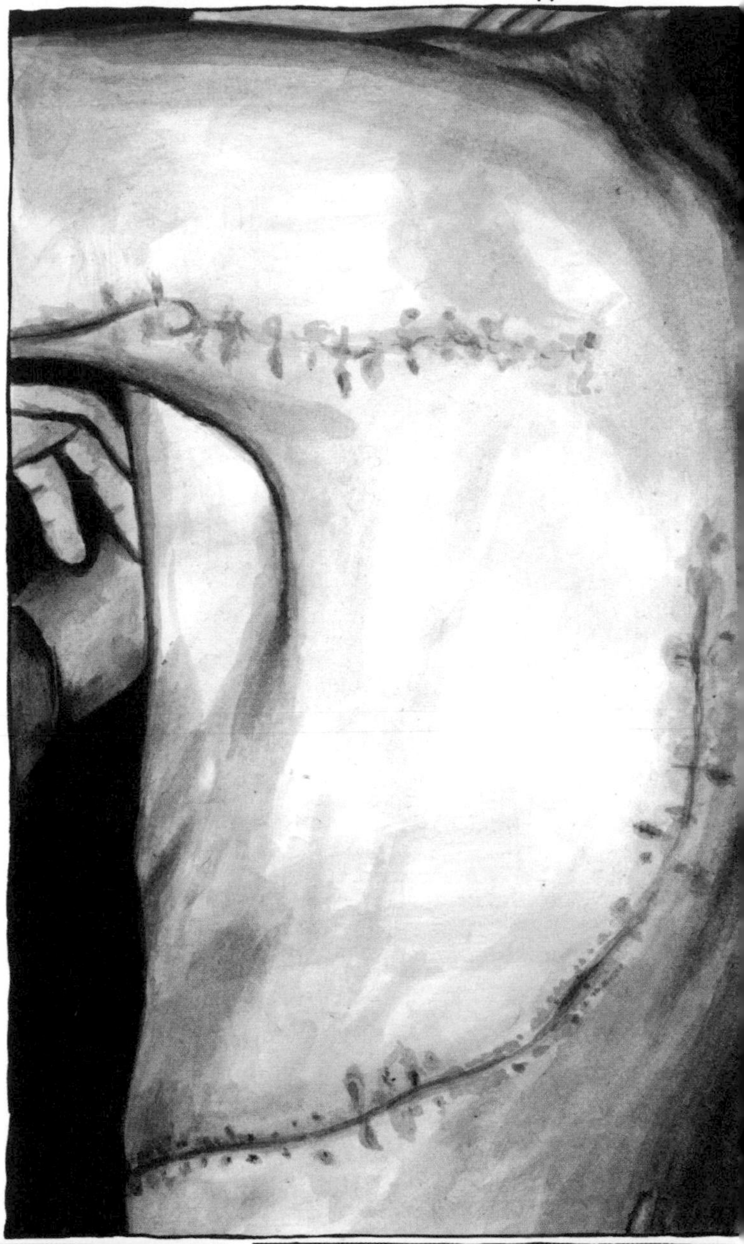

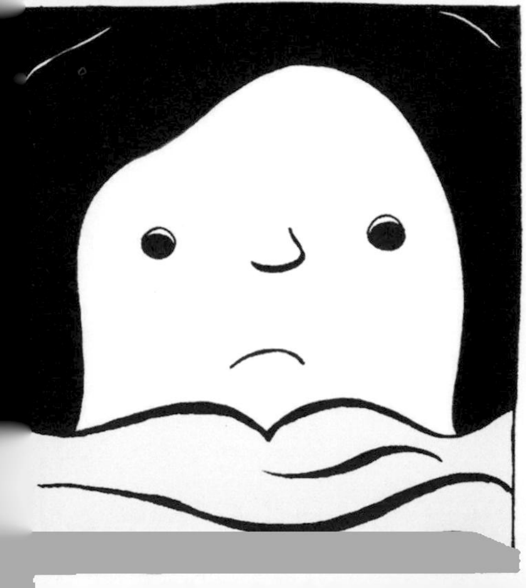

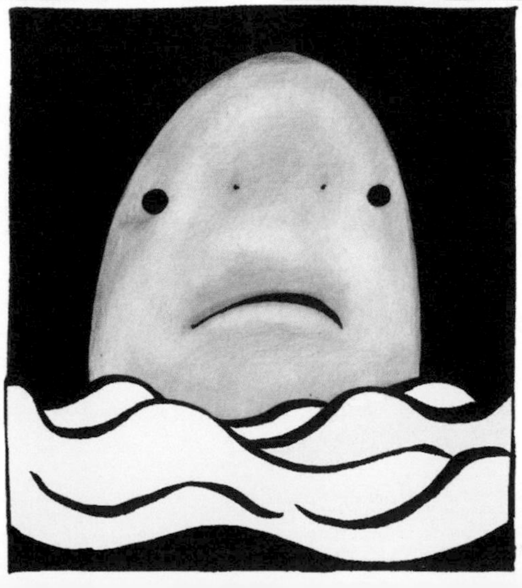

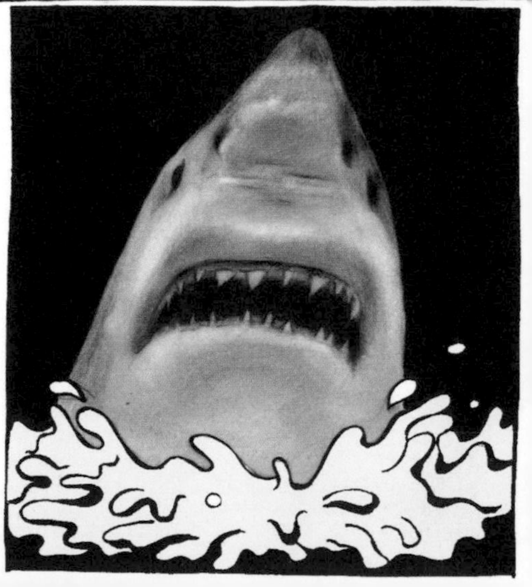

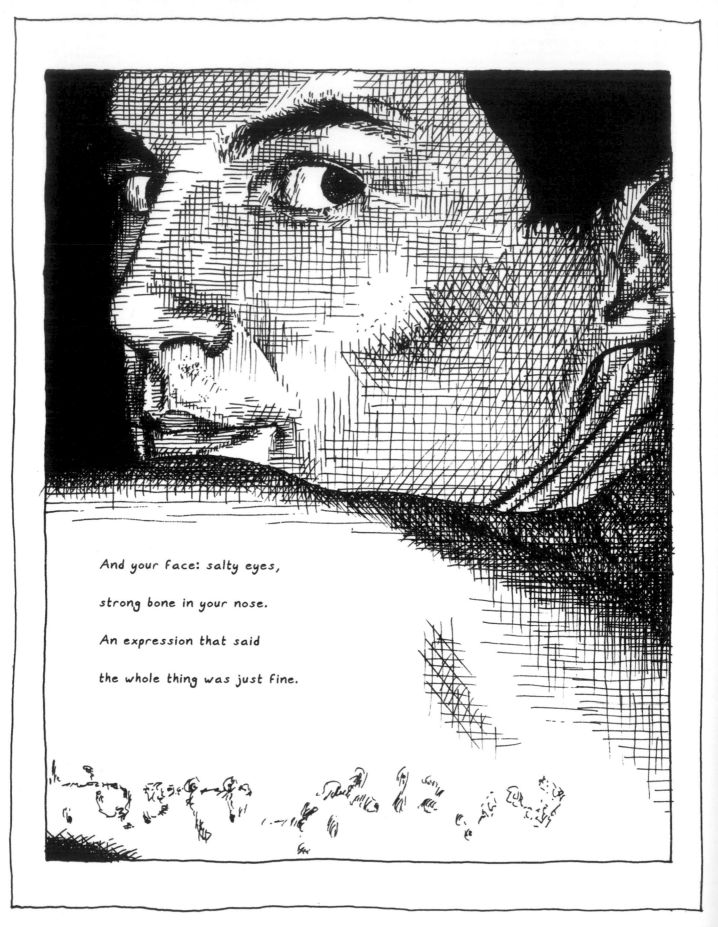

And your face: salty eyes,

strong bone in your nose.

An expression that said

the whole thing was just fine.

Stuck in the mouth, wrestling your thumbs into its eyes till it lets go,
and you feel yourself loose in your skin suit.

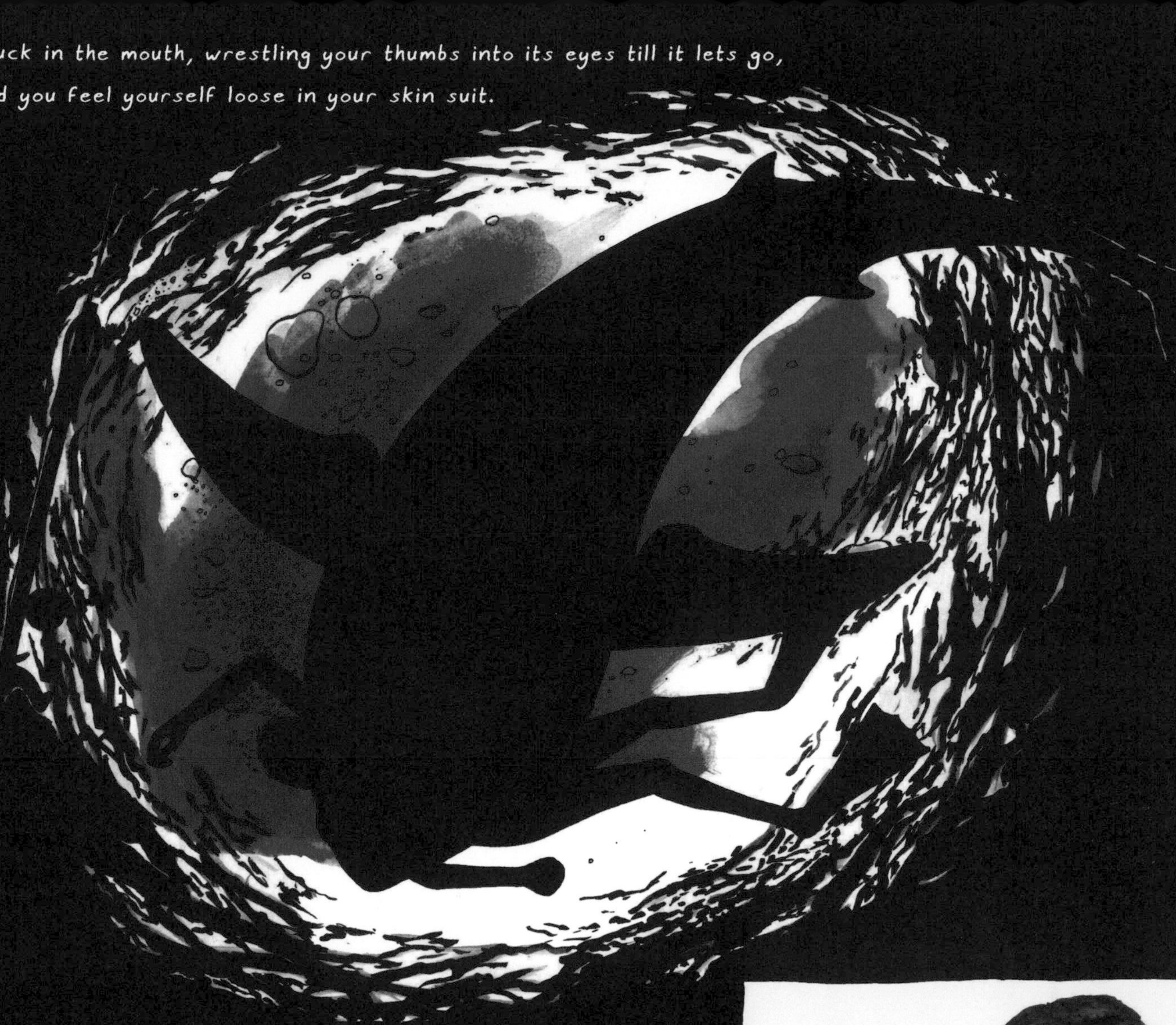

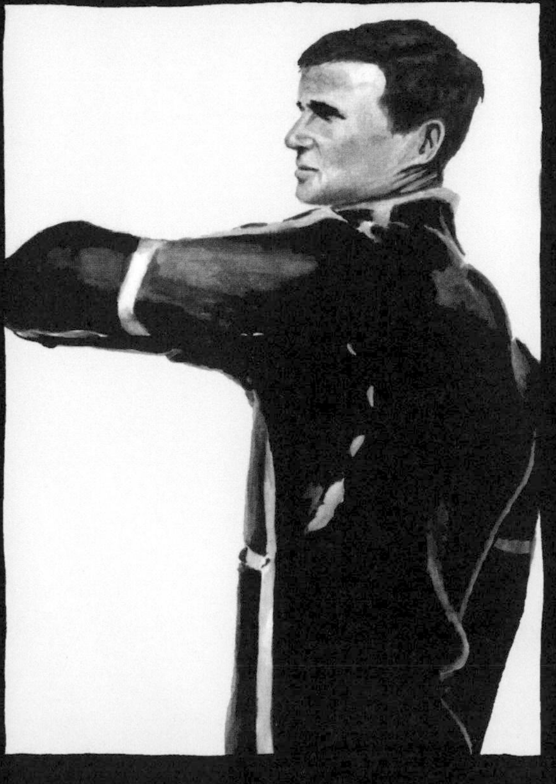

The shark is gone and people are nudging your guts back inside,
and when you wake again it hasn't changed your face.
It is all fine.

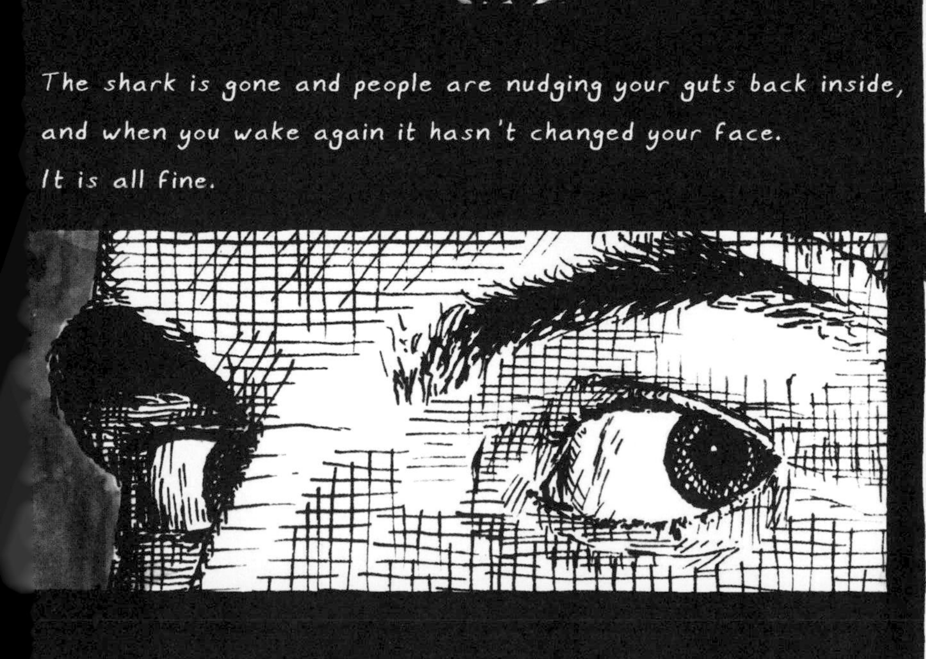

I solemnly understand you to be the greatest living man.

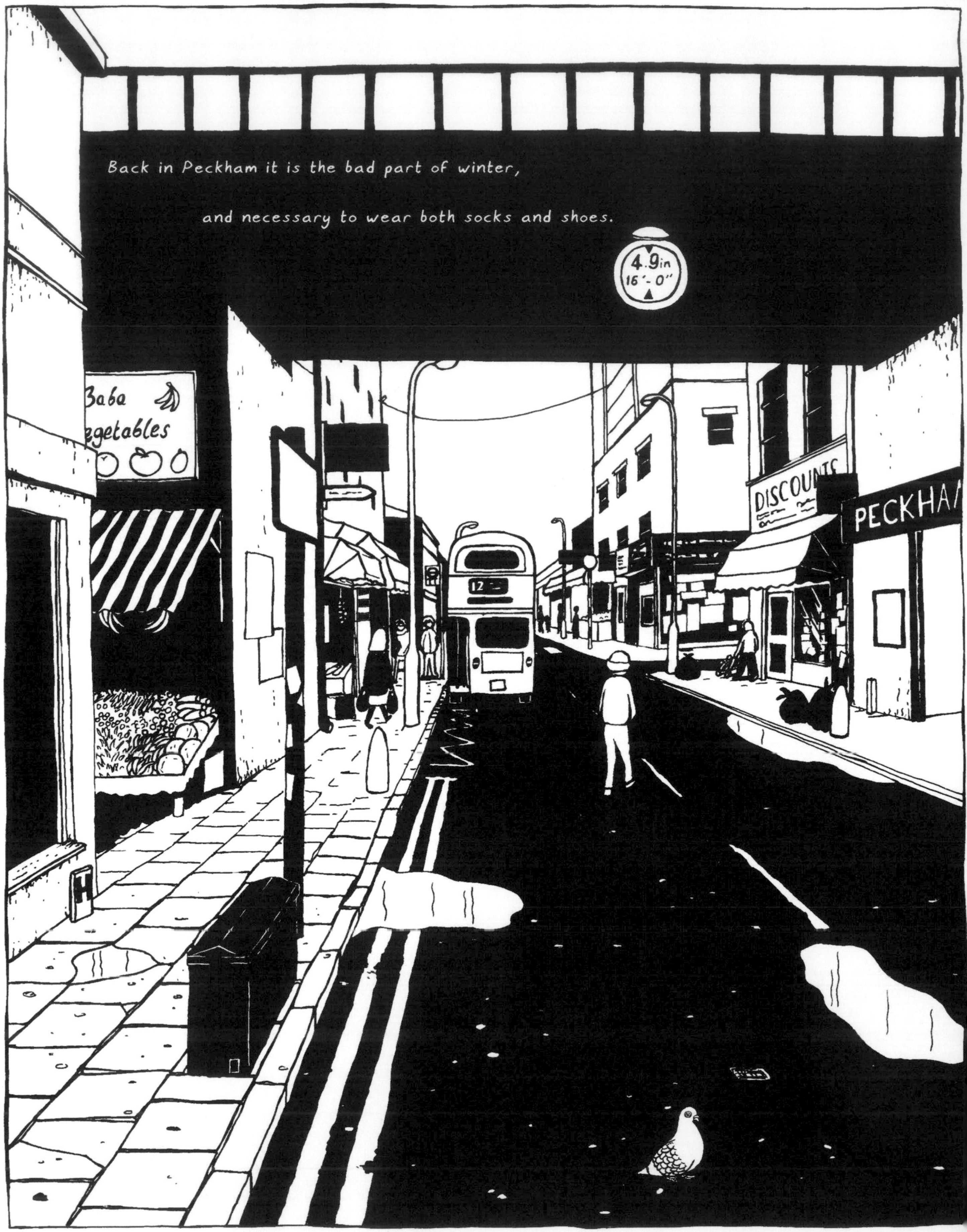
Back in Peckham it is the bad part of winter,
and necessary to wear both socks and shoes.
4.9in
15'-0''
Baba
12

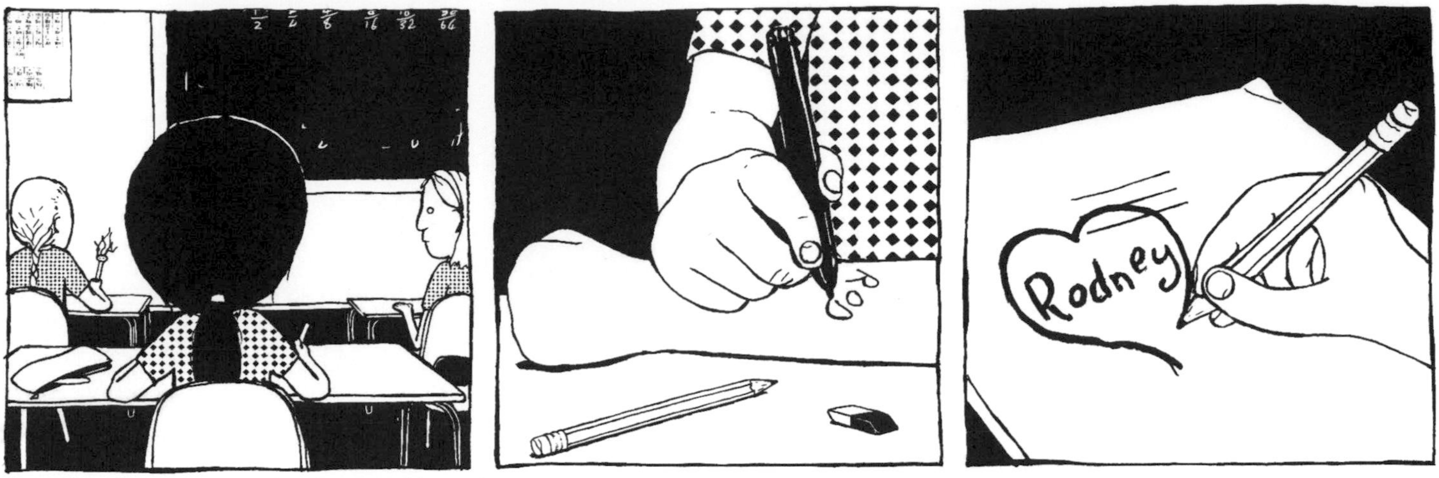
Rodney

I make up stories about myself and my schoolmates getting attacked by sharks.

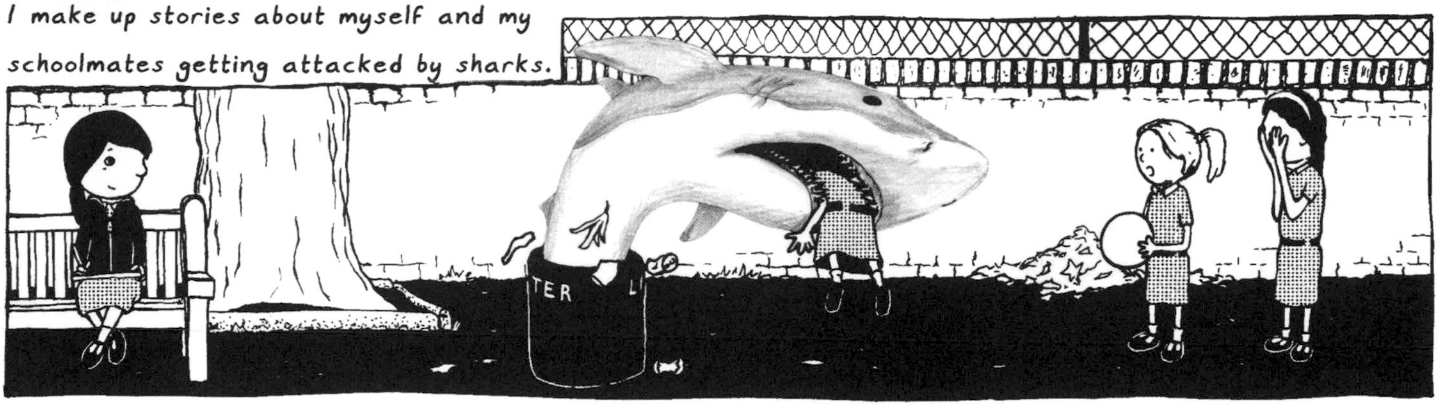

I sit in the library scrutinizing the shark books. But this is Sydenham, not Sydney, and there are just two books, thin and hardbacked, with drawings, not photographs, and there are no descriptions of attacks, no mentions of Rodney Fox, just diagrams and graphs. In England they are more interested in whales.

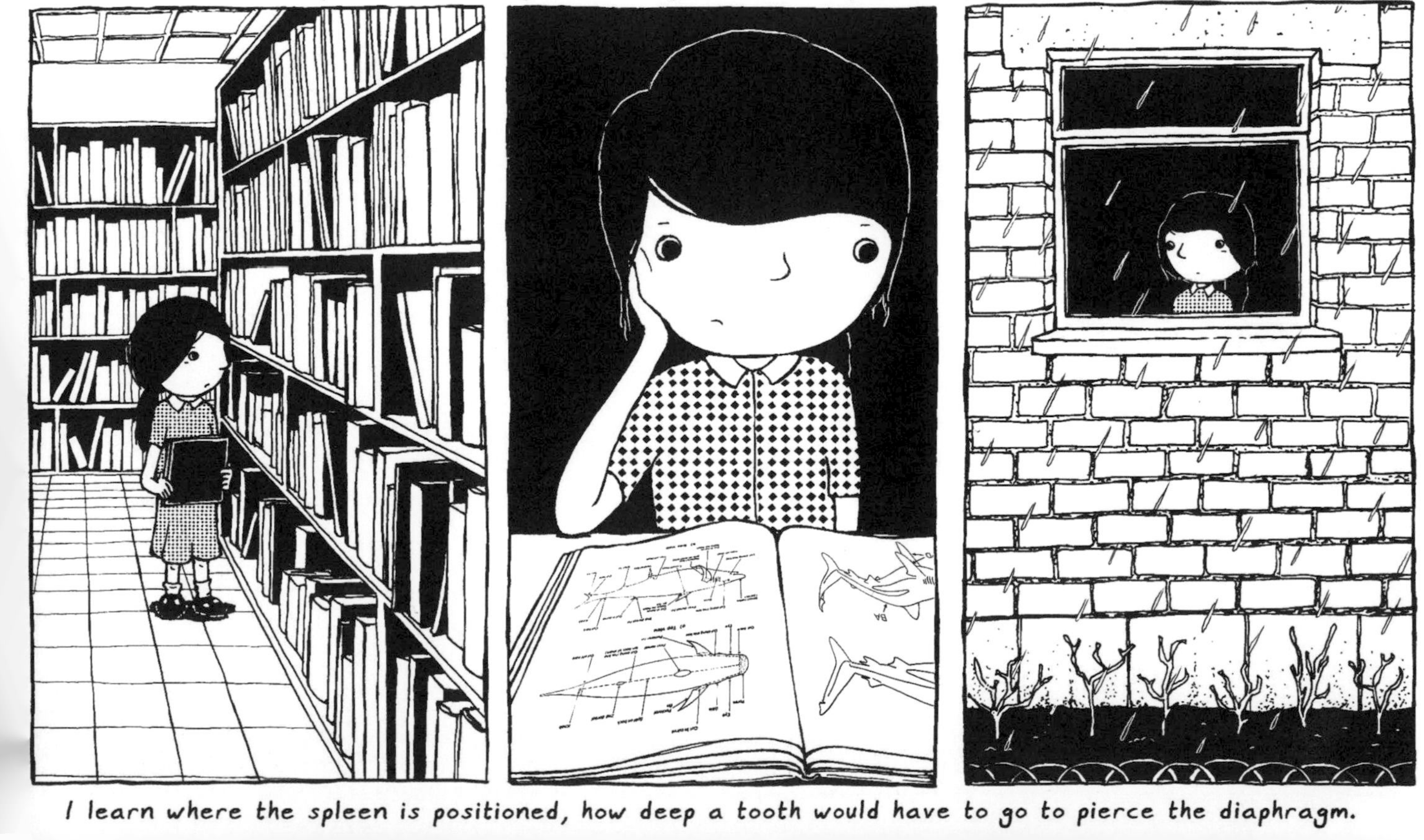

I learn where the spleen is positioned, how deep a tooth would have to go to pierce the diaphragm.

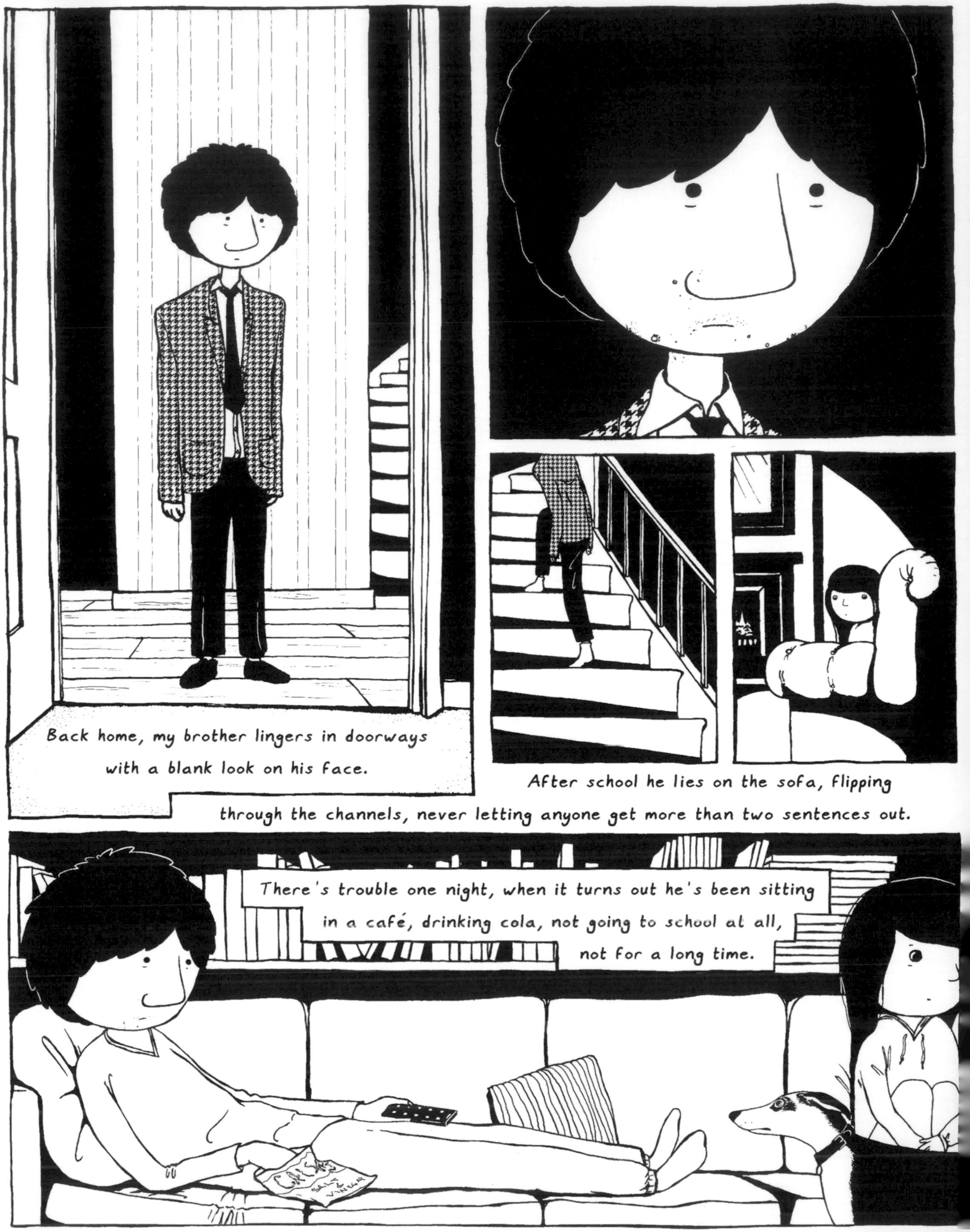
Back home, my brother lingers in doorways with a blank look on his face.
After school he lies on the sofa, flipping through the channels, never letting anyone get more than two sentences out.
There's trouble one night, when it turns out he's been sitting in a café, drinking cola, not going to school at all, not for a long time.

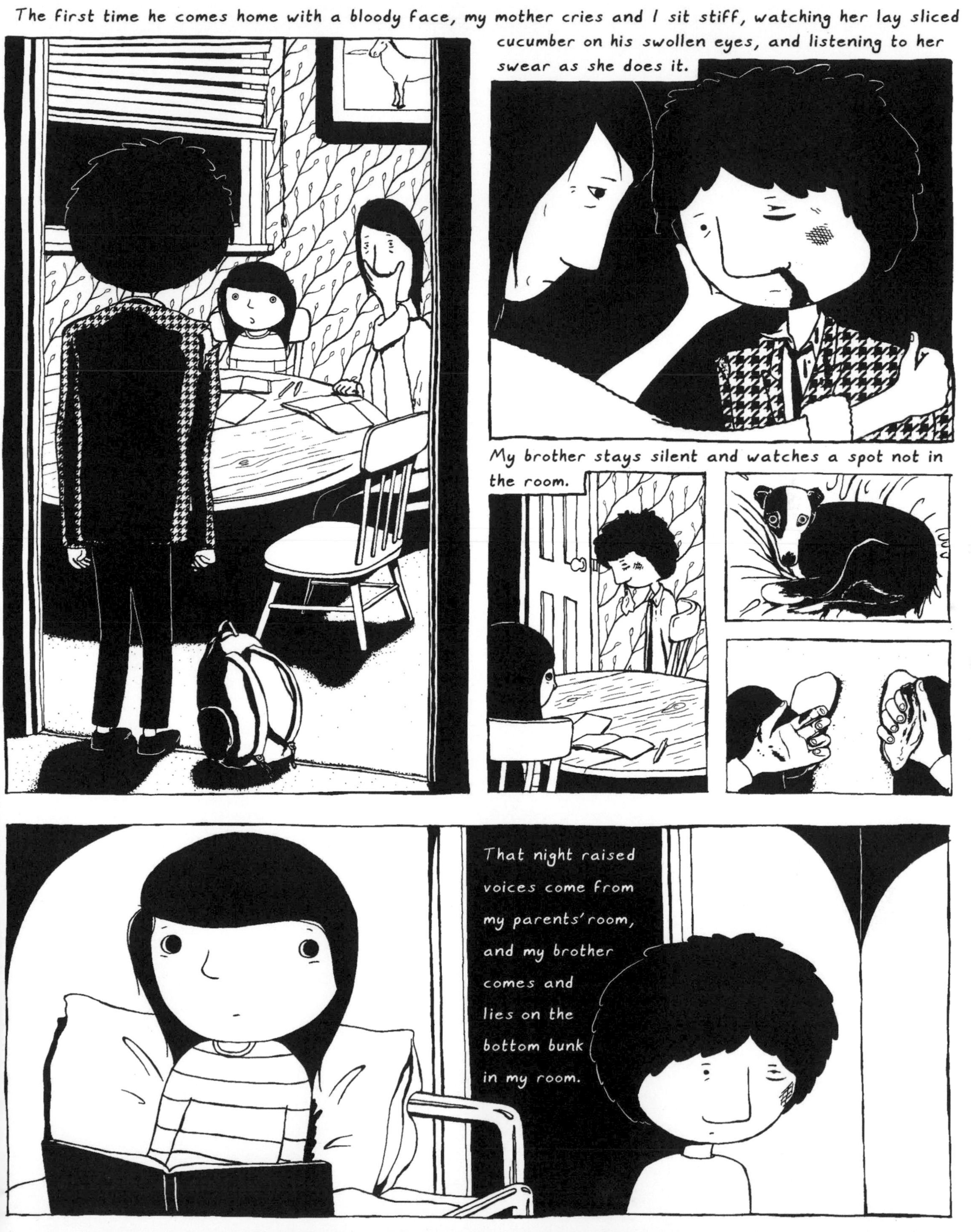
The first time he comes home with a bloody face, my mother cries and I sit stiff, watching her lay sliced cucumber on his swollen eyes, and listening to her swear as she does it.
My brother stays silent and watches a spot not in the room.
That night raised voices come from my parents' room, and my brother comes and lies on the bottom bunk in my room.

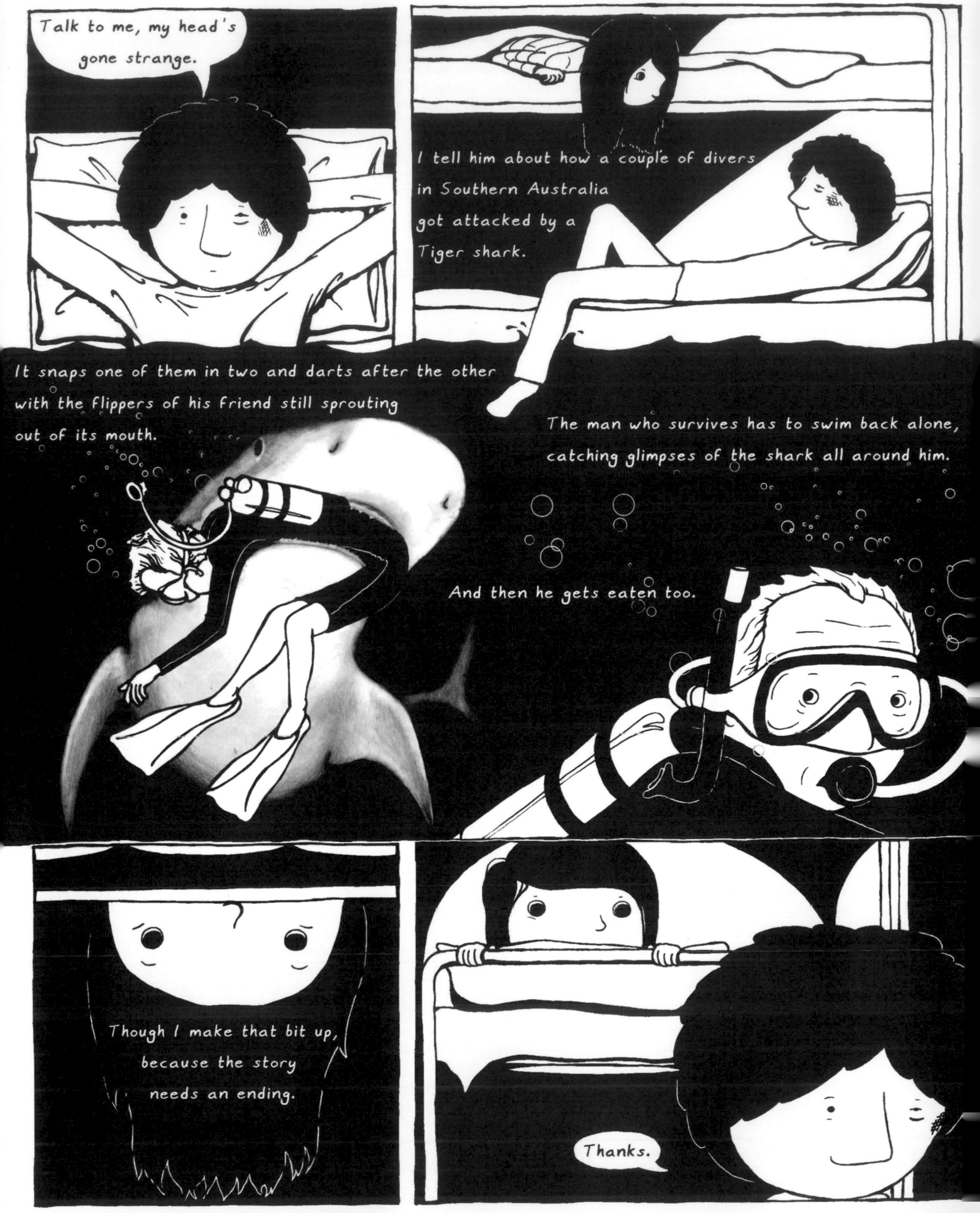
Talk to me, my head's gone strange.
I tell him about how a couple of divers in Southern Australia got attacked by a Tiger shark.
It snaps one of them in two and darts after the other with the flippers of his friend still sprouting out of its mouth.
The man who survives has to swim back alone, catching glimpses of the shark all around him.
And then he gets eaten too.
Though I make that bit up, because the story needs an ending.
Thanks.

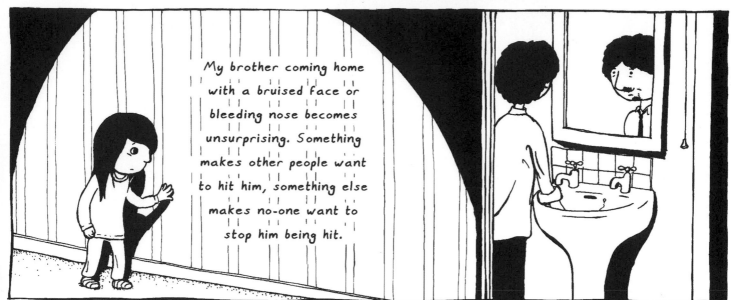

My brother coming home with a bruised face or bleeding nose becomes unsurprising. Something makes other people want to hit him, something else makes no-one want to stop him being hit.

My father shouts at the police down the phone, and they can't help. My brother remains silent on the matter, but continues coming into my room and listening to shark stories. Once I start to tell him about a girl at school who'd lost her finger to a rottweiler, but he shakes his head...

Stick to shark stories.

So I tell him about the Mako at Burning Palms that was found with a pair of expensive stilettos in its stomach.

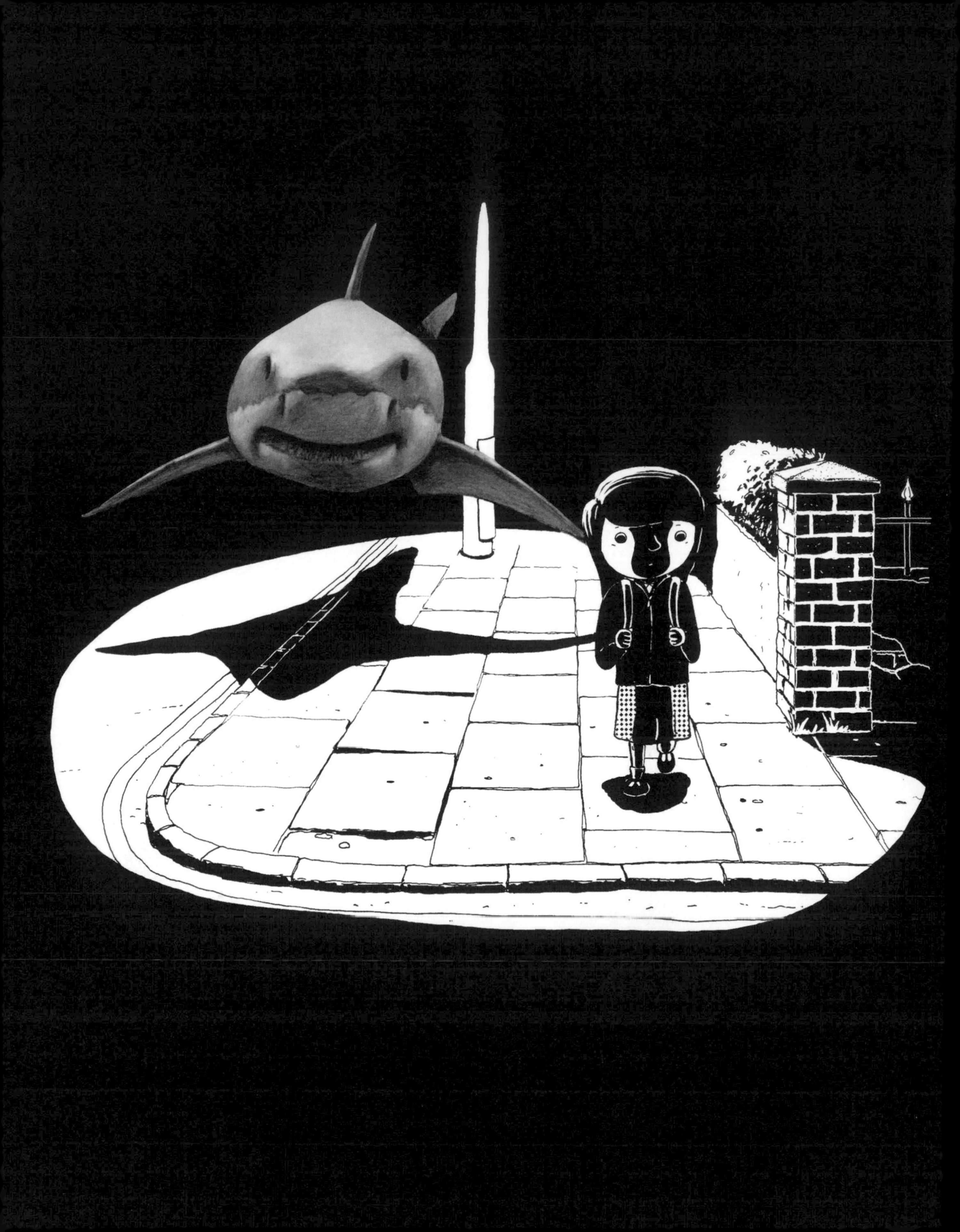

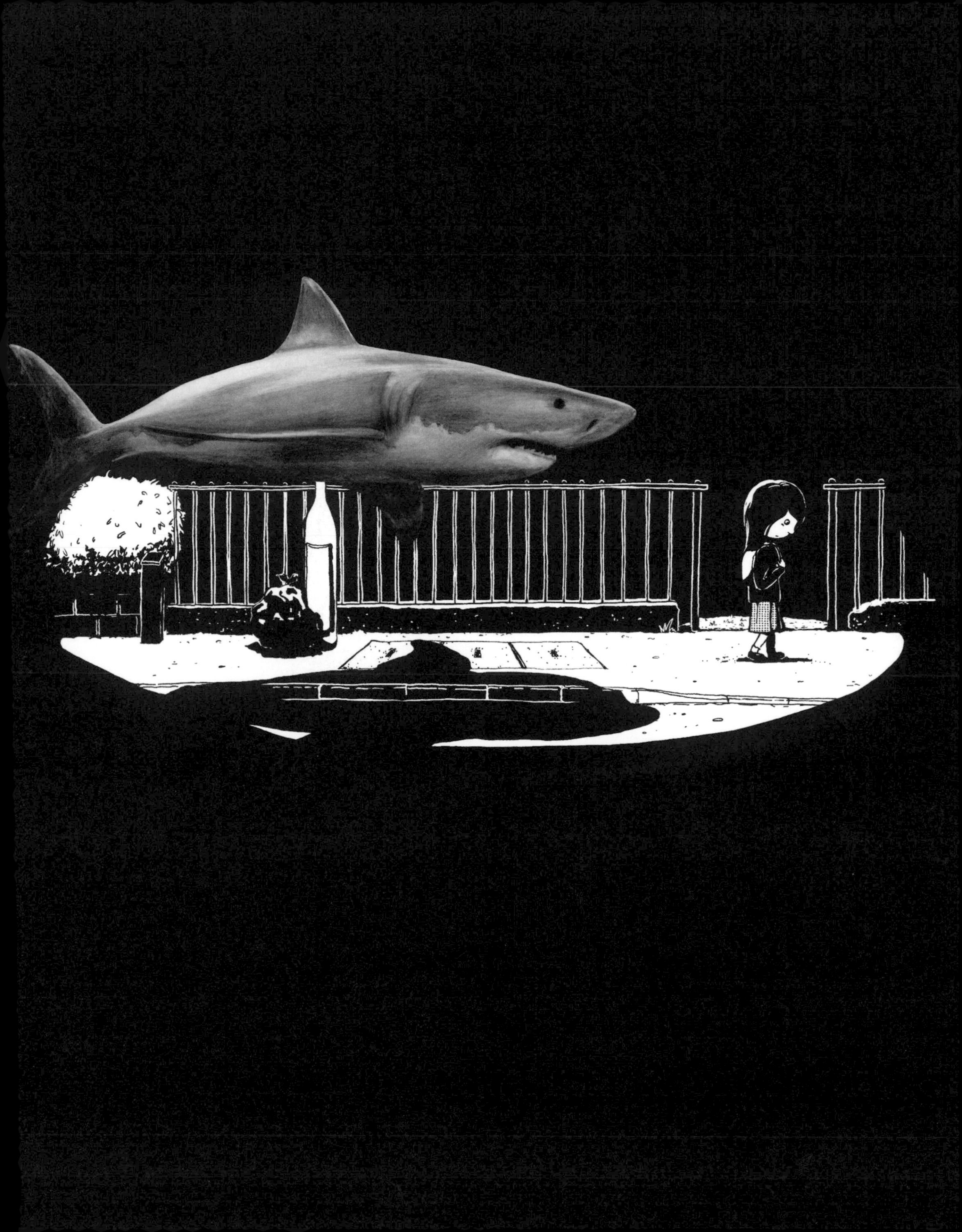

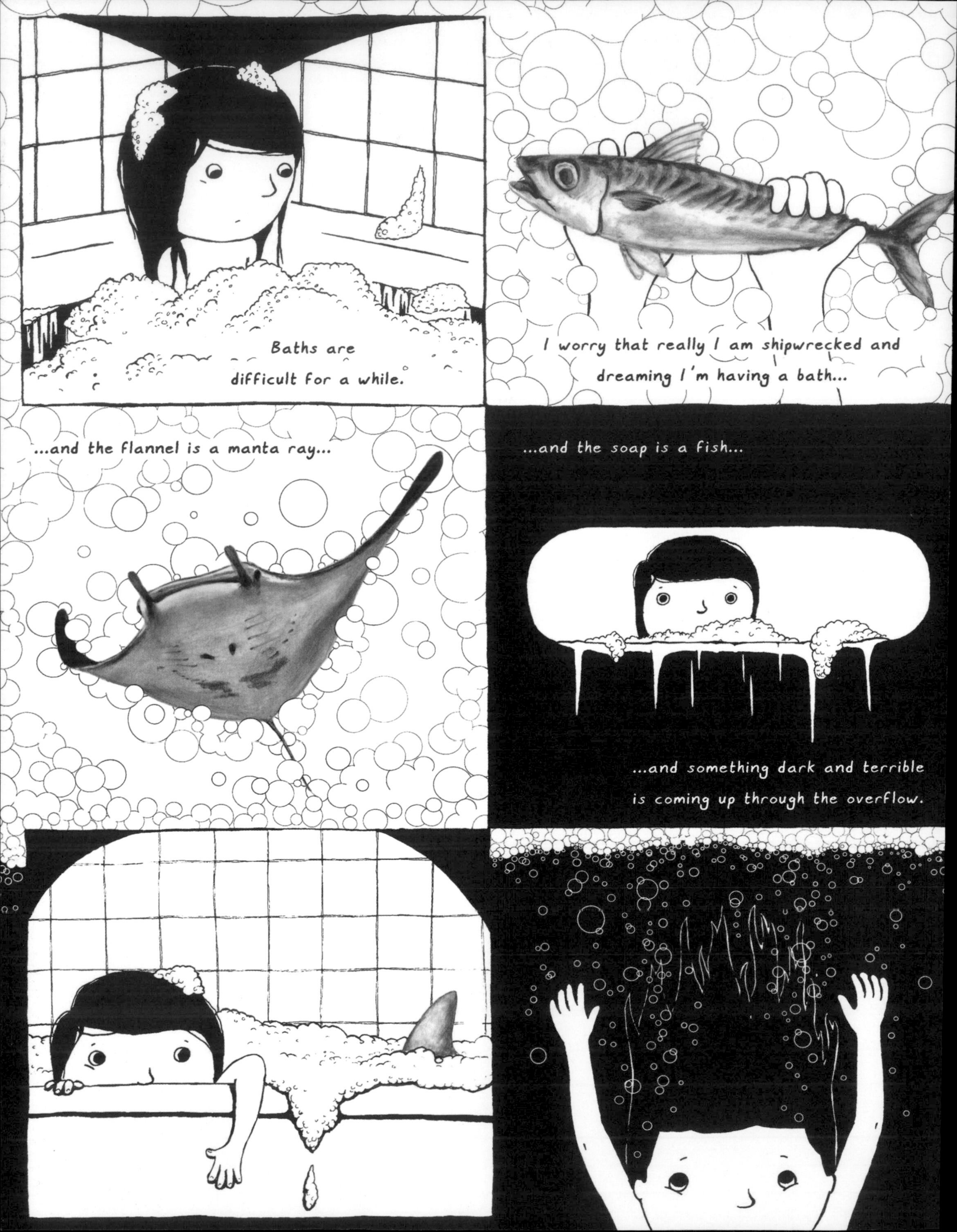
Baths are difficult for a while.
I worry that really I am shipwrecked and dreaming I'm having a bath...
...and the flannel is a manta ray...
...and the soap is a fish...
...and something dark and terrible is coming up through the overflow.

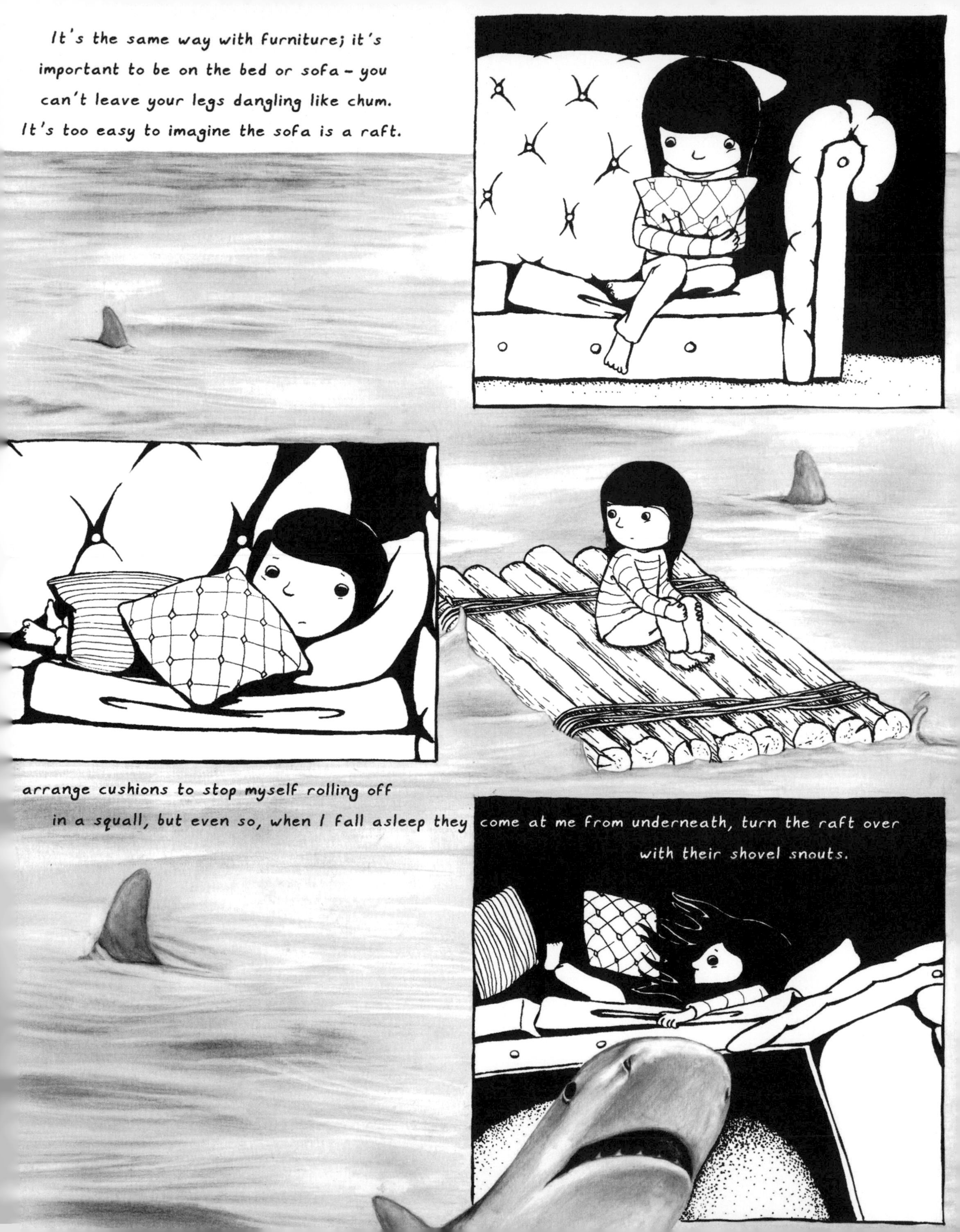
It's the same way with furniture; it's important to be on the bed or sofa - you can't leave your legs dangling like chum. It's too easy to imagine the sofa is a raft.
arrange cushions to stop myself rolling off
in a squall, but even so, when I fall asleep they
come at me from underneath, turn the raft over with their shovel snouts.

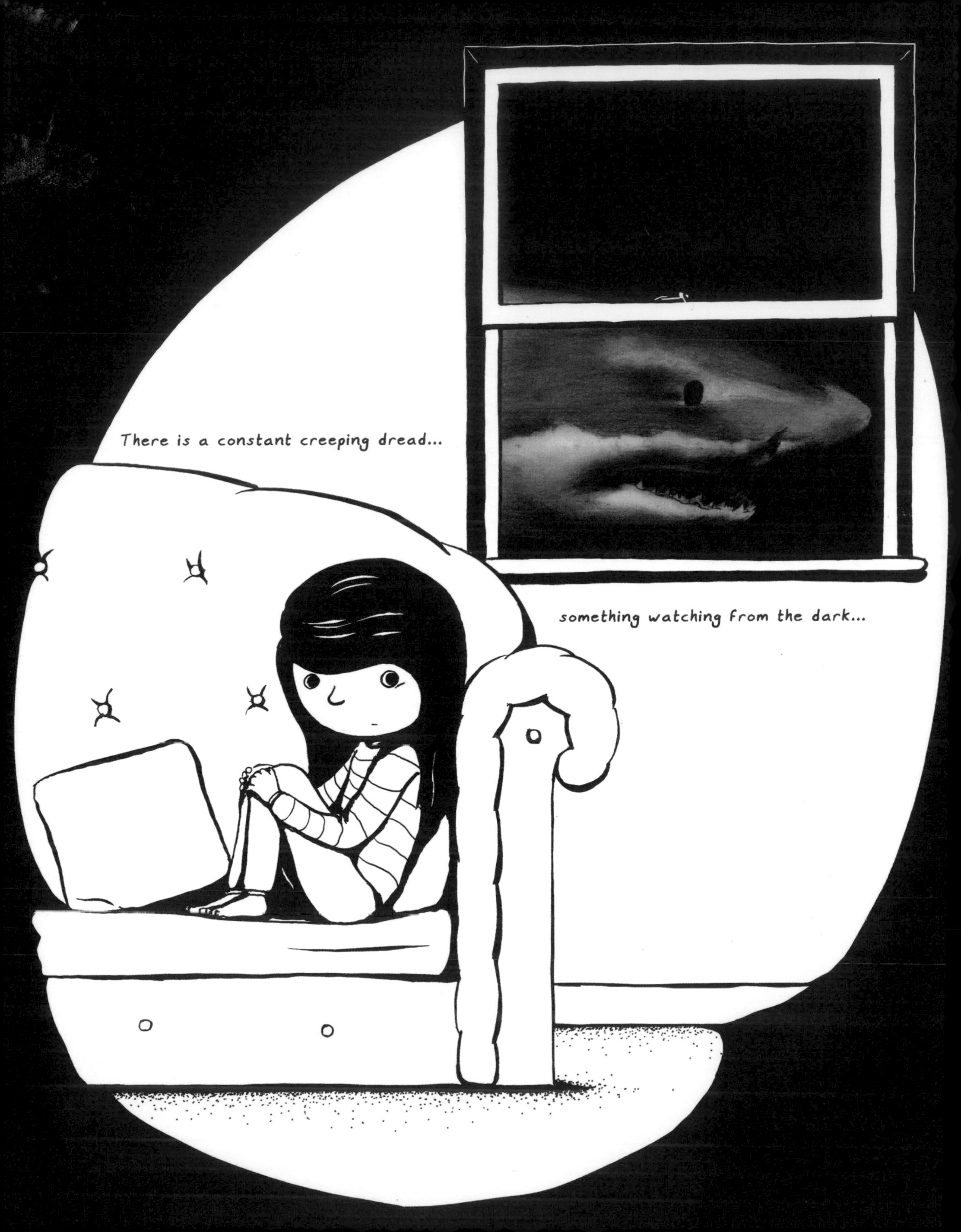
There is a constant creeping dread...
something watching from the dark...

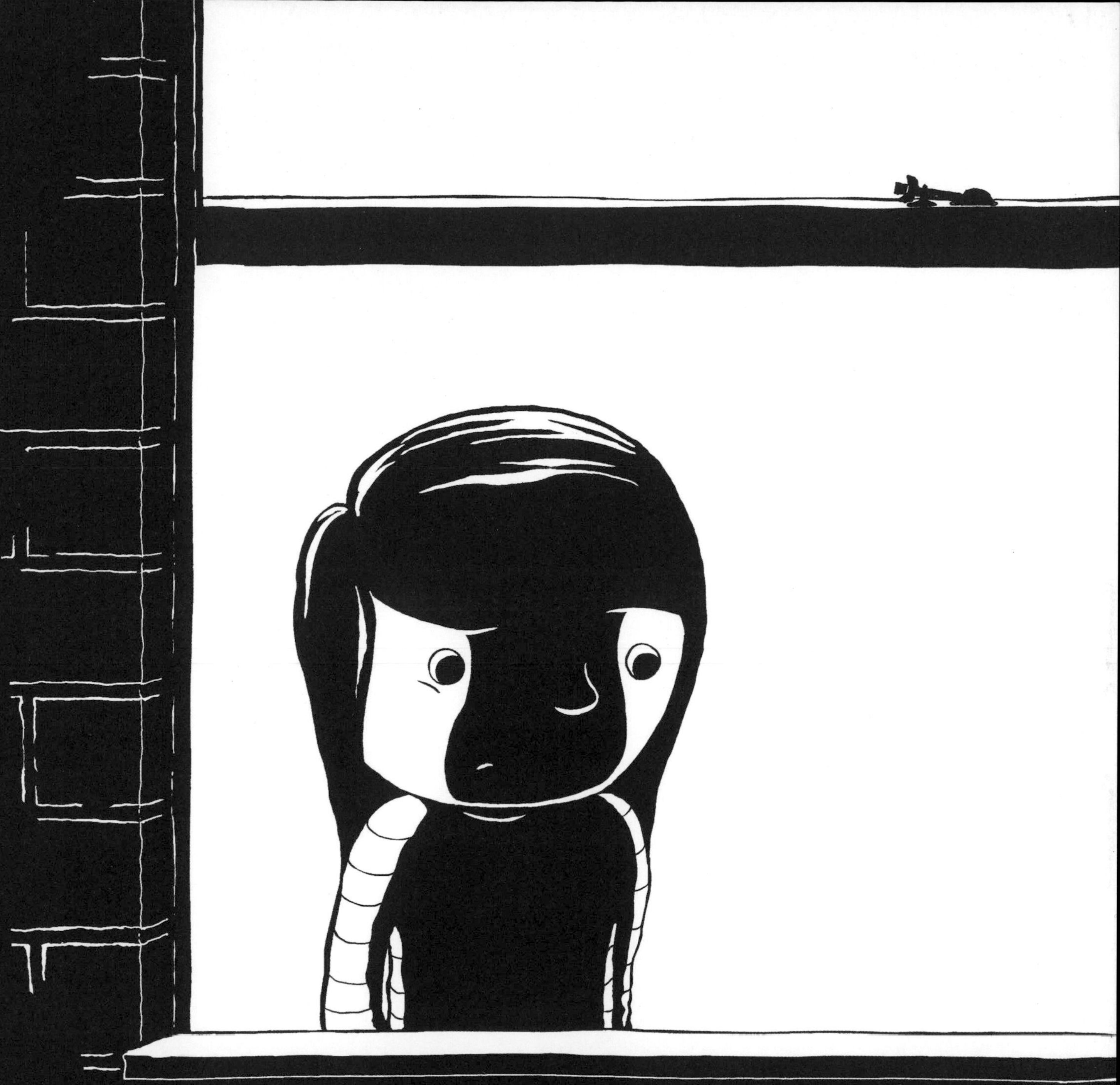

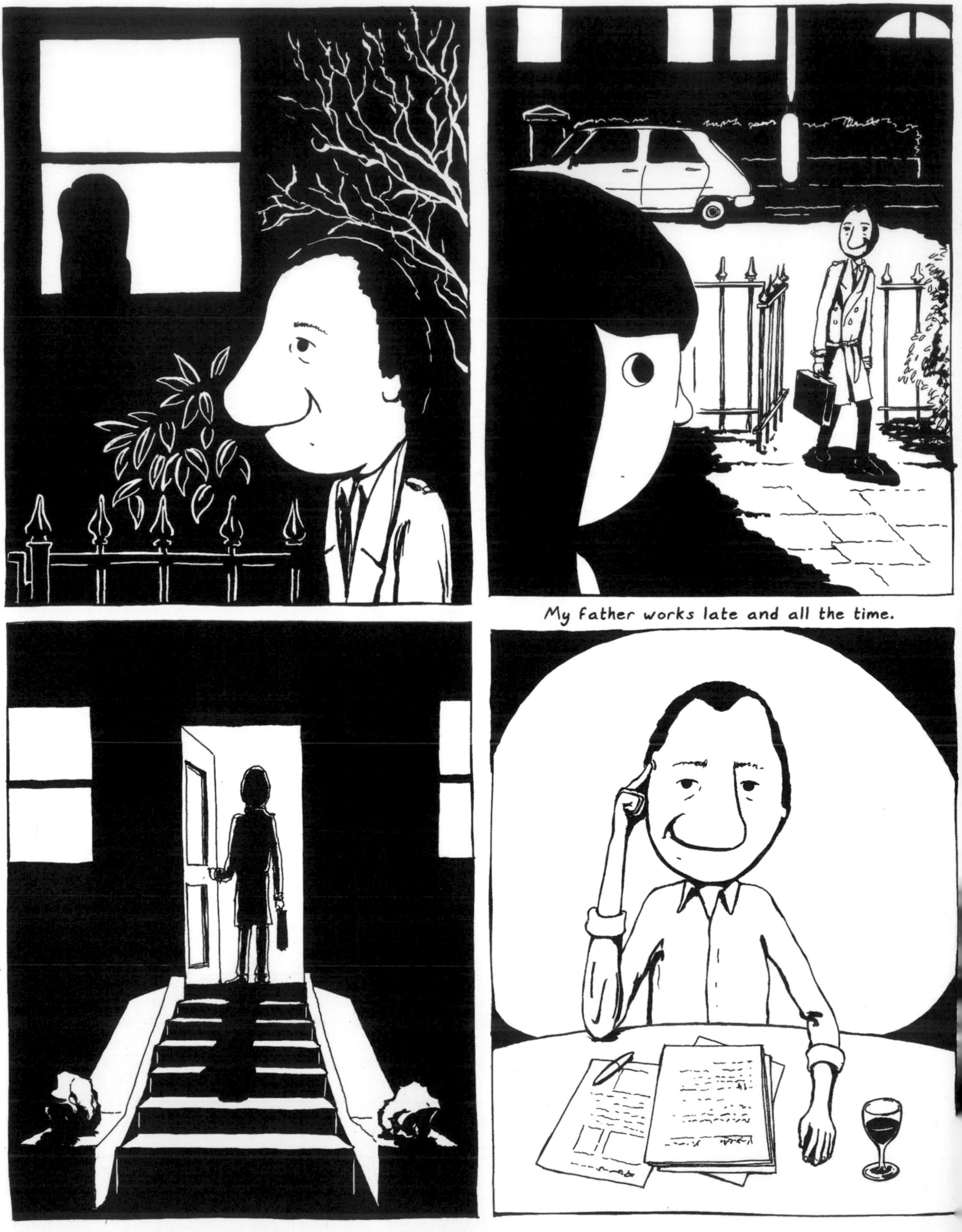
My father works late and all the time.

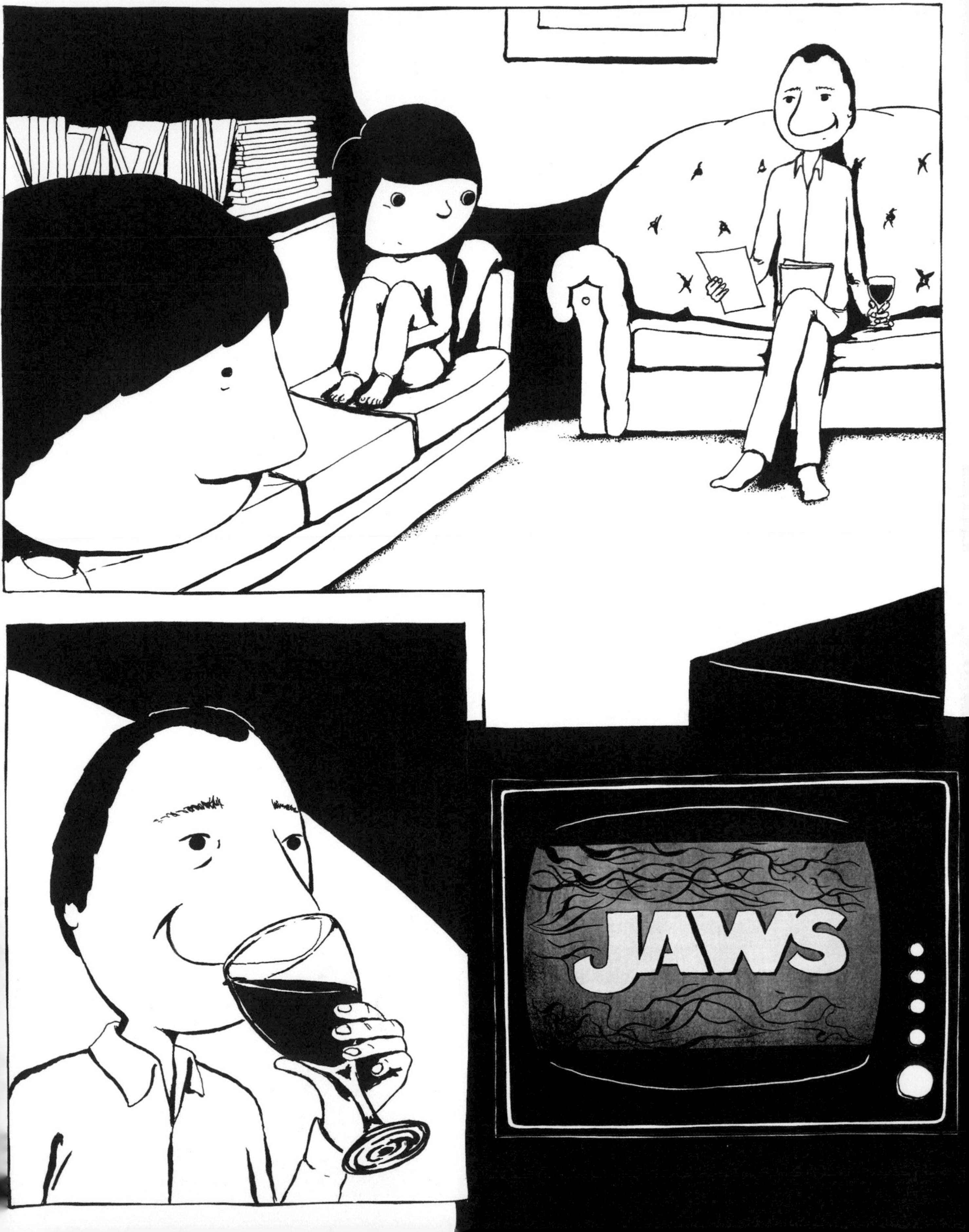
JAWS

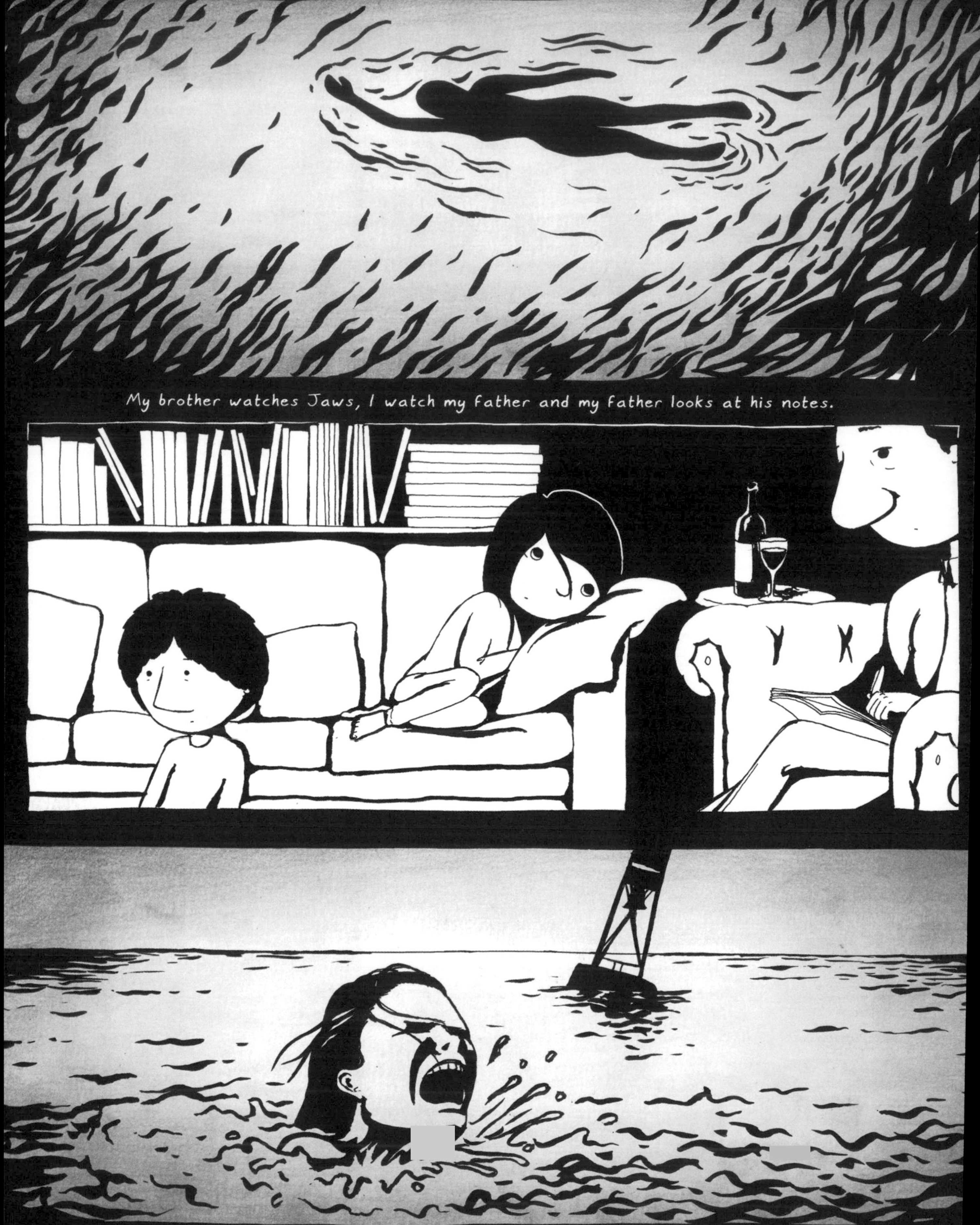
My brother watches Jaws, I watch my father and my father looks at his notes.

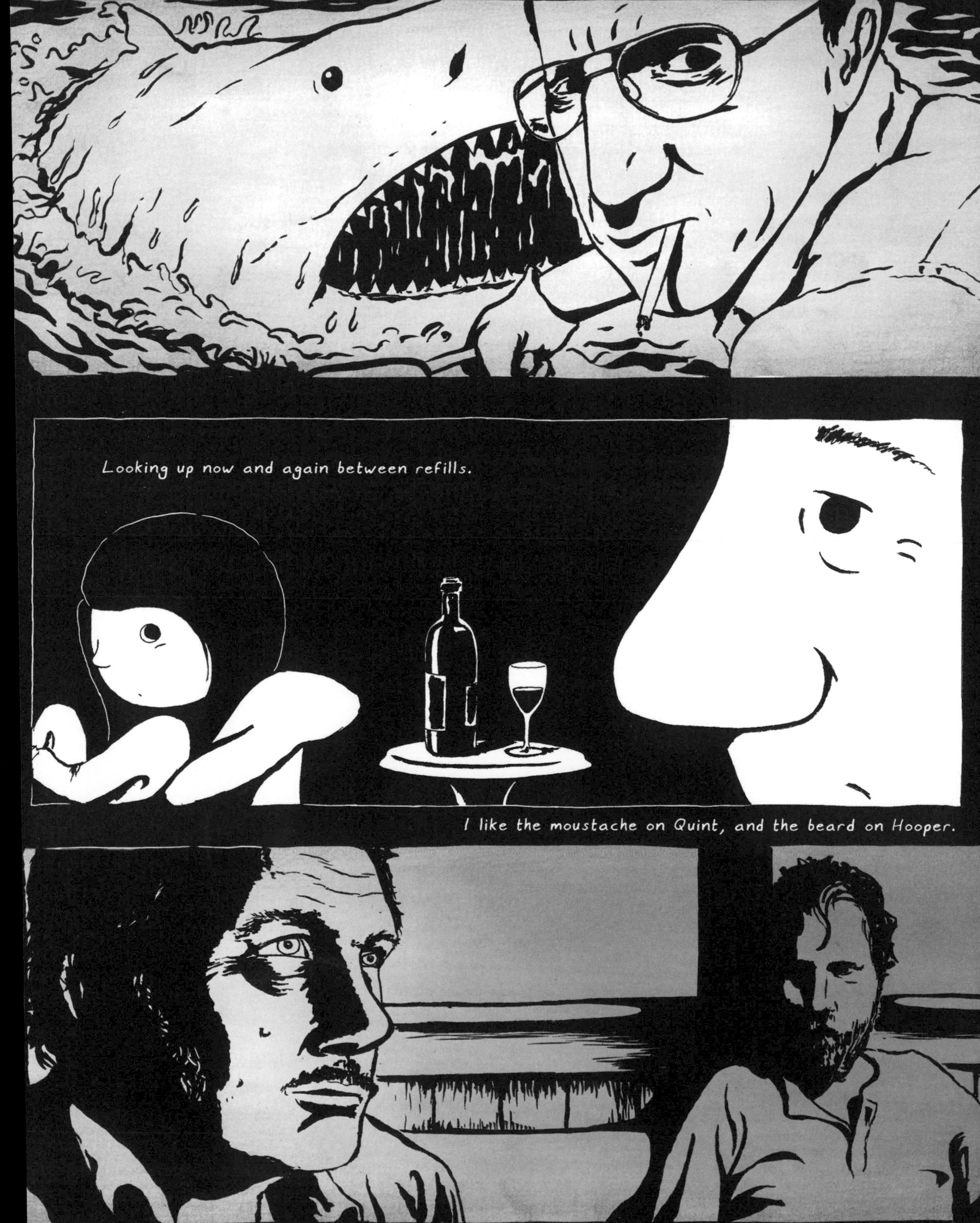
Looking up now and again between refills.
I like the moustache on Quint, and the beard on Hooper.

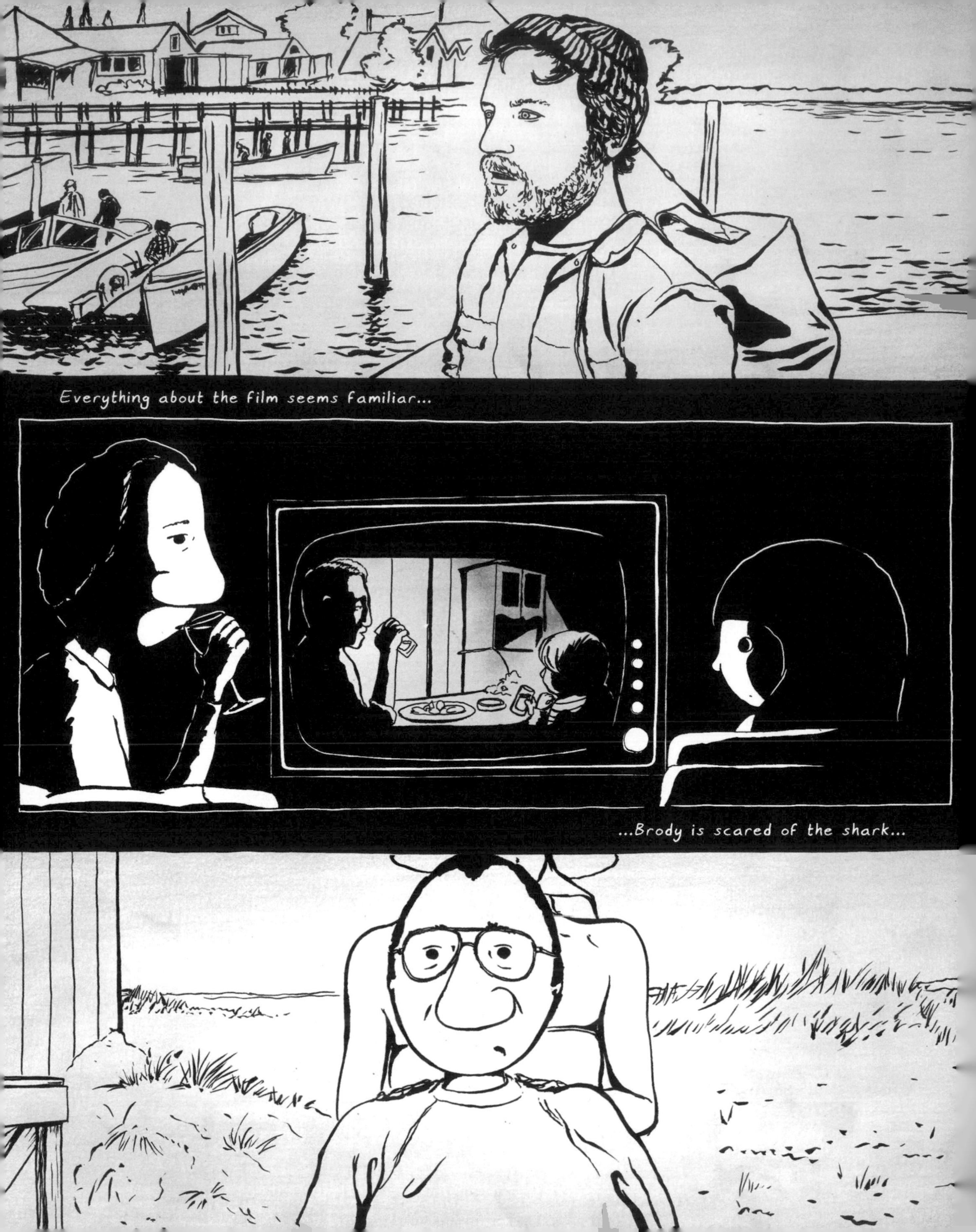
Everything about the film seems familiar...
...Brody is scared of the shark...

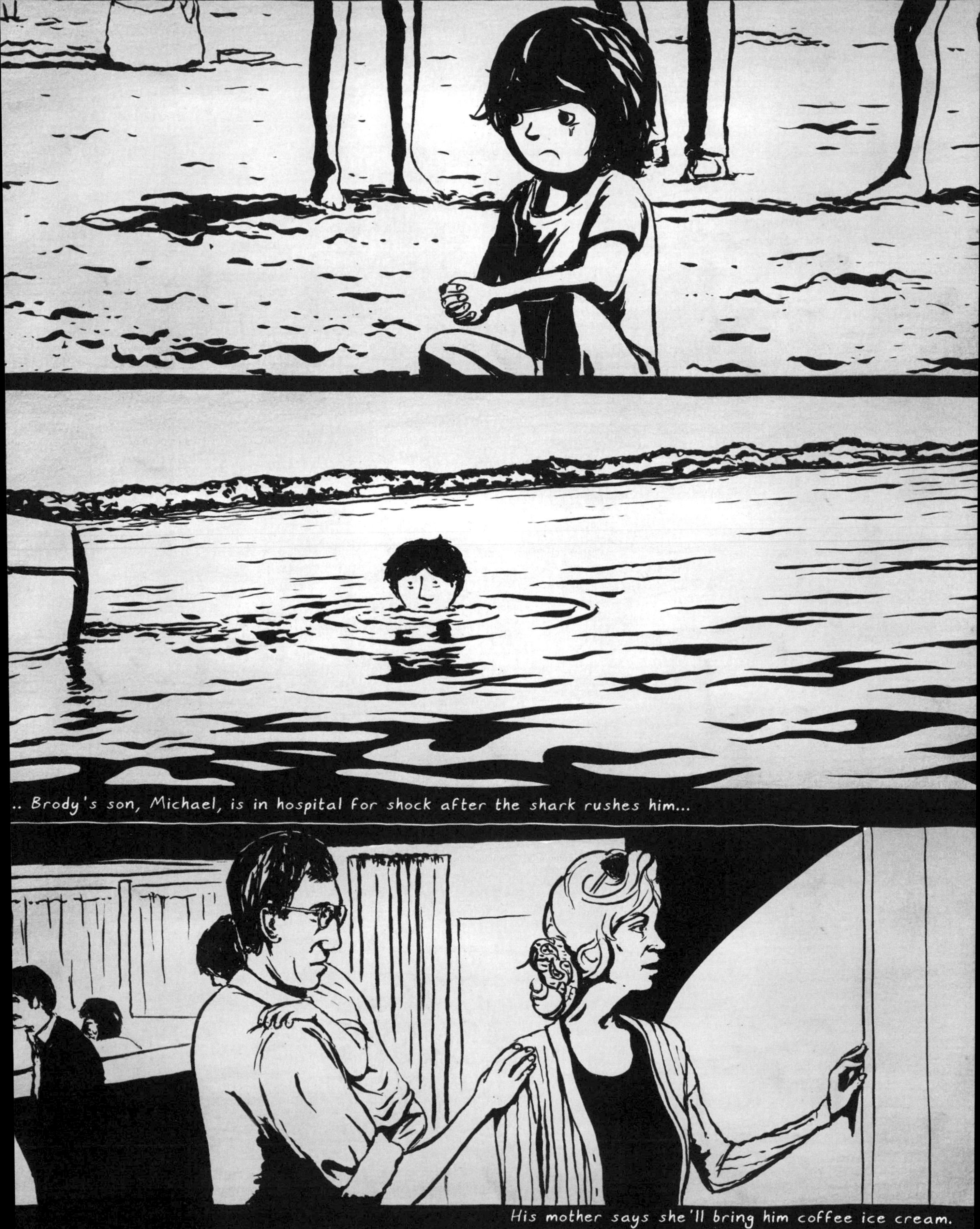
.. Brody's son, Michael, is in hospital for shock after the shark rushes him...
His mother says she'll bring him coffee ice cream.

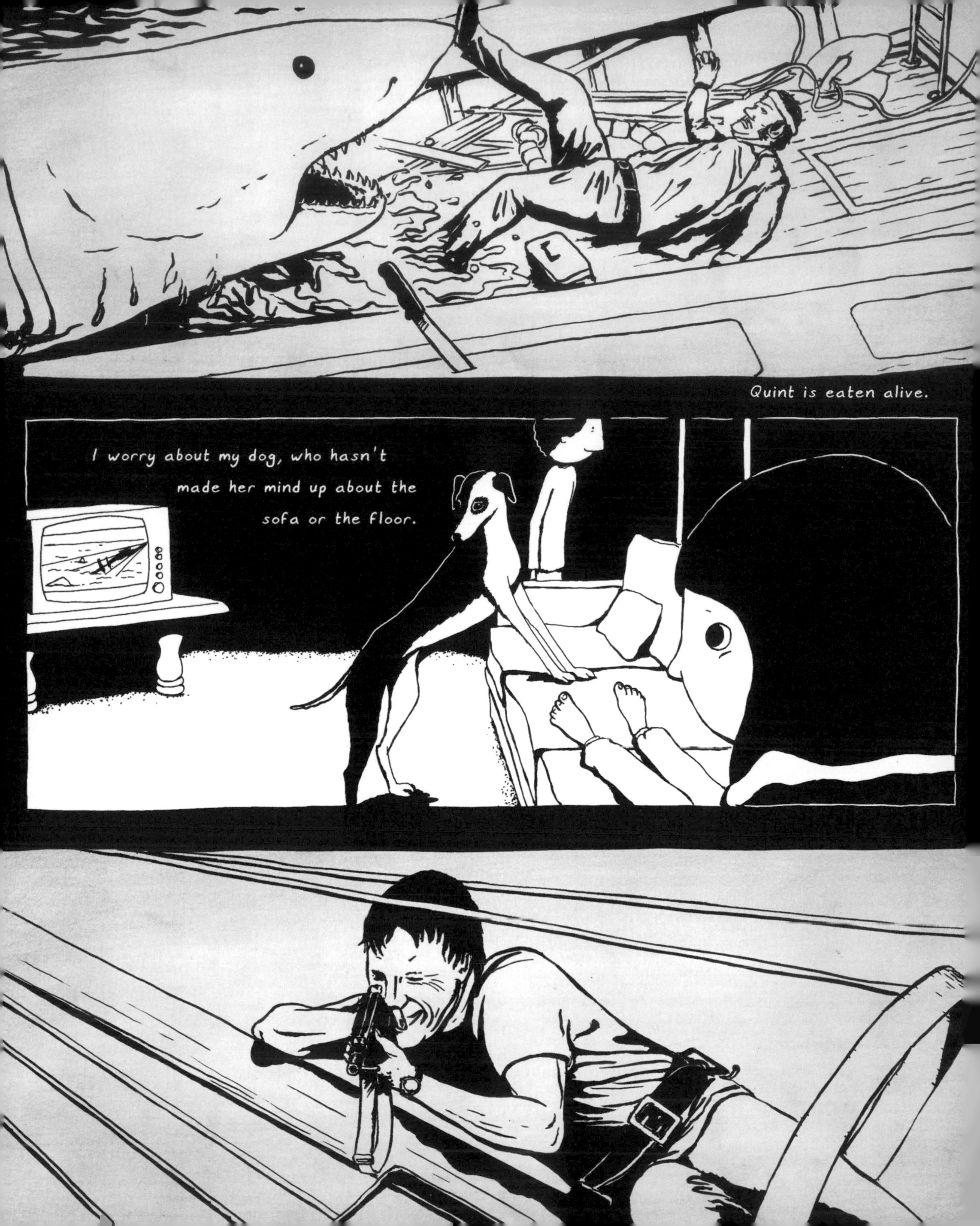
Quint is eaten alive.
I worry about my dog, who hasn't made her mind up about the sofa or the floor.

When Brody explodes the shark, my father looks up from his work and pumps a fist in the air.

Then pours himself another glass of wine to celebrate.

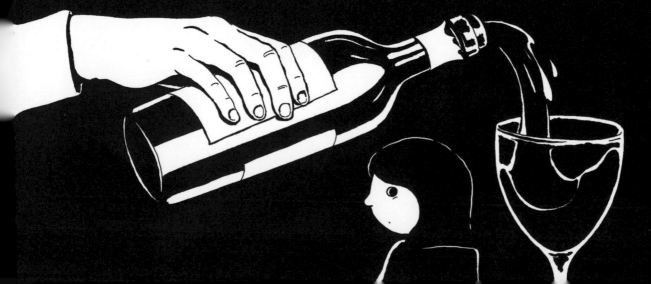

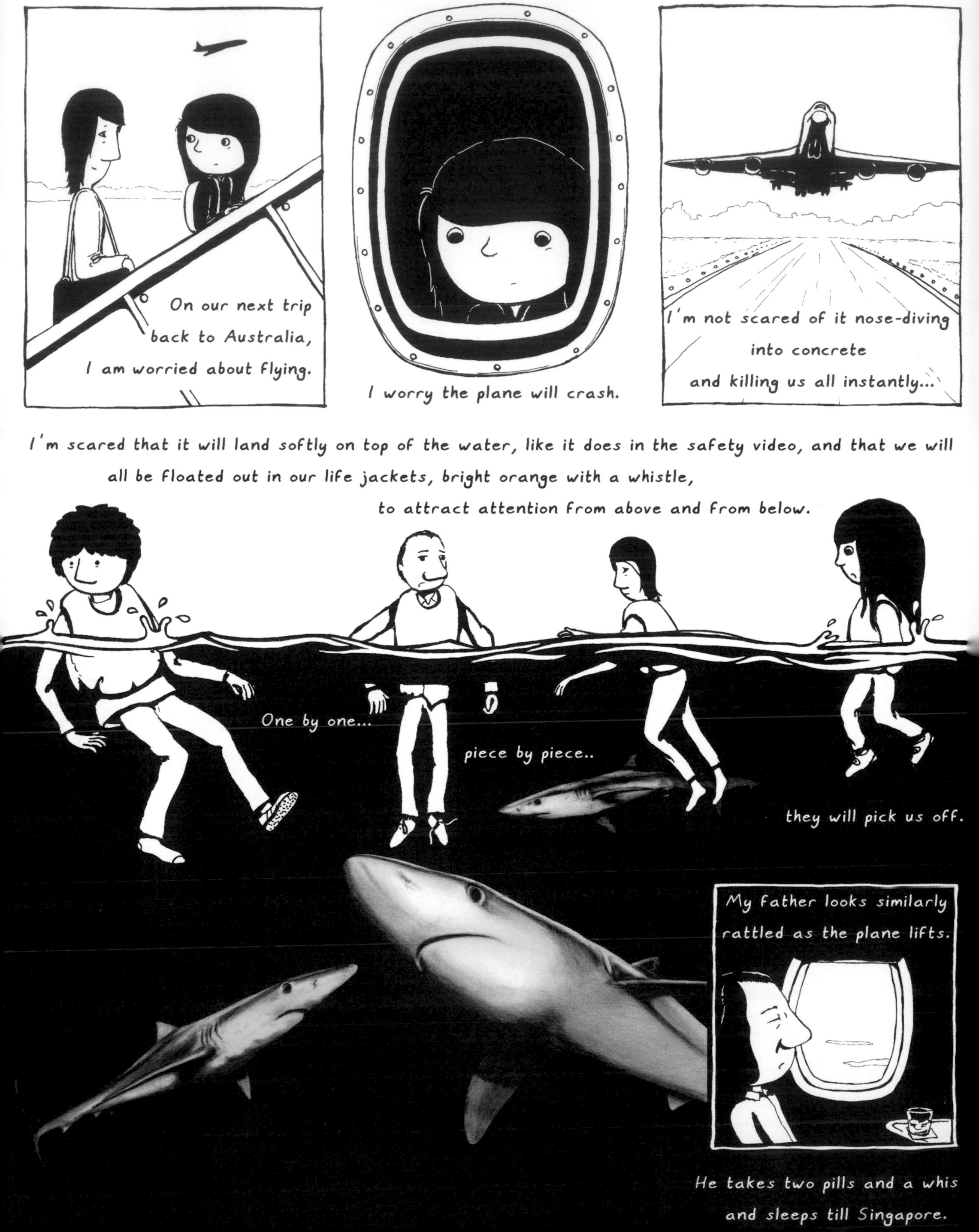
On our next trip
back to Australia,
I am worried about flying.
I worry the plane will crash.
I'm not scared of it nose-diving
into concrete
and killing us all instantly...
I'm scared that it will land softly on top of the water, like it does in the safety video, and that we will
all be floated out in our life jackets, bright orange with a whistle,
to attract attention from above and from below.
One by one...
piece by piece..
they will pick us off.
My father looks similarly
rattled as the plane lifts.
He takes two pills and a whis
and sleeps till Singapore.

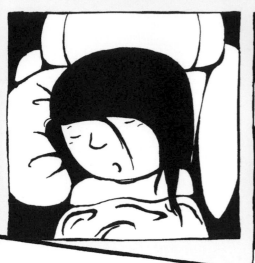

From Sydney we take the small plane to Ballina and arrive at the farm red-nosed and static-haired.

There is a welcome meal of butterfly prawns and mud crab from the river.

There is a large huntsman in our room.

Everything is as it should be.

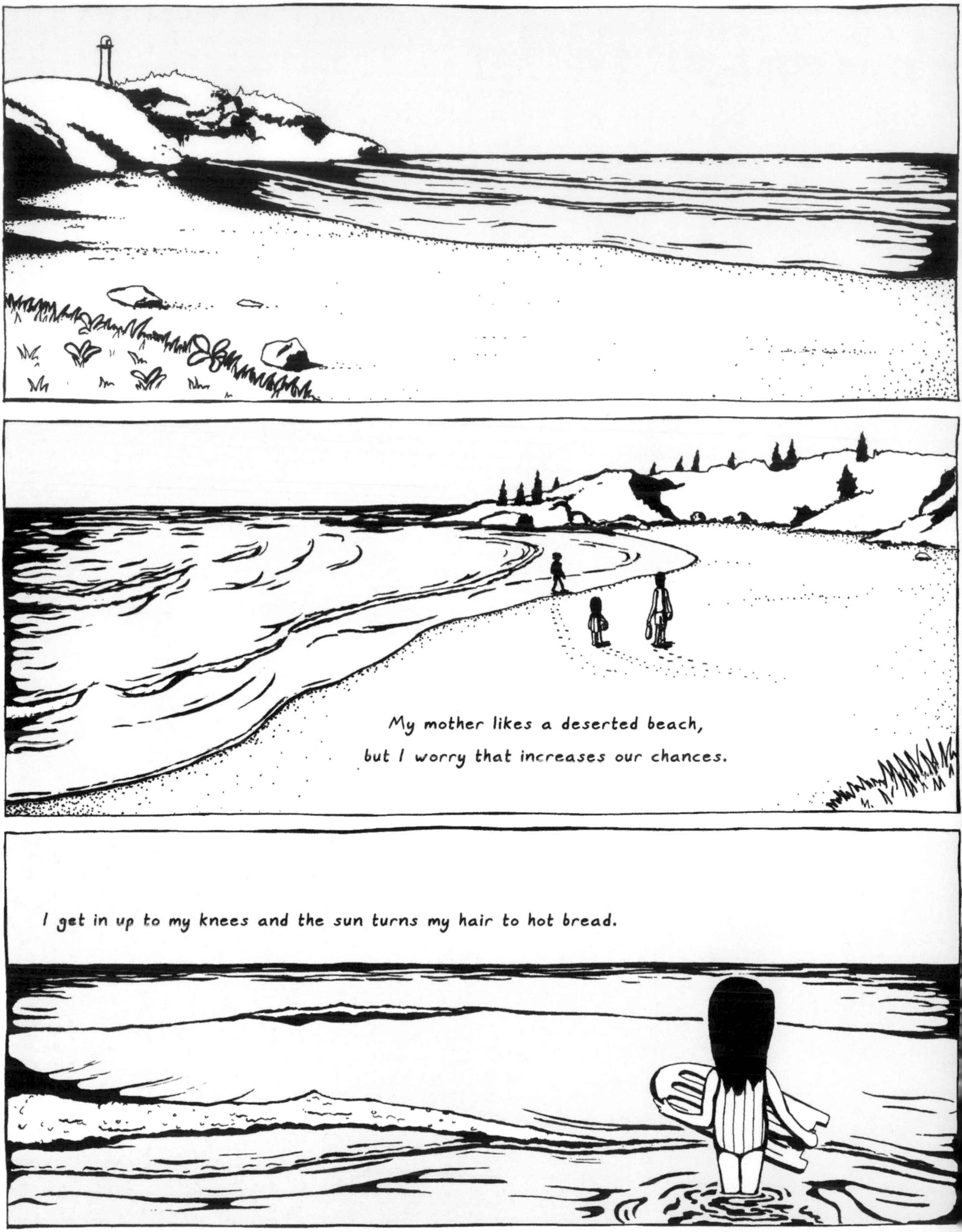
My mother likes a deserted beach,
but I worry that increases our chances.
I get in up to my knees and the sun turns my hair to hot bread.

I watch my brother up—and—under waves, spurting water like a whale from his mouth each time.

He is far out.

My feet twitch in the sand.

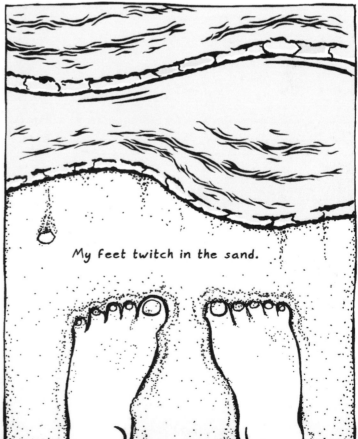

Later, my uncle takes my brother and me to see a dead shark that's been washed up downriver.

We mess with it, my brother sits on it rodeo style. I run a hand over the sandpaper skin I've read about.

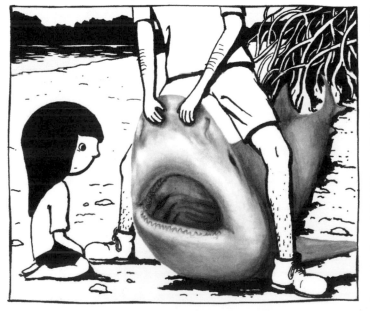

Survivors find themselves grazed from it when the shark glides by.

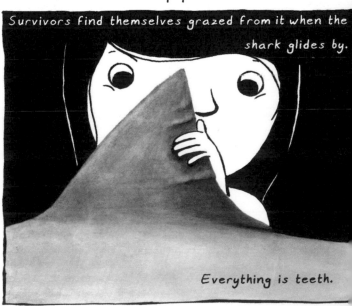

Everything is teeth.

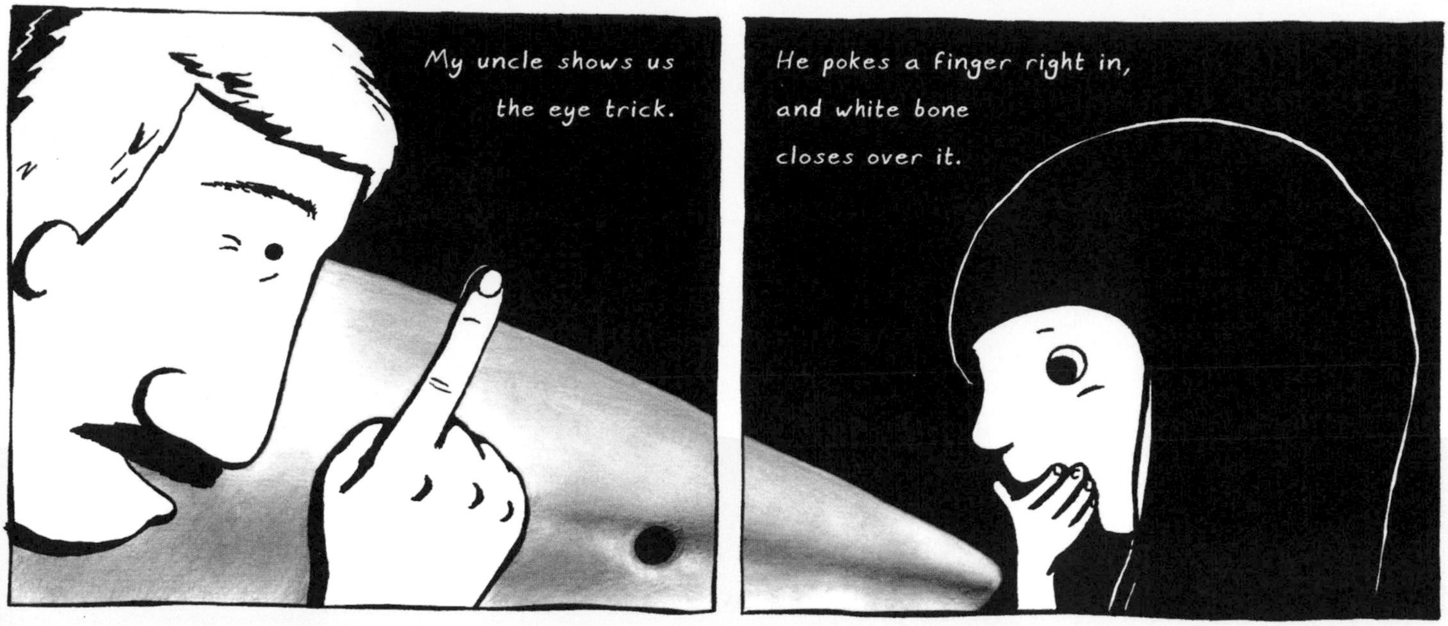
My uncle shows us the eye trick.
He pokes a finger right in, and white bone closes over it.

I think of you, Rodney Fox – did that bone close over your finger?

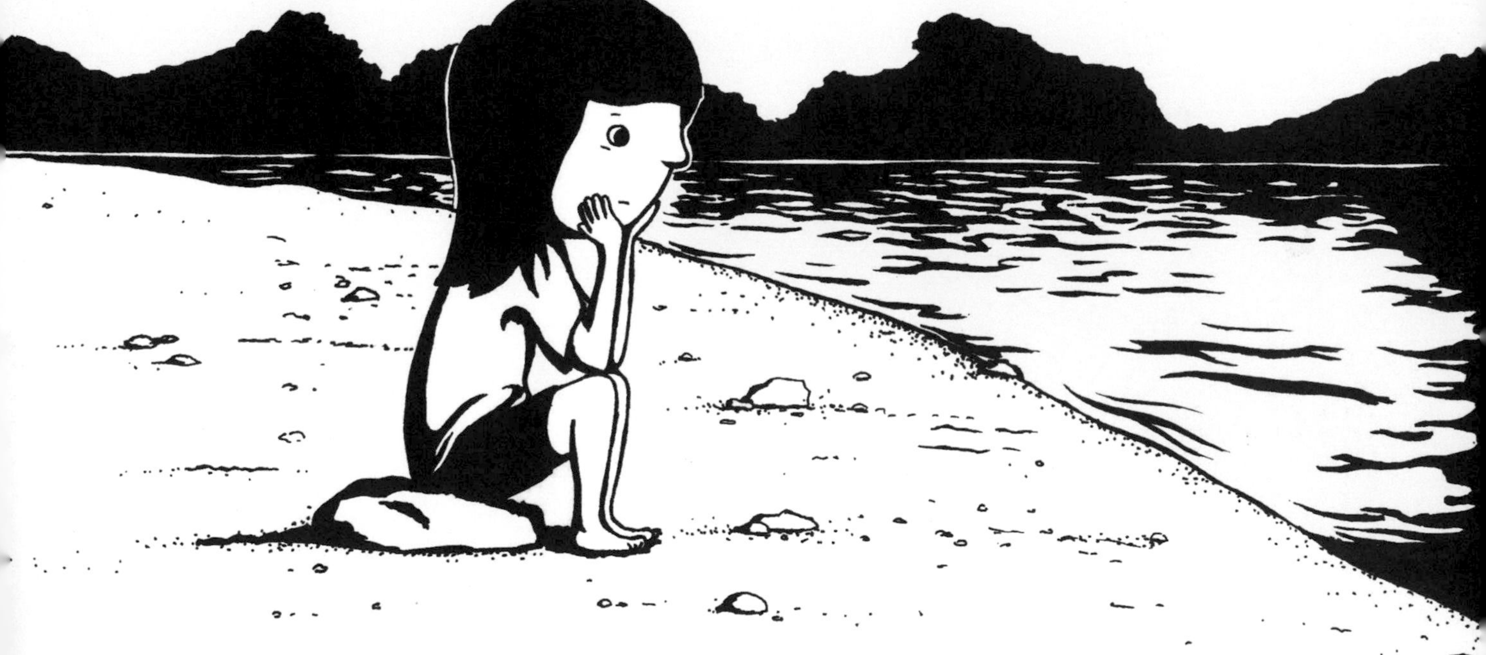

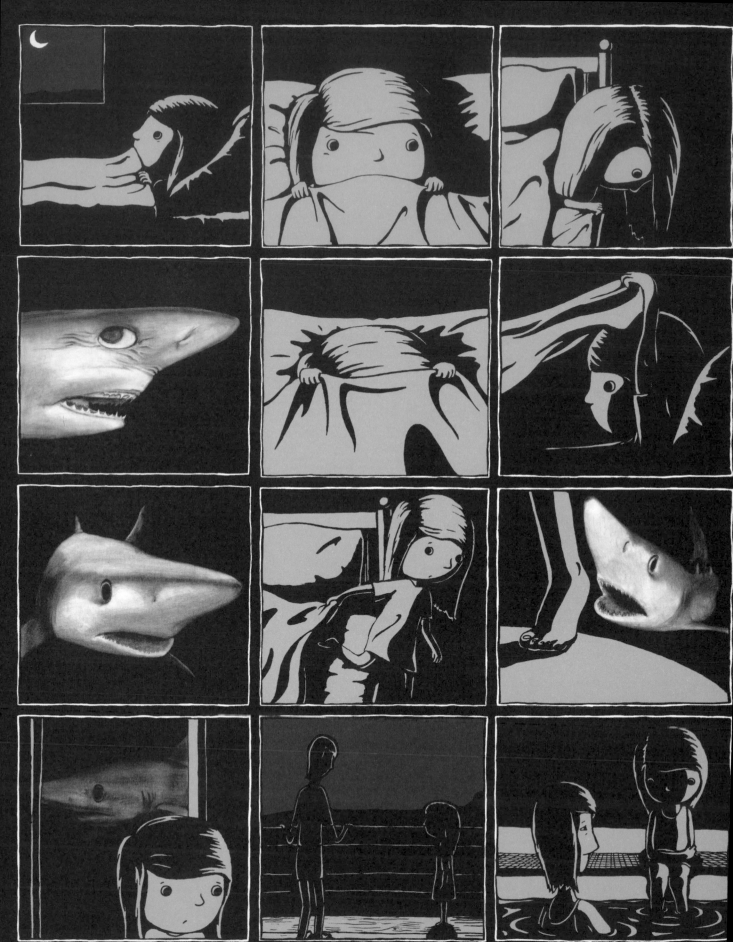

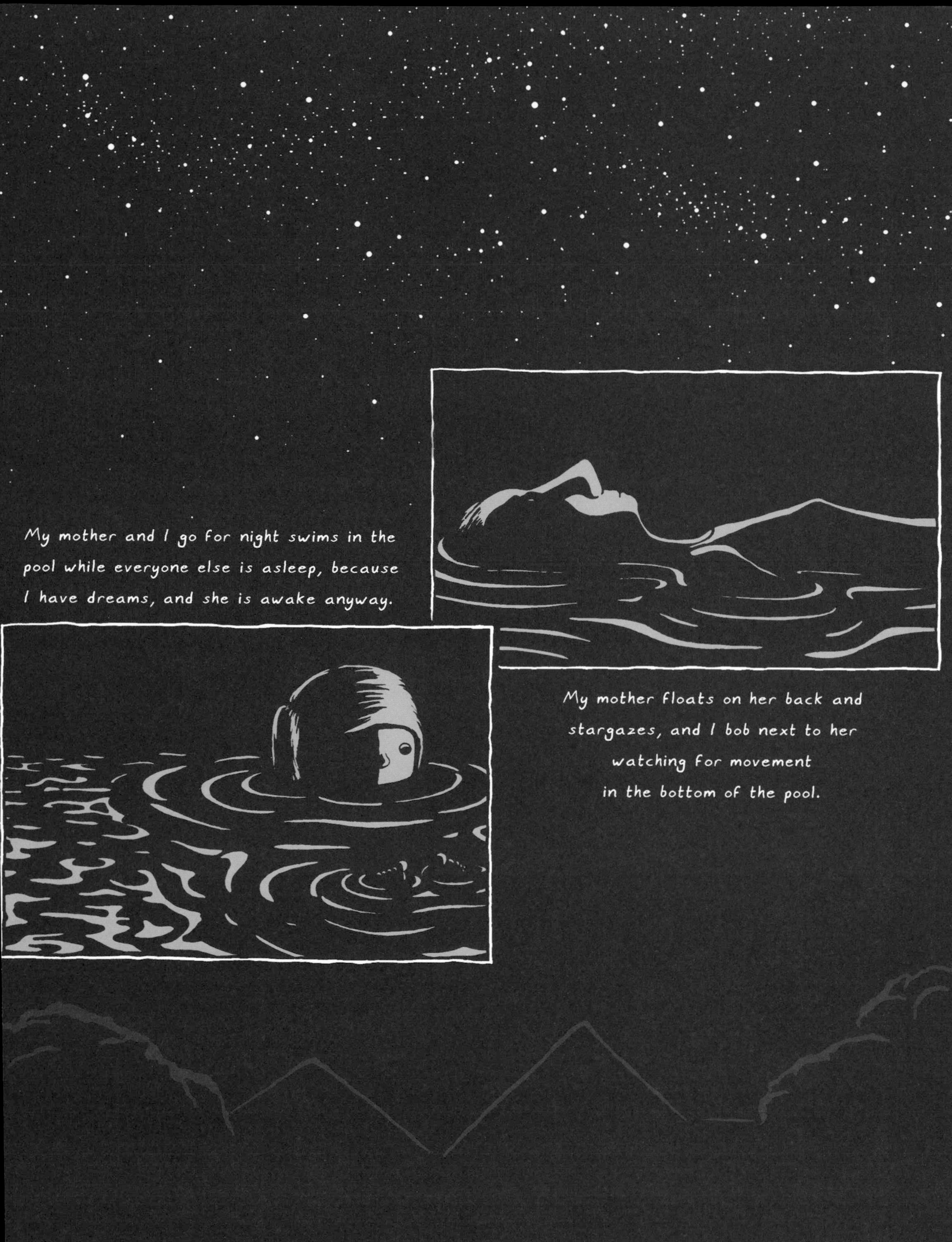
My mother and I go for night swims in the pool while everyone else is asleep, because I have dreams, and she is awake anyway.
My mother floats on her back and stargazes, and I bob next to her watching for movement in the bottom of the pool.

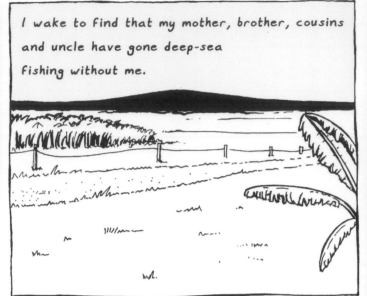
I wake to find that my mother, brother, cousins and uncle have gone deep-sea fishing without me.

They have deliberately snuck out because there isn't room for me in the boat.

And I am too small to be anything but in the way.

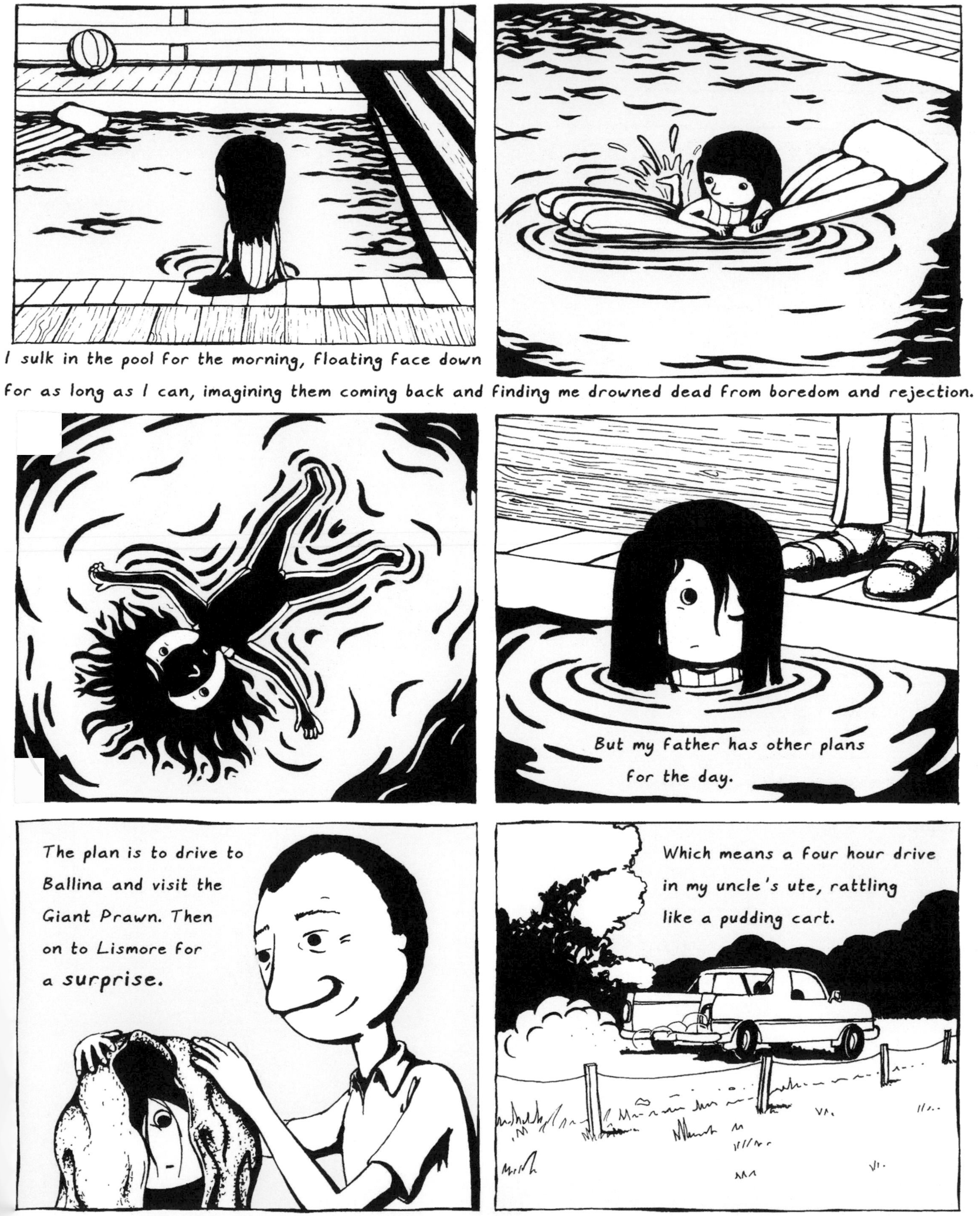
I sulk in the pool for the morning, floating face down
for as long as I can, imagining them coming back and finding me drowned dead from boredom and rejection.
But my father has other plans for the day.
The plan is to drive to Ballina and visit the Giant Prawn. Then on to Lismore for a surprise.
Which means a four hour drive in my uncle's ute, rattling like a pudding cart.

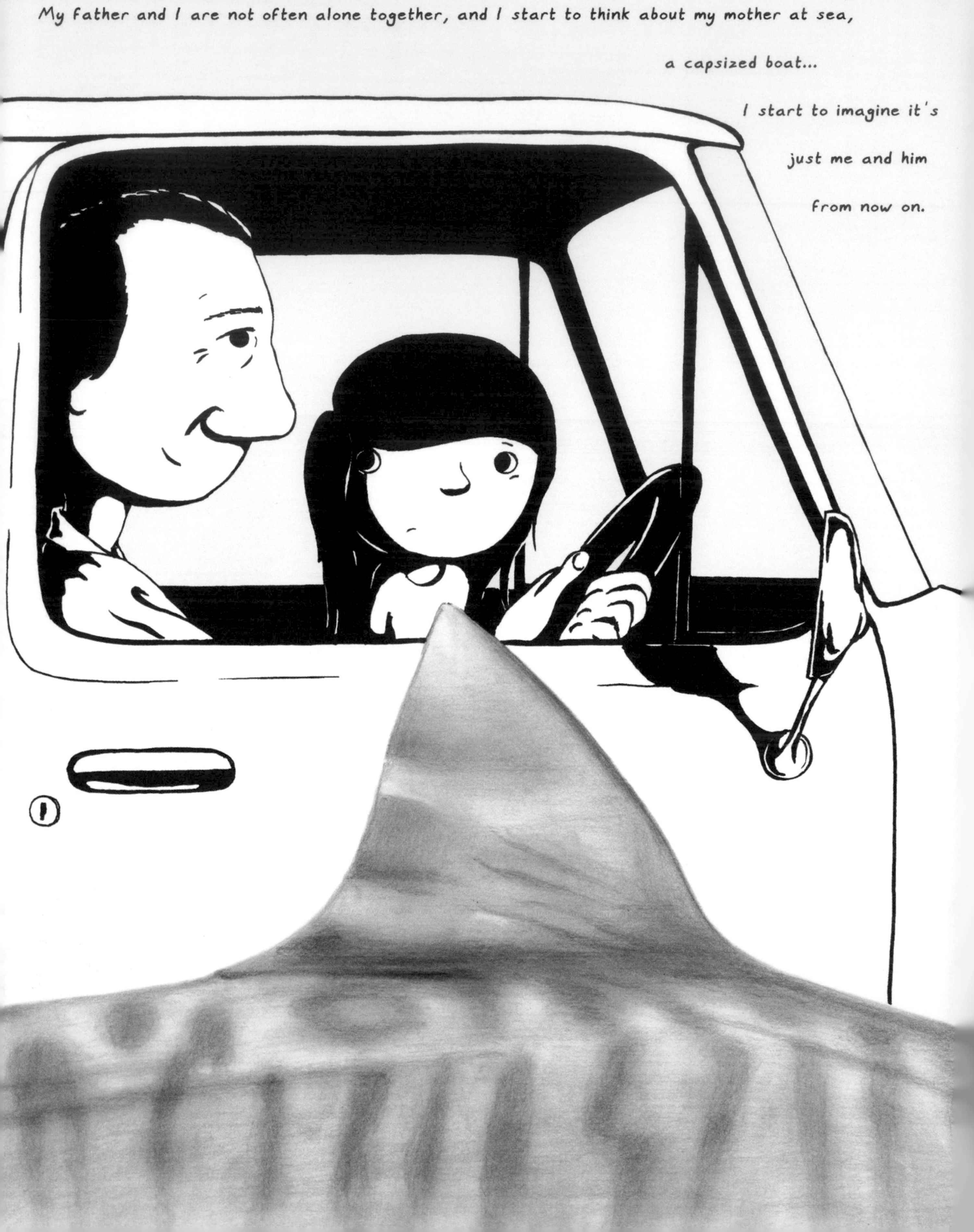
My father and I are not often alone together, and I start to think about my mother at sea,
a capsized boat...
I start to imagine it's
just me and him
from now on.

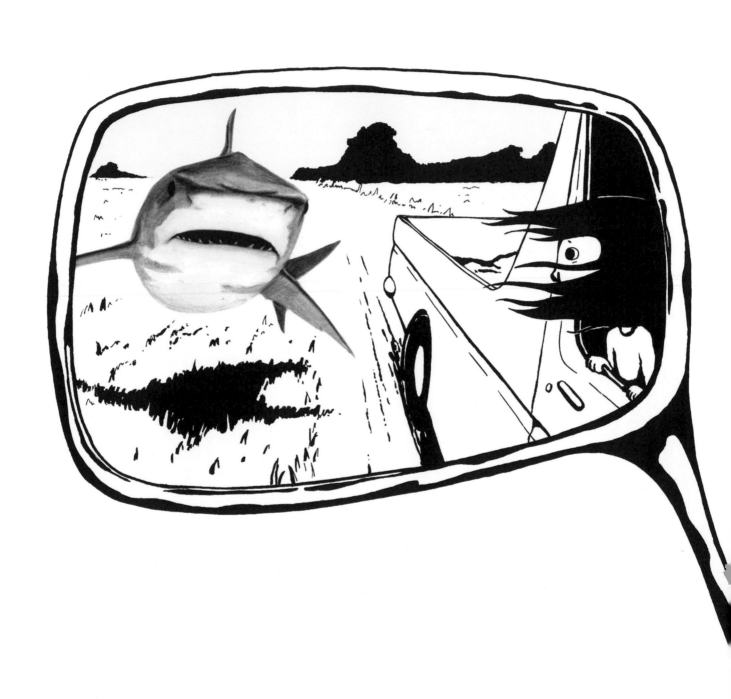

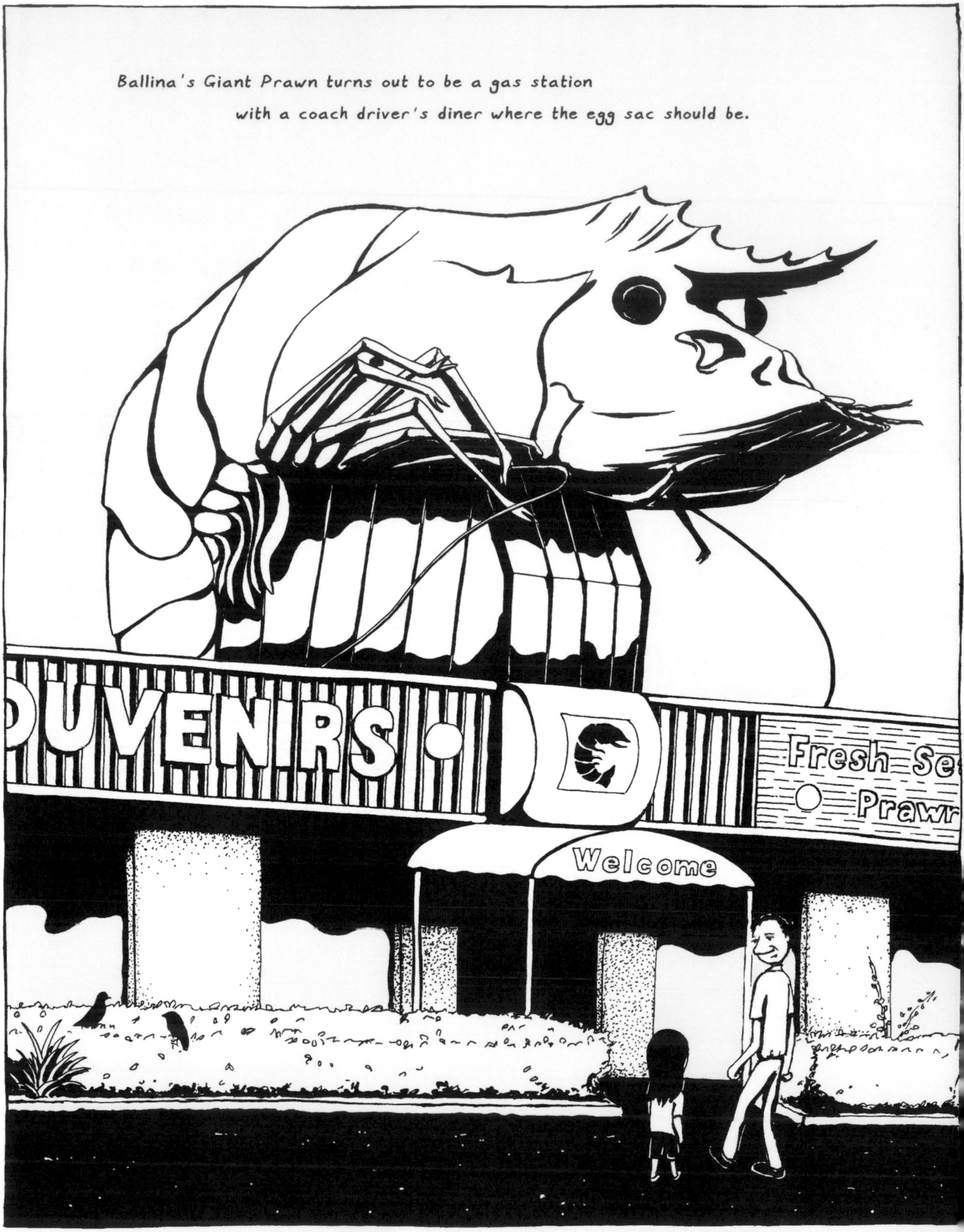
Ballina's Giant Prawn turns out to be a gas station
with a coach driver's diner where the egg sac should be.
UVENIRS
Fresh Se
Prawn
Welcome

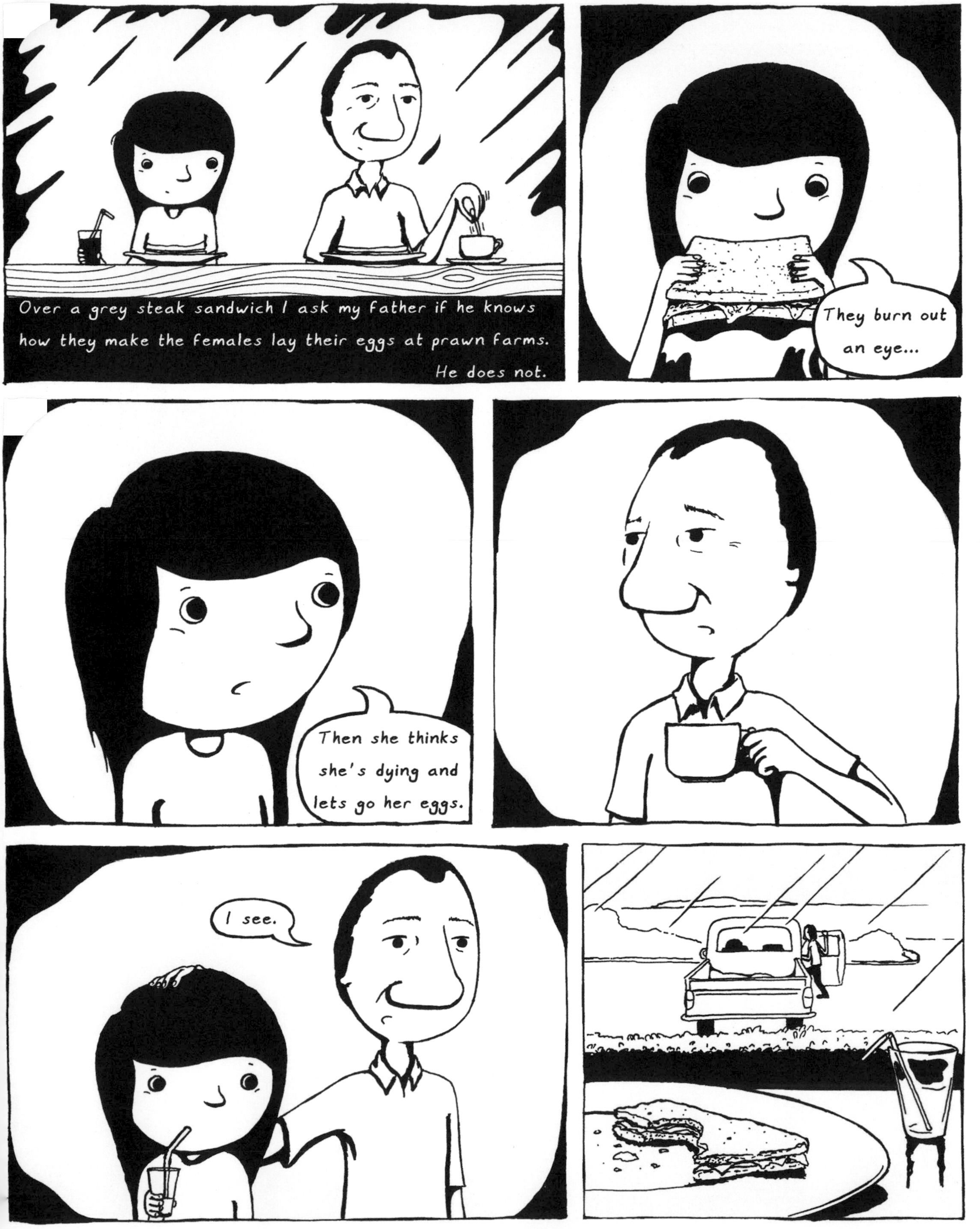
Over a grey steak sandwich I ask my father if he knows how they make the females lay their eggs at prawn farms.
He does not.
They burn out an eye...
Then she thinks she's dying and lets go her eggs.
I see.

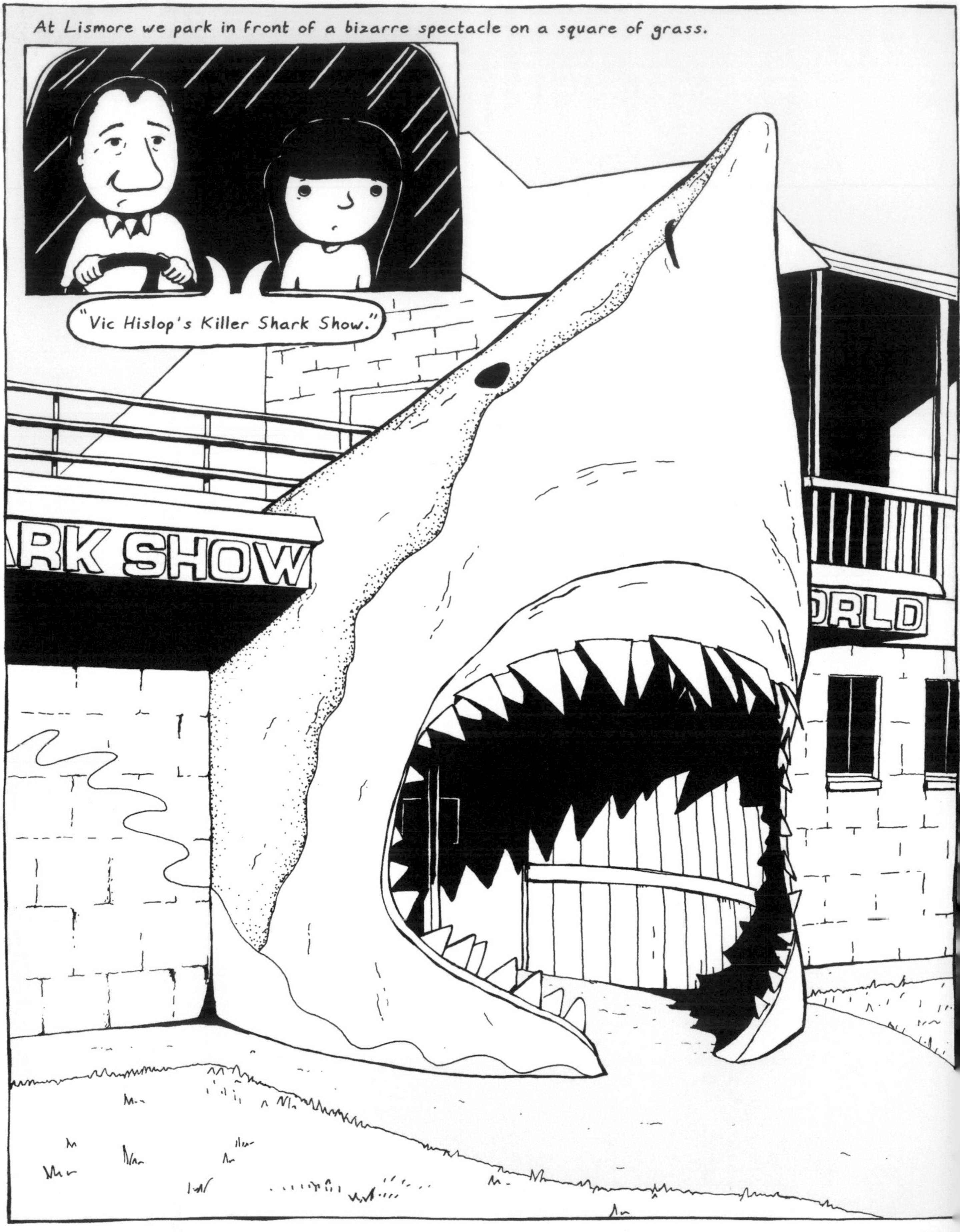
At Lismore we park in front of a bizarre spectacle on a square of grass.
"Vic Hislop's Killer Shark Show."
RK SHOW
ORLD

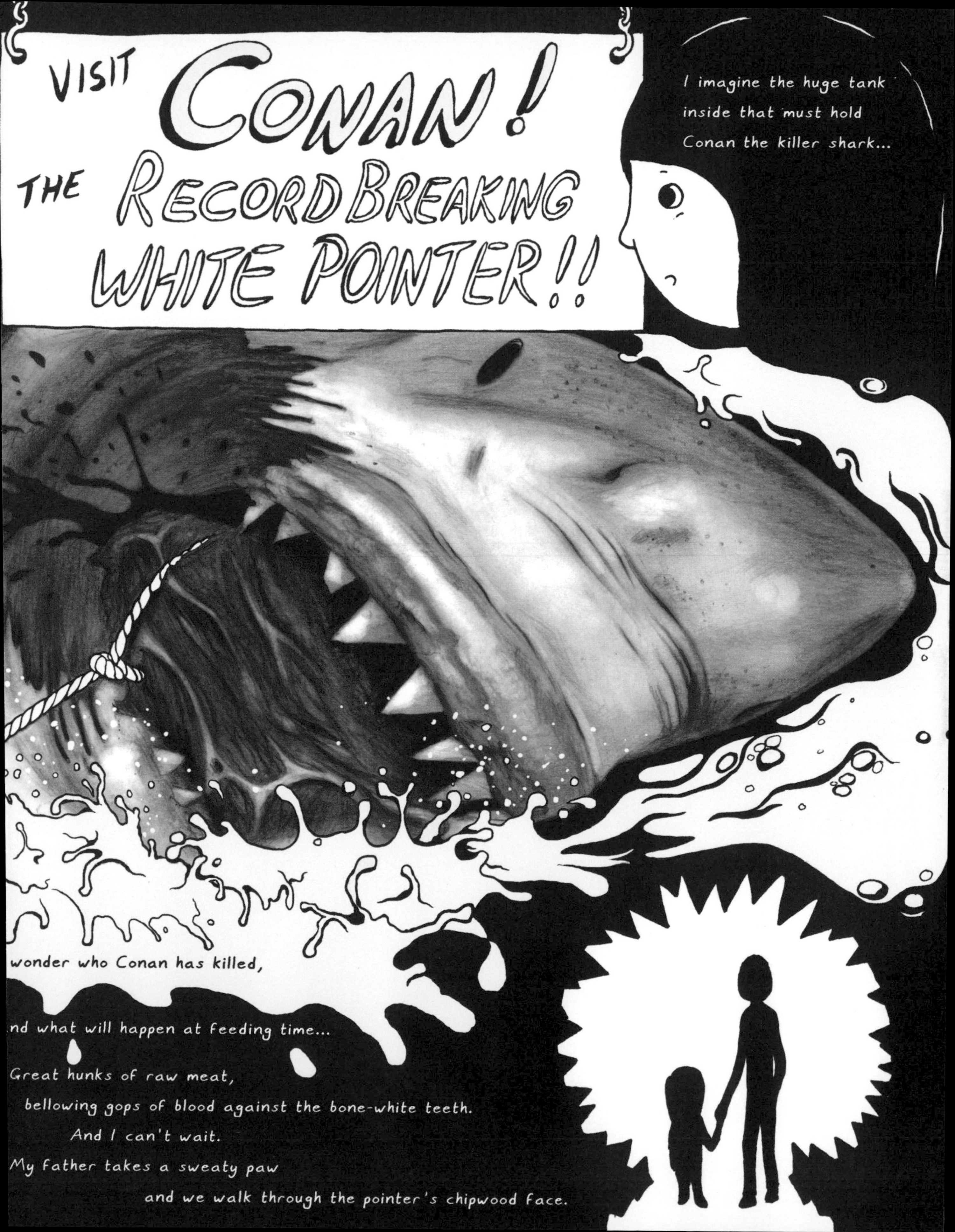
VISIT CONAN! THE RECORD BREAKING WHITE POINTER!!
I imagine the huge tank inside that must hold Conan the killer shark...
wonder who Conan has killed,
nd what will happen at feeding time...
Great hunks of raw meat,
bellowing gops of blood against the bone-white teeth.
And I can't wait.
My father takes a sweaty paw
and we walk through the pointer's chipwood face.

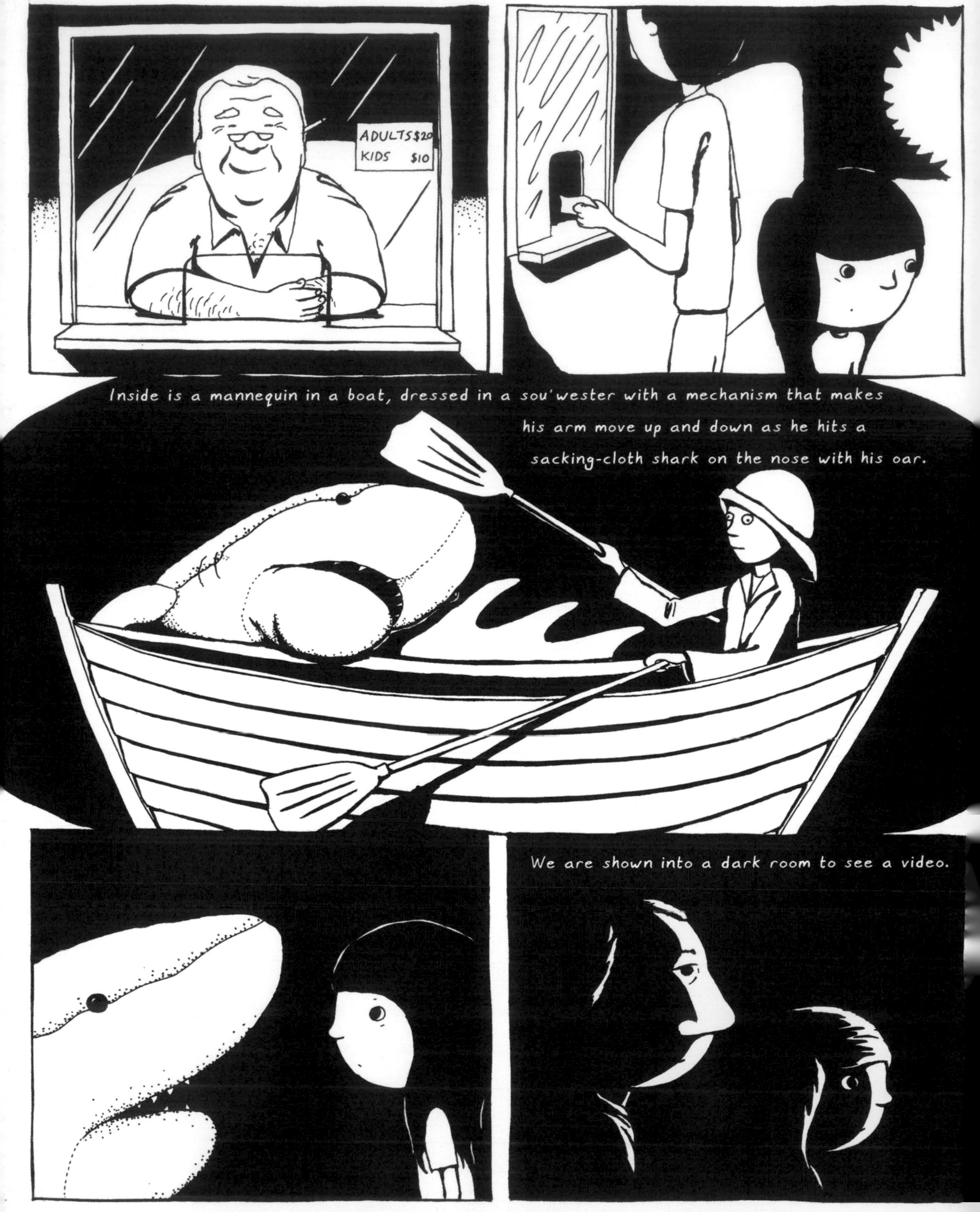
ADULTS $20
KIDS $10
Inside is a mannequin in a boat, dressed in a sou'wester with a mechanism that makes his arm move up and down as he hits a sacking-cloth shark on the nose with his oar.
We are shown into a dark room to see a video.

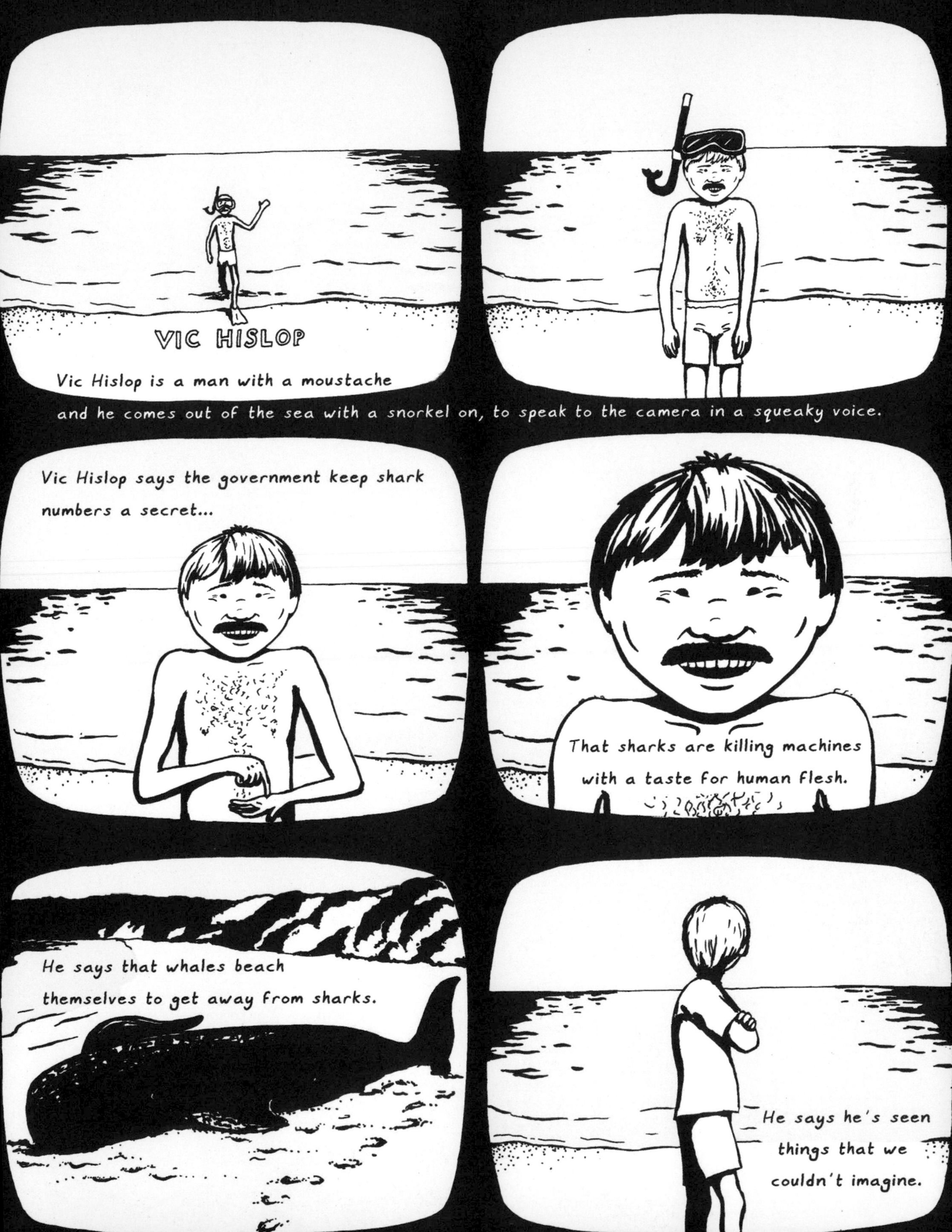
VIC HISLOP
Vic Hislop is a man with a moustache
and he comes out of the sea with a snorkel on, to speak to the camera in a squeaky voice.
Vic Hislop says the government keep shark numbers a secret...
That sharks are killing machines with a taste for human flesh.
He says that whales beach themselves to get away from sharks.
He says he's seen things that we couldn't imagine.

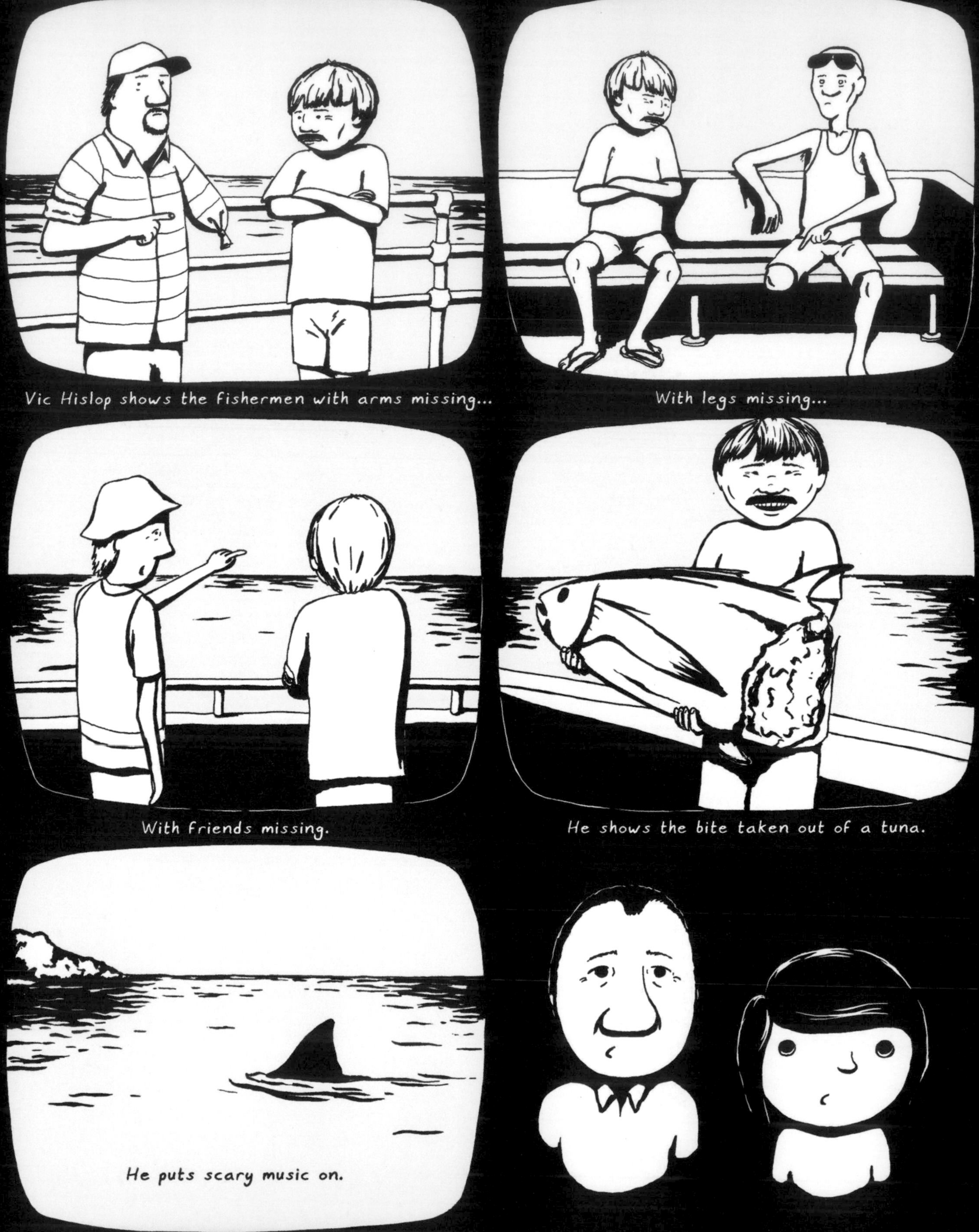
Vic Hislop shows the fishermen with arms missing...
With legs missing...
With friends missing.
He shows the bite taken out of a tuna.
He puts scary music on.

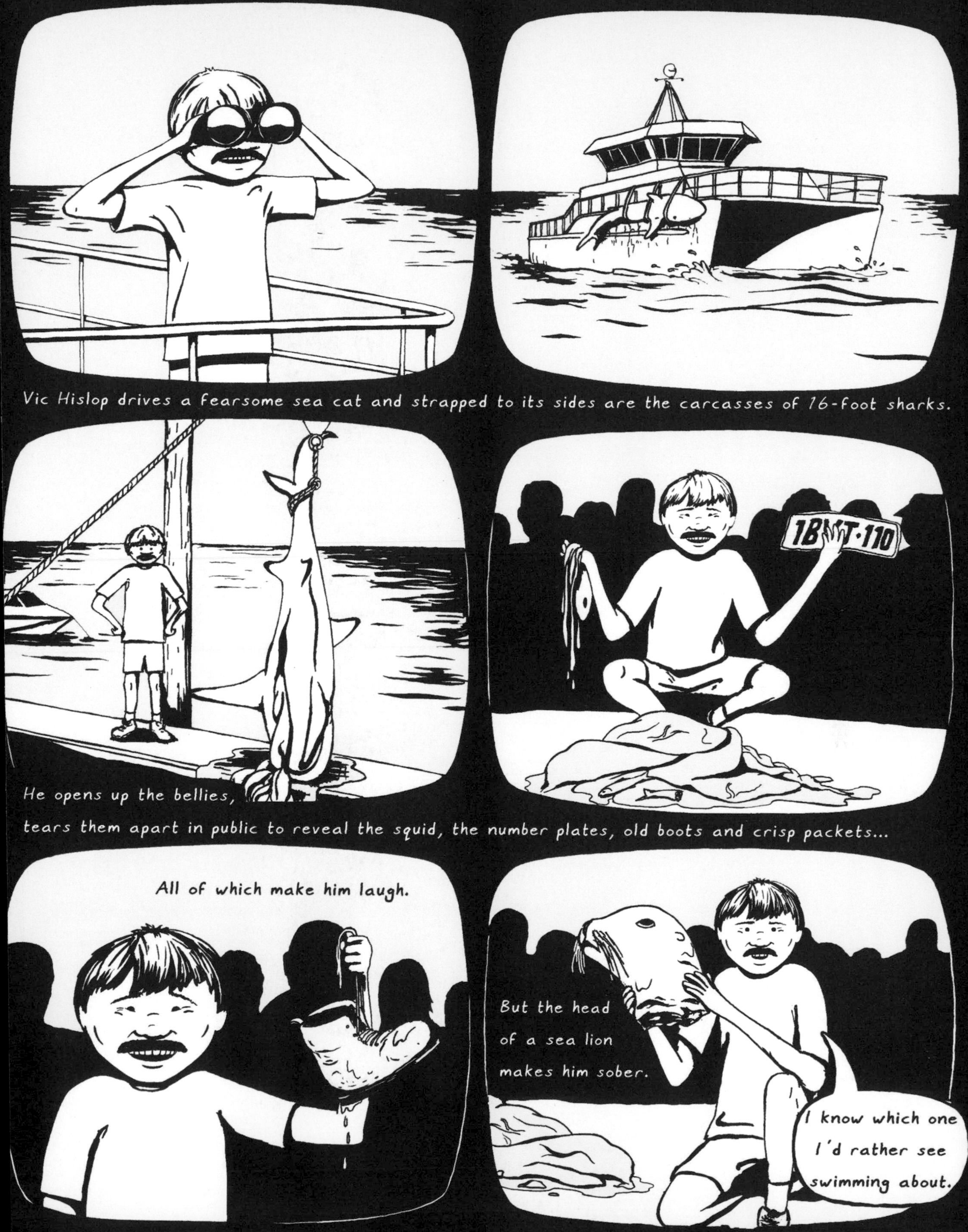
Vic Hislop drives a fearsome sea cat and strapped to its sides are the carcasses of 16-foot sharks.
He opens up the bellies,
tears them apart in public to reveal the squid, the number plates, old boots and crisp packets...
All of which make him laugh.
But the head of a sea lion makes him sober.
I know which one I'd rather see swimming about.

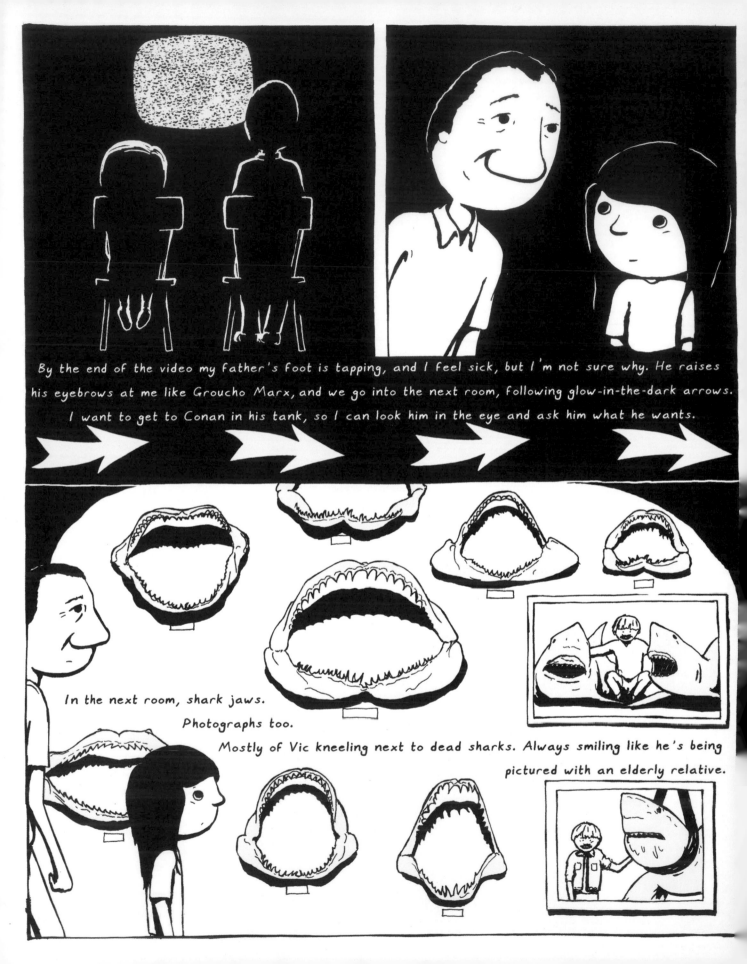

By the end of the video my father's foot is tapping, and I feel sick, but I'm not sure why. He raises his eyebrows at me like Groucho Marx, and we go into the next room, following glow-in-the-dark arrows. I want to get to Conan in his tank, so I can look him in the eye and ask him what he wants.

In the next room, shark jaws.

Photographs too.

Mostly of Vic kneeling next to dead sharks. Always smiling like he's being pictured with an elderly relative.

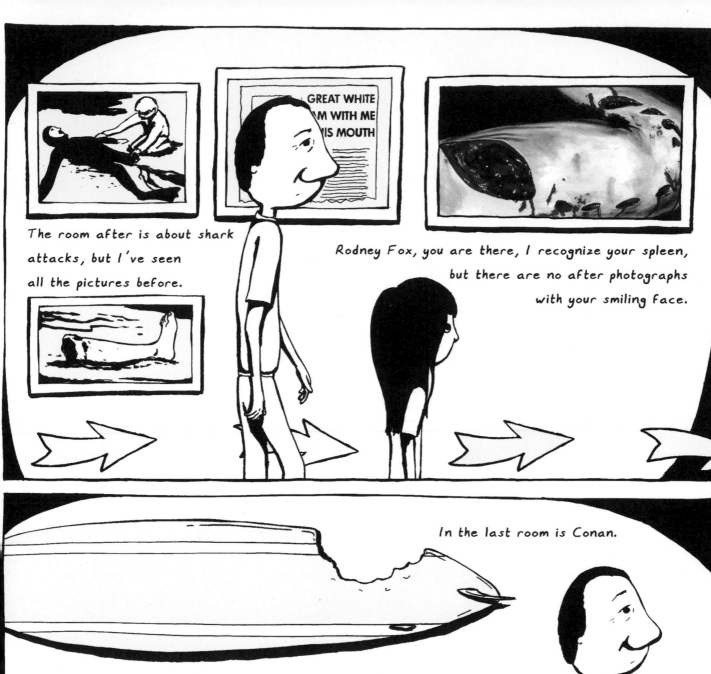

The room after is about shark attacks, but I've seen all the pictures before.

Rodney Fox, you are there, I recognize your spleen, but there are no after photographs with your smiling face.

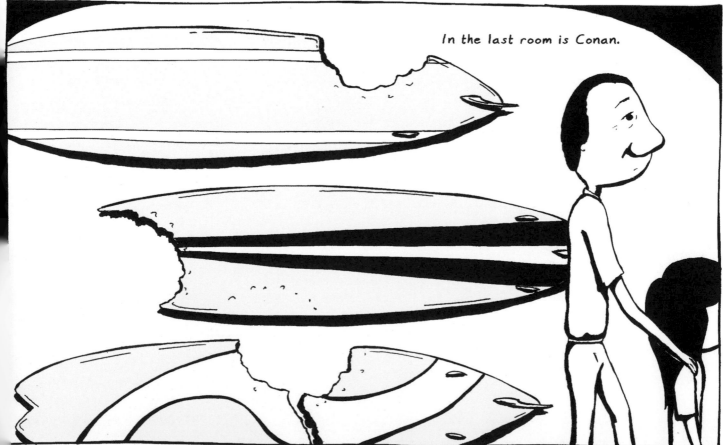

In the last room is Conan.

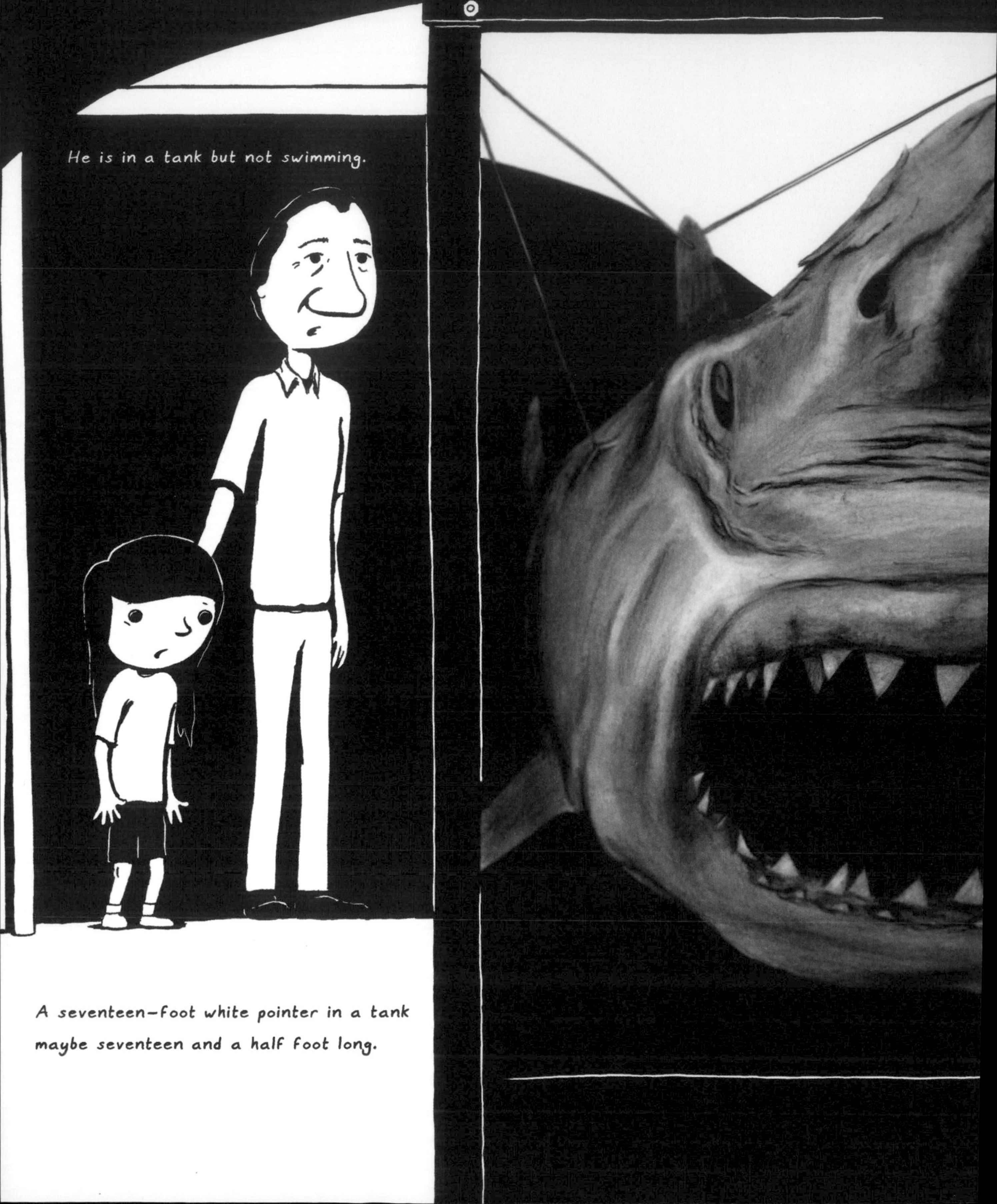
He is in a tank but not swimming.
A seventeen-foot white pointer in a tank maybe seventeen and a half foot long.

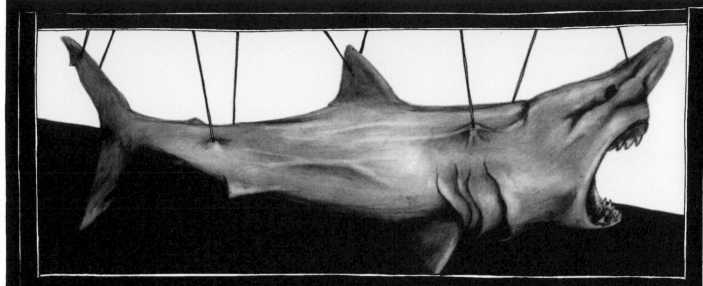

Wires shot into his head, back and tail keep him suspended in a liquid the colour of tobacco teeth. Parts of him have flaked away, and his skin has turned from grey blue to brown.

There's a bad smell in the room.

I don't feel good.

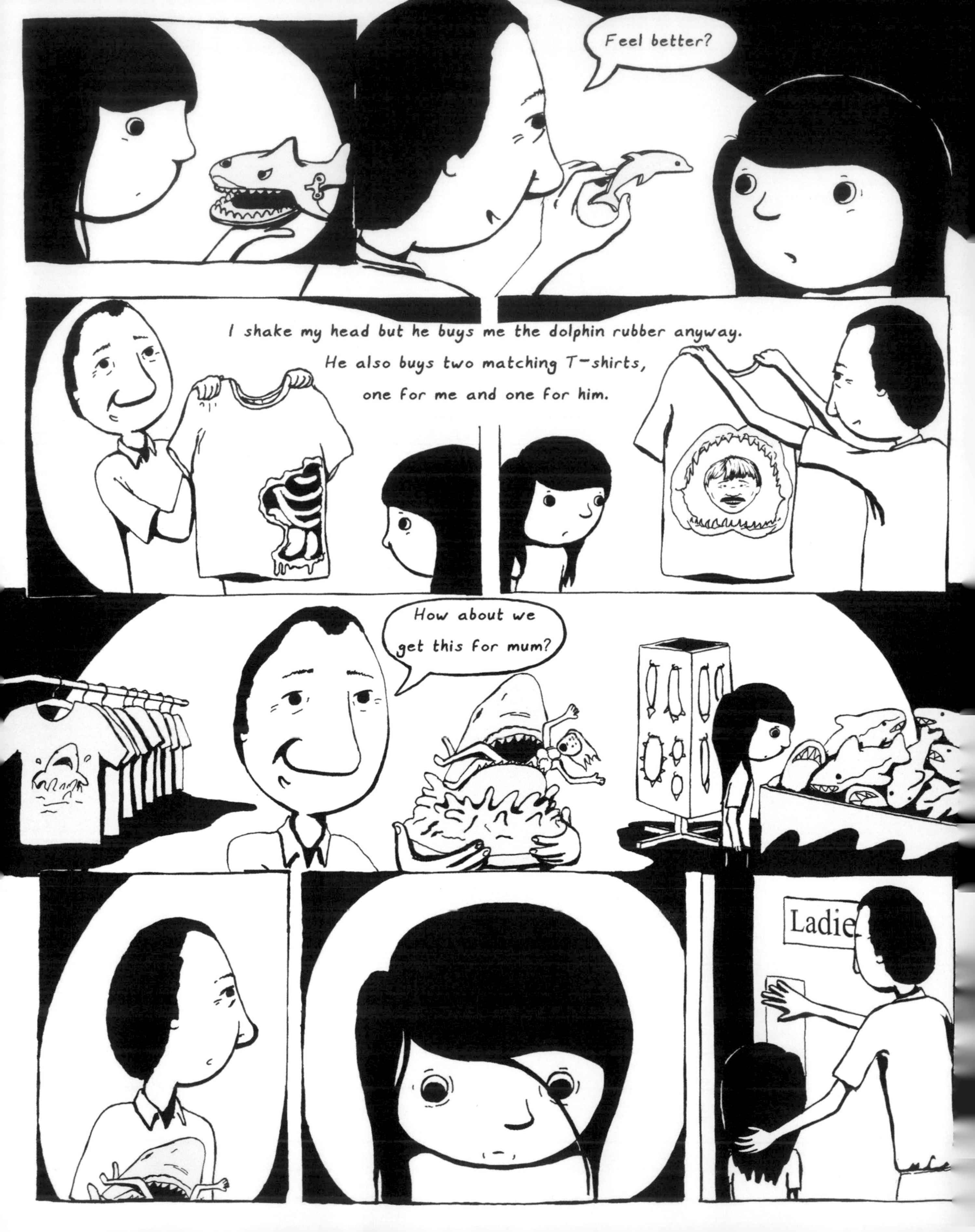
Feel better?
I shake my head but he buys me the dolphin rubber anyway.
He also buys two matching T-shirts,
one for me and one for him.
How about we get this for mum?
Ladie

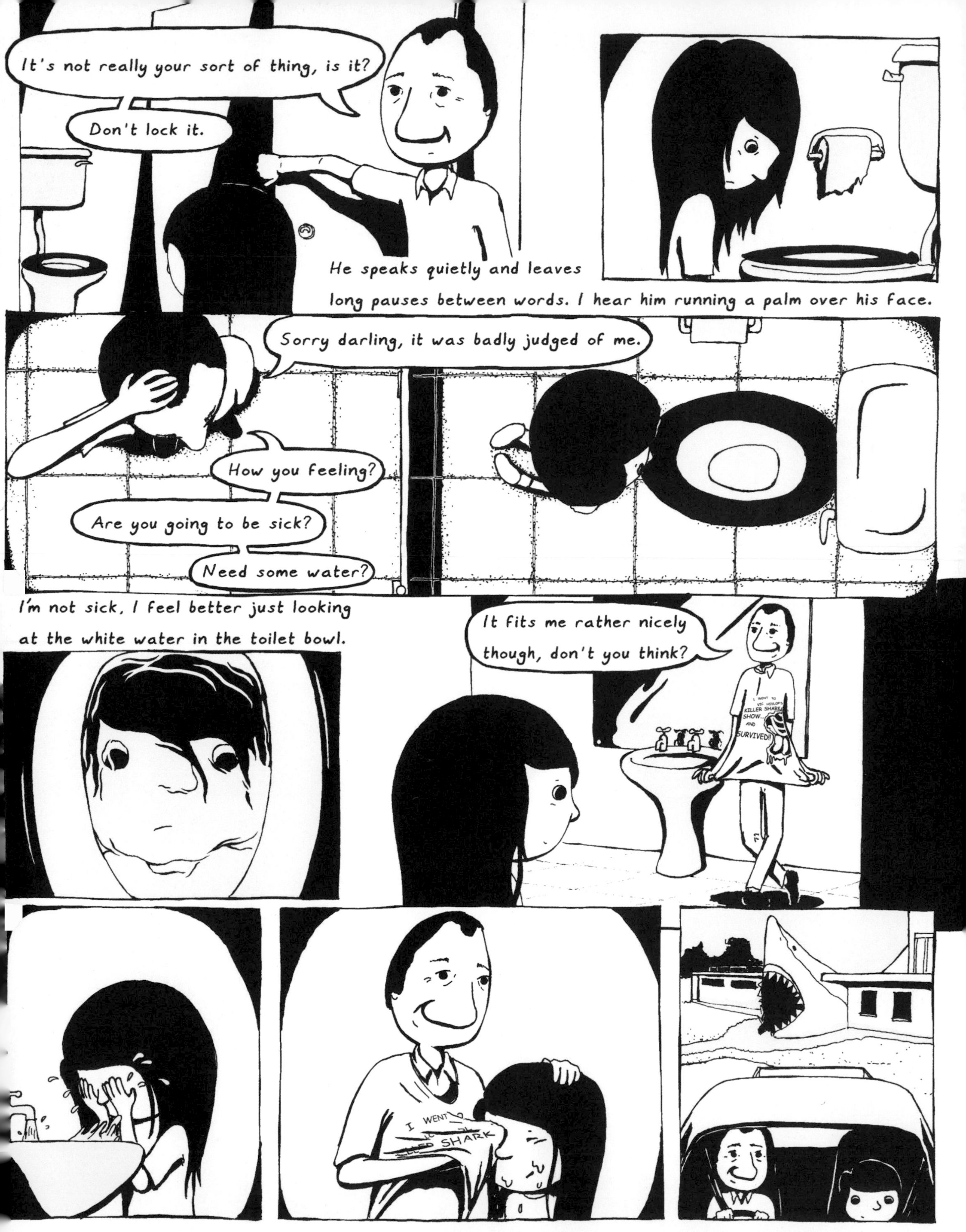
It's not really your sort of thing, is it?
Don't lock it.
He speaks quietly and leaves long pauses between words. I hear him running a palm over his face.
Sorry darling, it was badly judged of me.
How you feeling?
Are you going to be sick?
Need some water?
I'm not sick, I feel better just looking at the white water in the toilet bowl.
It fits me rather nicely though, don't you think?
I WENT TO VIC HISLOP'S KILLER SHARK SHOW... AND SURVIVED!!

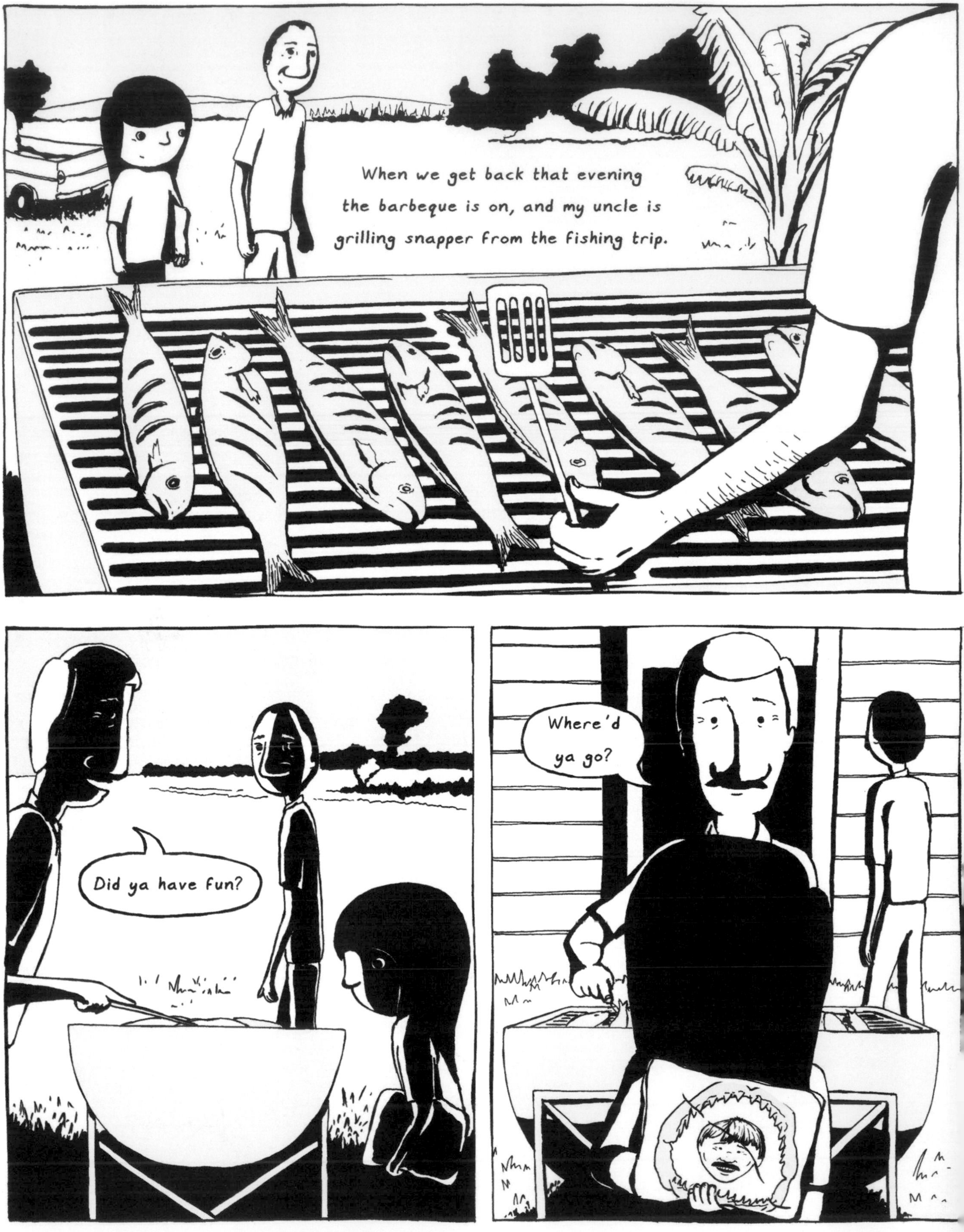
When we get back that evening the barbeque is on, and my uncle is grilling snapper from the fishing trip.
Did ya have fun?
Where'd ya go?

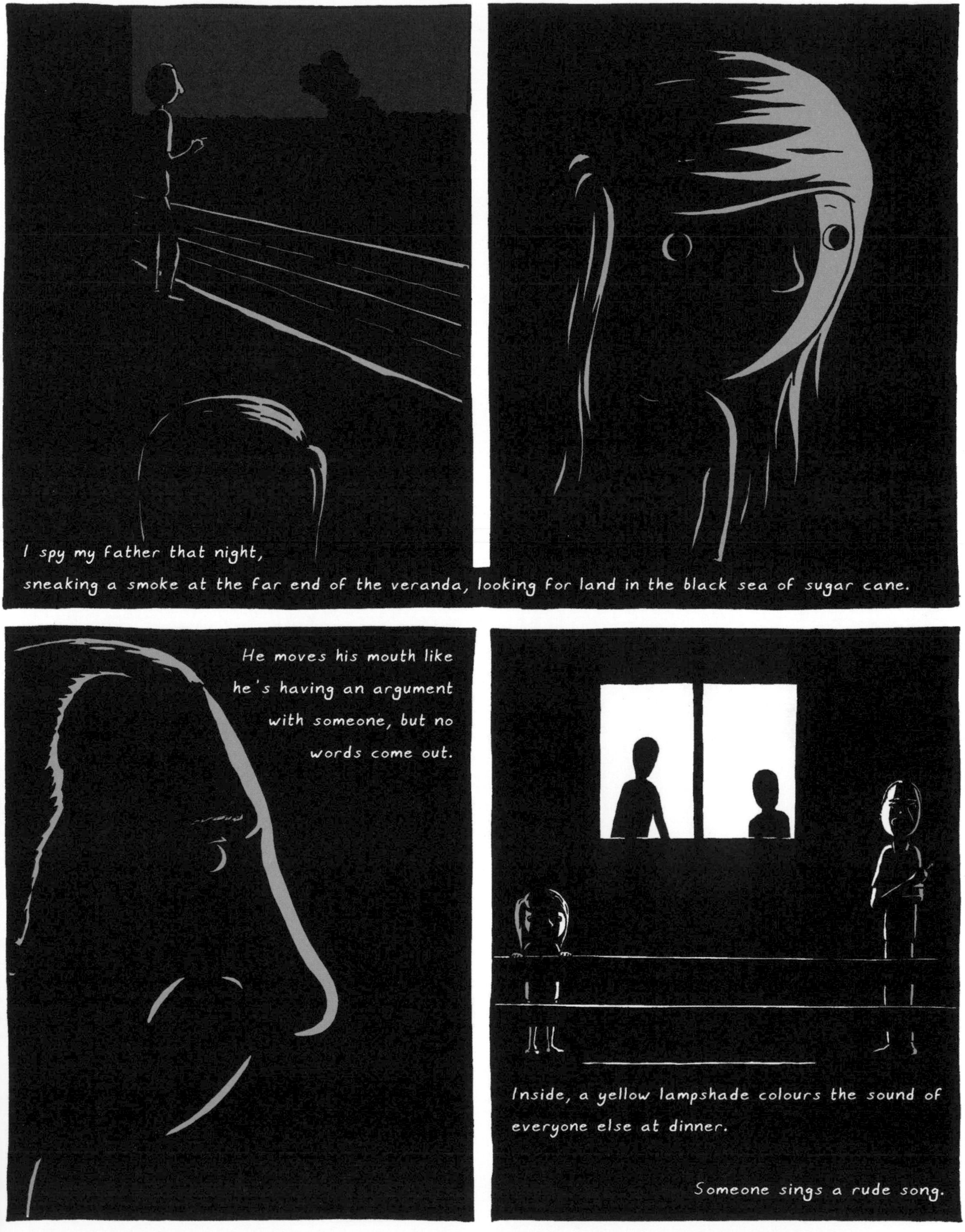
I spy my father that night,
sneaking a smoke at the far end of the veranda, looking for land in the black sea of sugar cane.
He moves his mouth like he's having an argument with someone, but no words come out.
Inside, a yellow lampshade colours the sound of everyone else at dinner.
Someone sings a rude song.

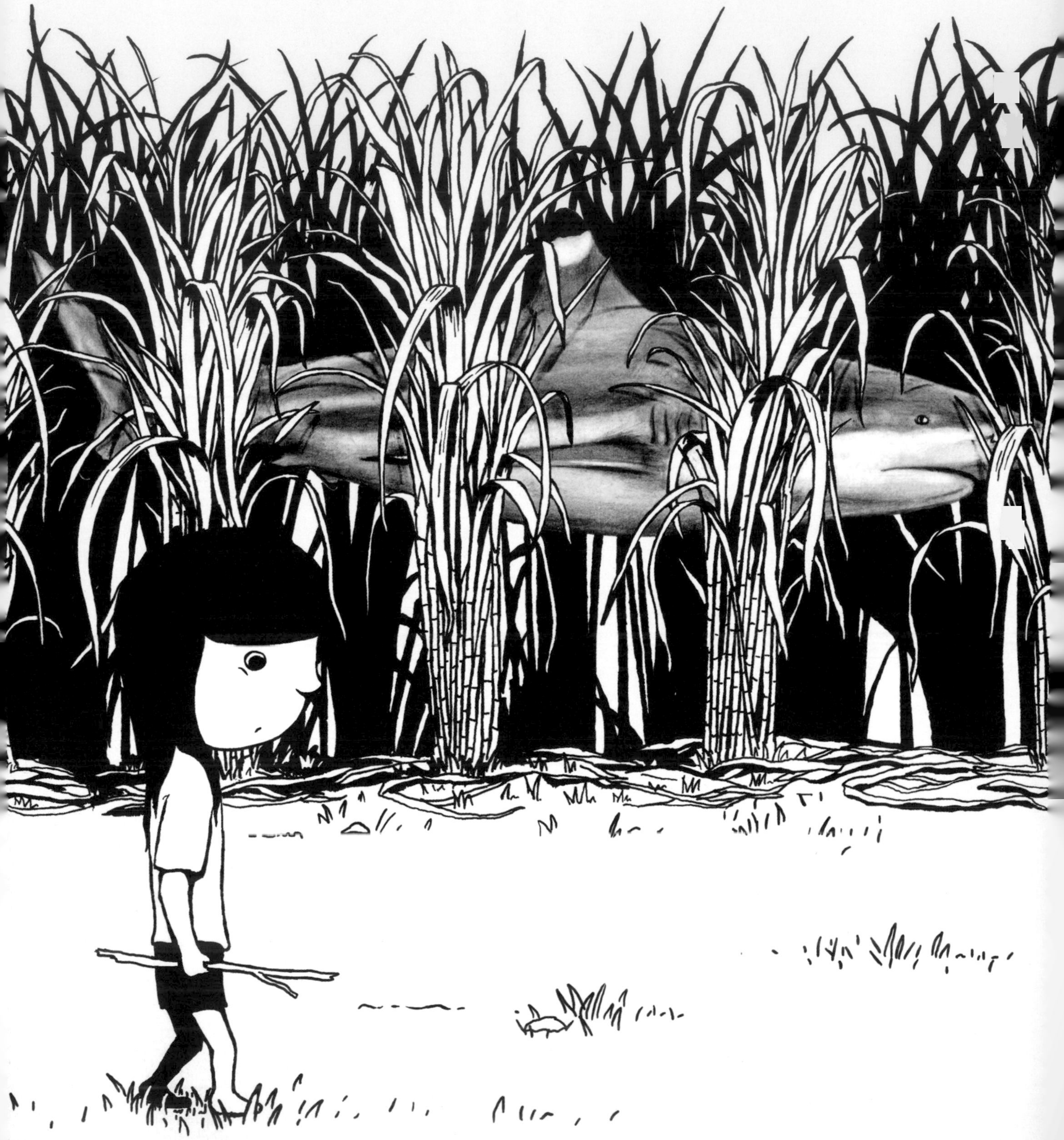

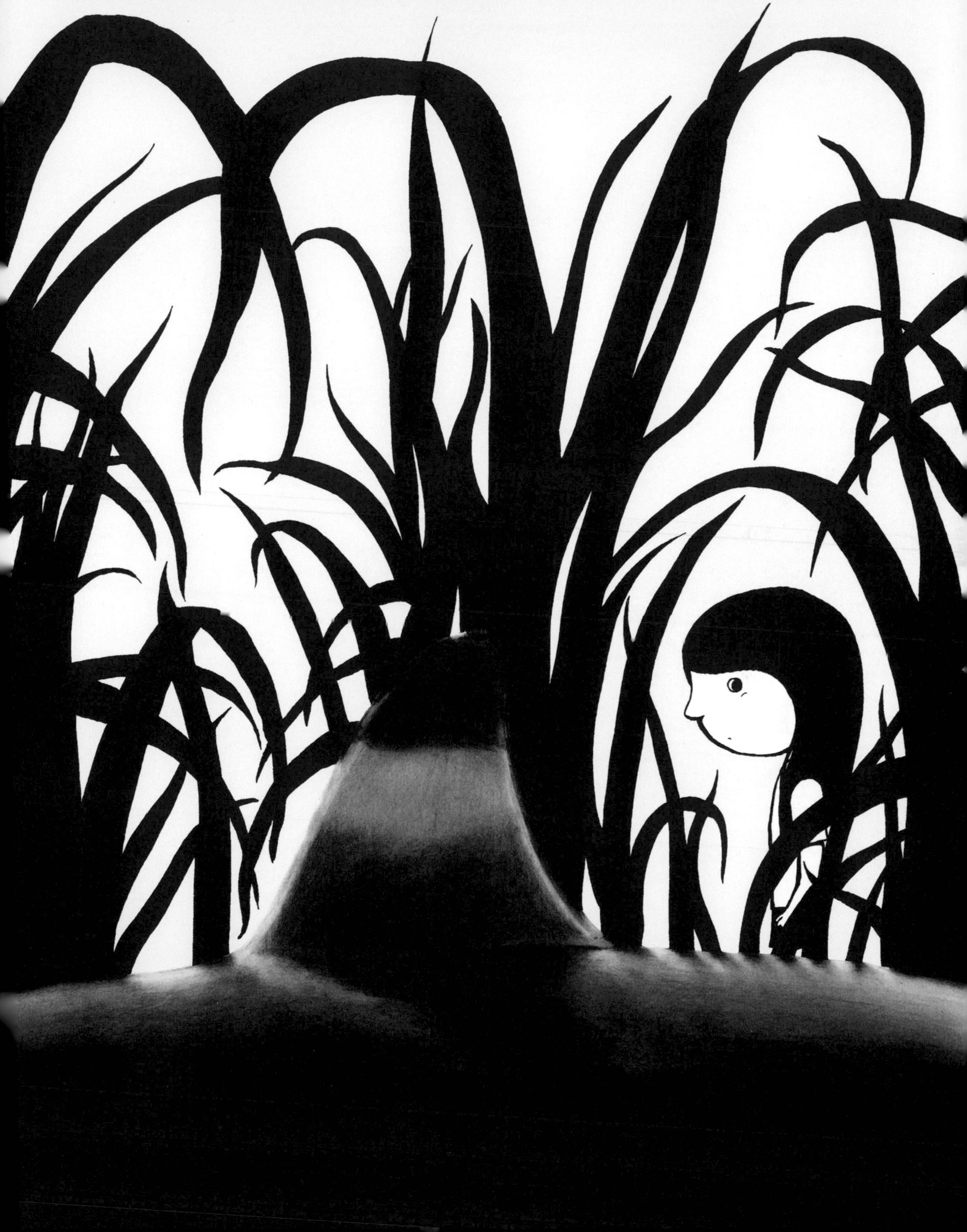

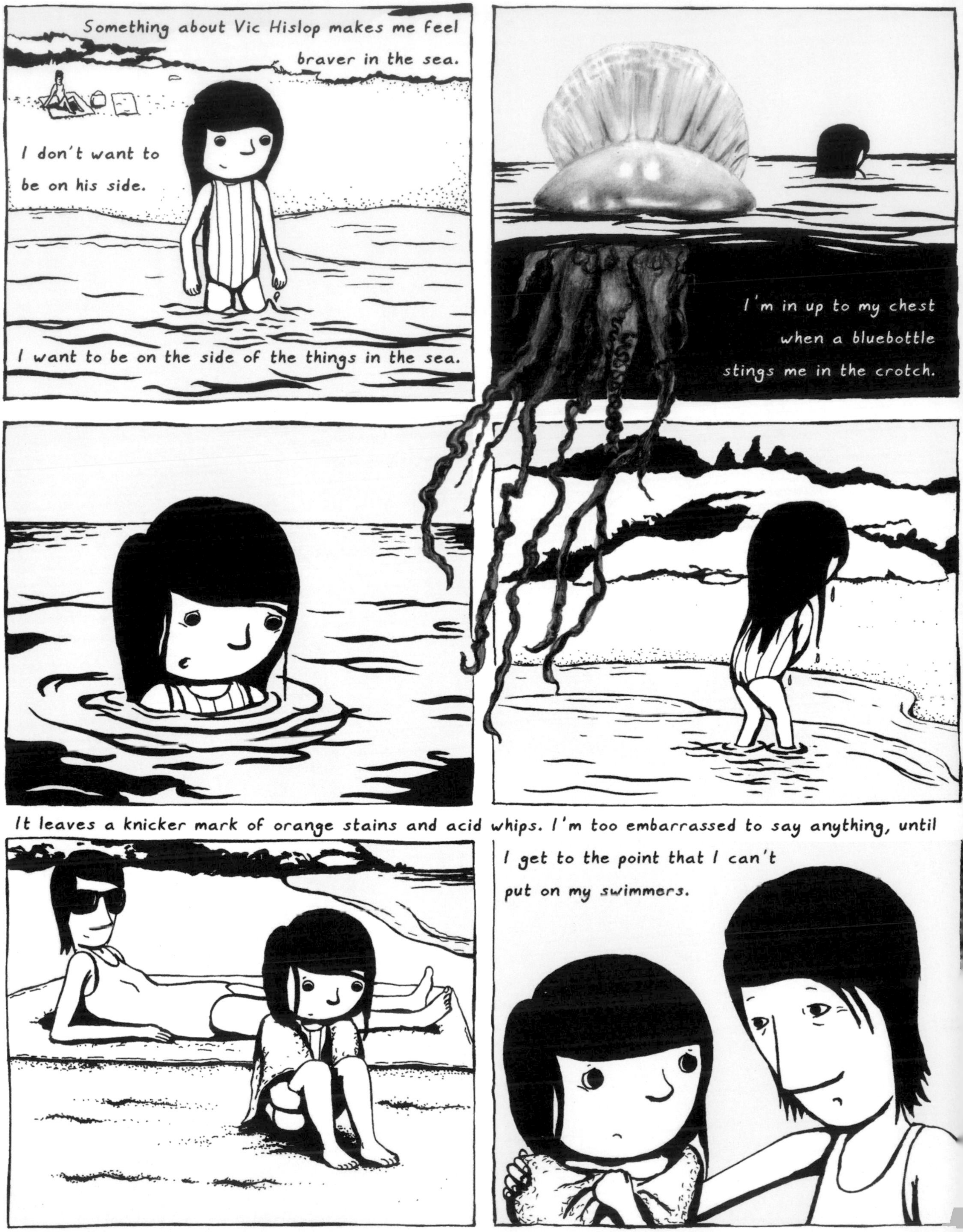
Something about Vic Hislop makes me feel
braver in the sea.
I don't want to be on his side.
I want to be on the side of the things in the sea.
I'm in up to my chest
when a bluebottle
stings me in the crotch.
It leaves a knicker mark of orange stains and acid whips. I'm too embarrassed to say anything, until
I get to the point that I can't
put on my swimmers.

What follows

is a humiliating trip to the doctor, who, in trying to get a smile out of me, suggests weeing on the stings.

I stare at him in silence, wondering if he will use his own urine.

In the end he gives us some cream, instructions not to go in the sea for a week, and a badge...

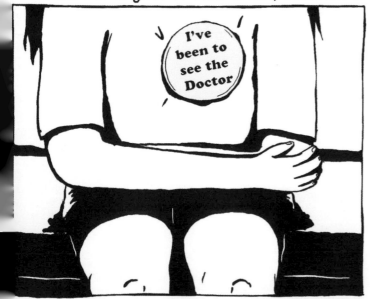

I've been to see the Doctor

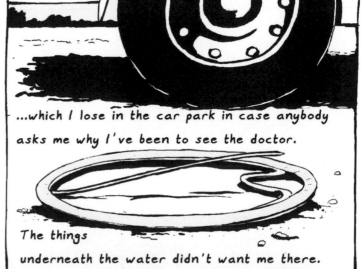

...which I lose in the car park in case anybody asks me why I've been to see the doctor.

The things underneath the water didn't want me there.

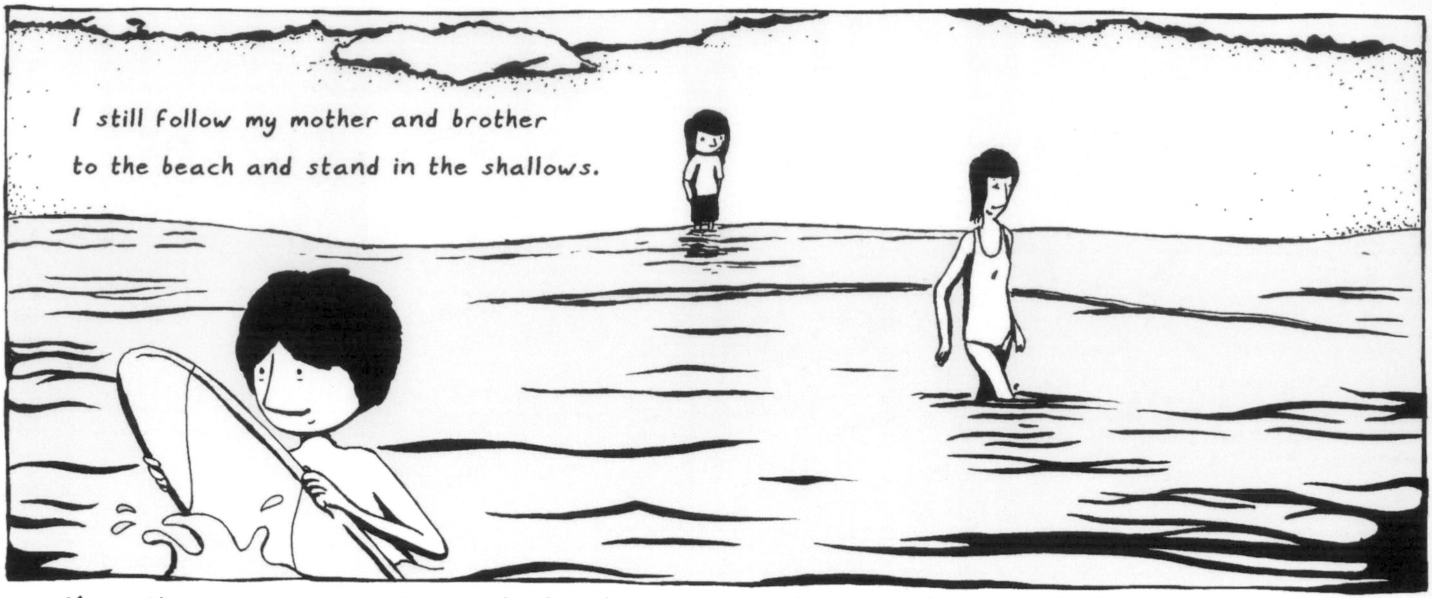
I still follow my mother and brother
to the beach and stand in the shallows.

My mother never goes out past the breakers, except this once, because she has turned forty.

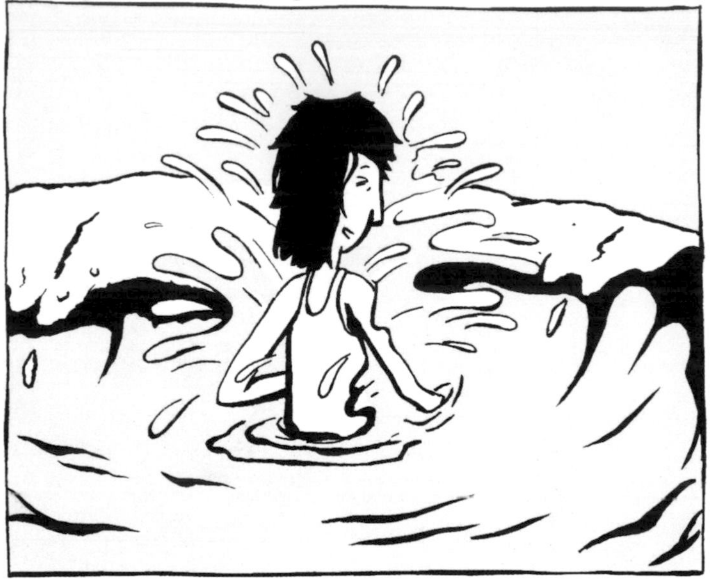

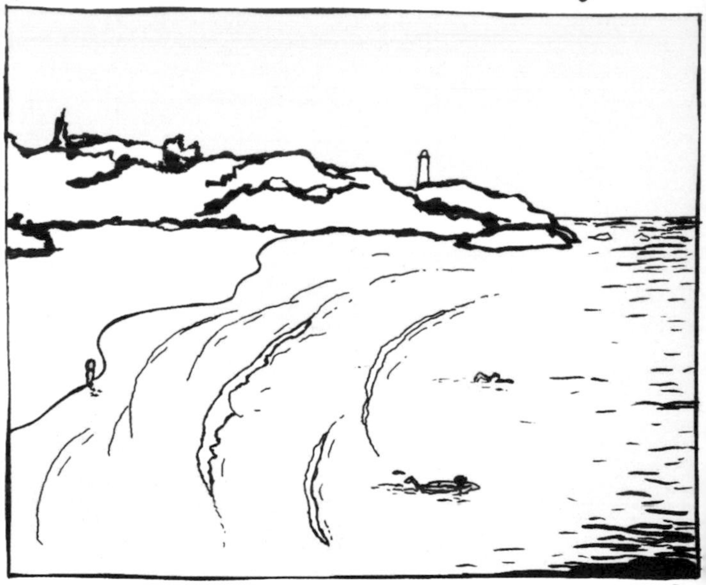

She strides out with my brother and catches a big wave in, her mouth a big rectangle of smile.

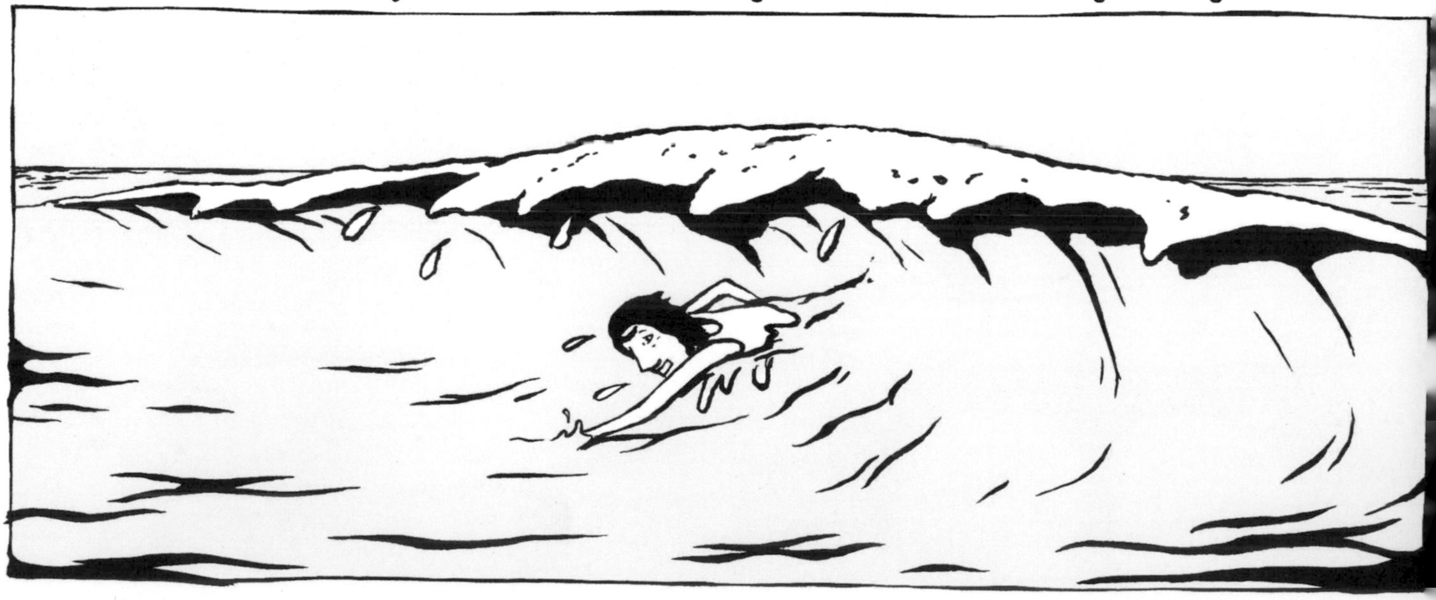

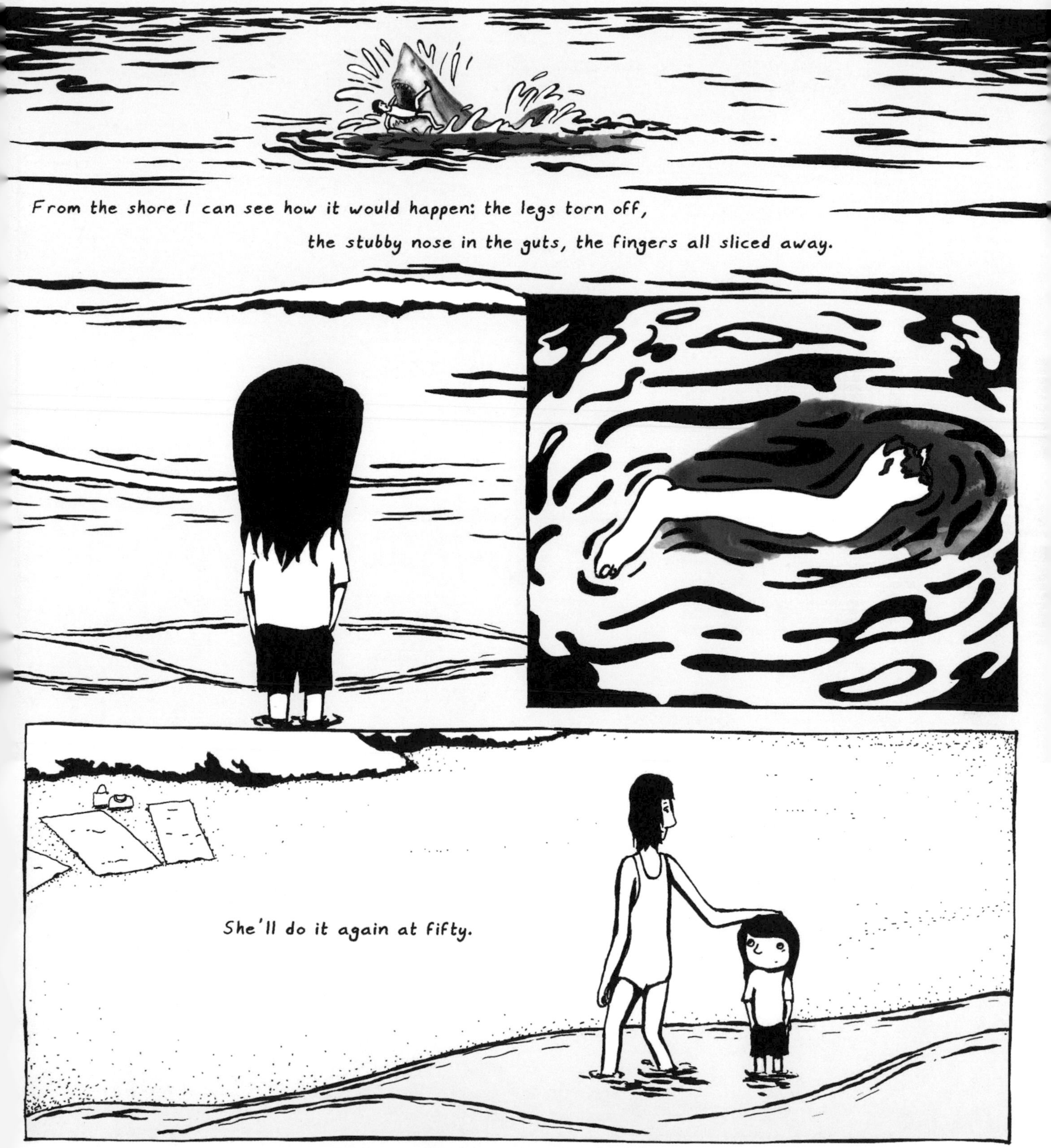
From the shore I can see how it would happen: the legs torn off,
the stubby nose in the guts, the fingers all sliced away.
She'll do it again at fifty.

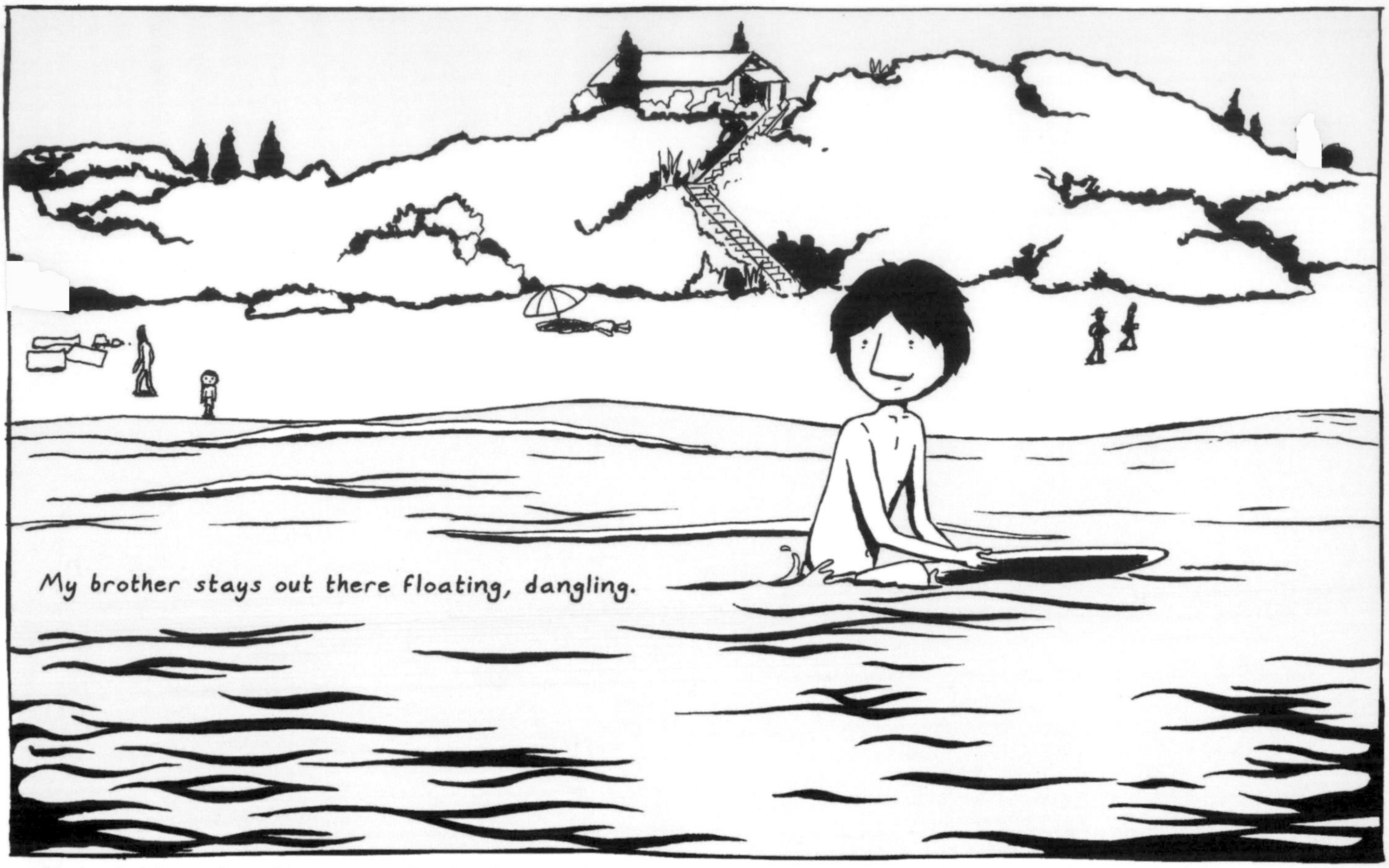
My brother stays out there floating, dangling.

He's told me he often sees dark shapes darting out of the corner of his eye, but they are porpoise.

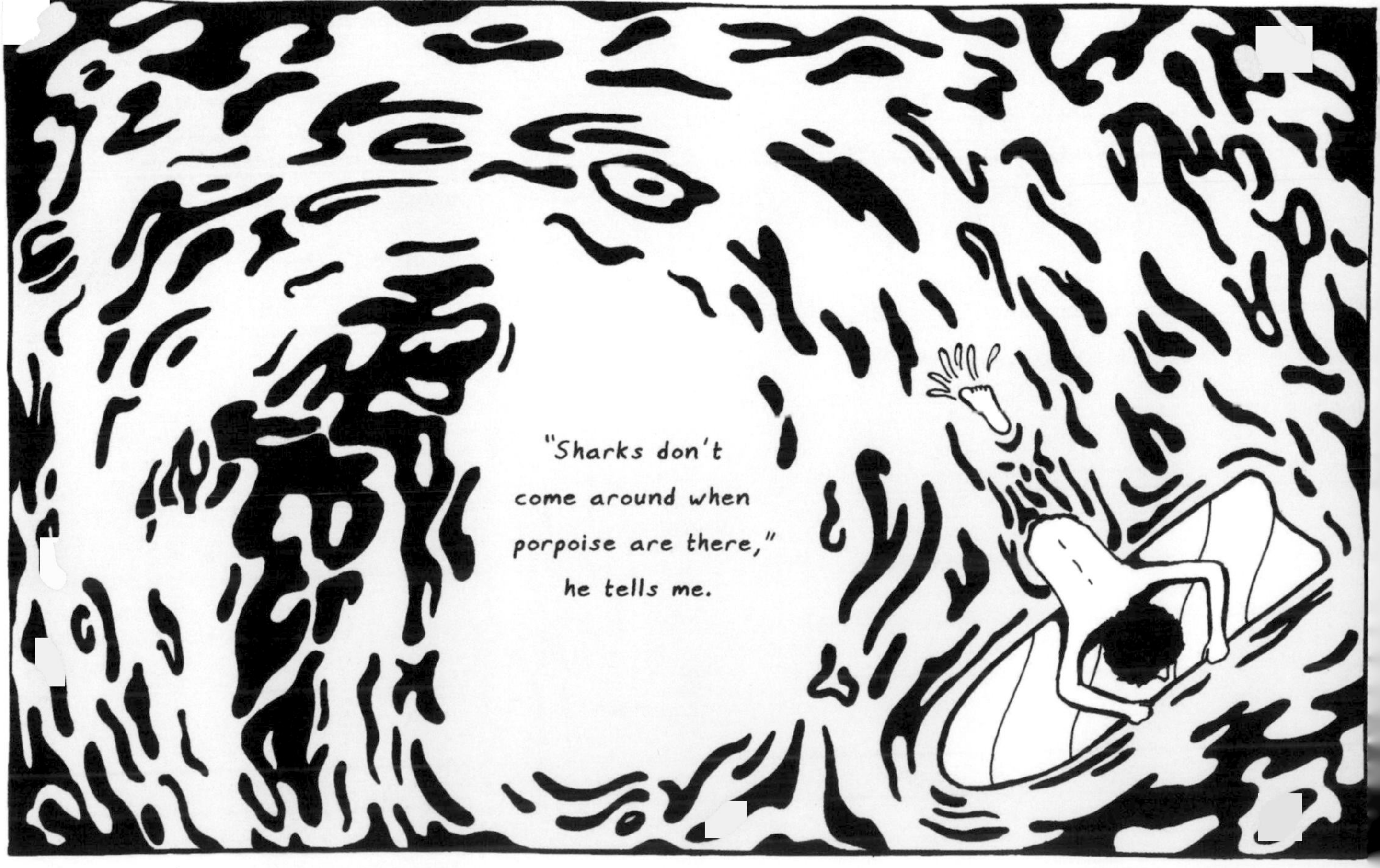
"Sharks don't come around when porpoise are there," he tells me.

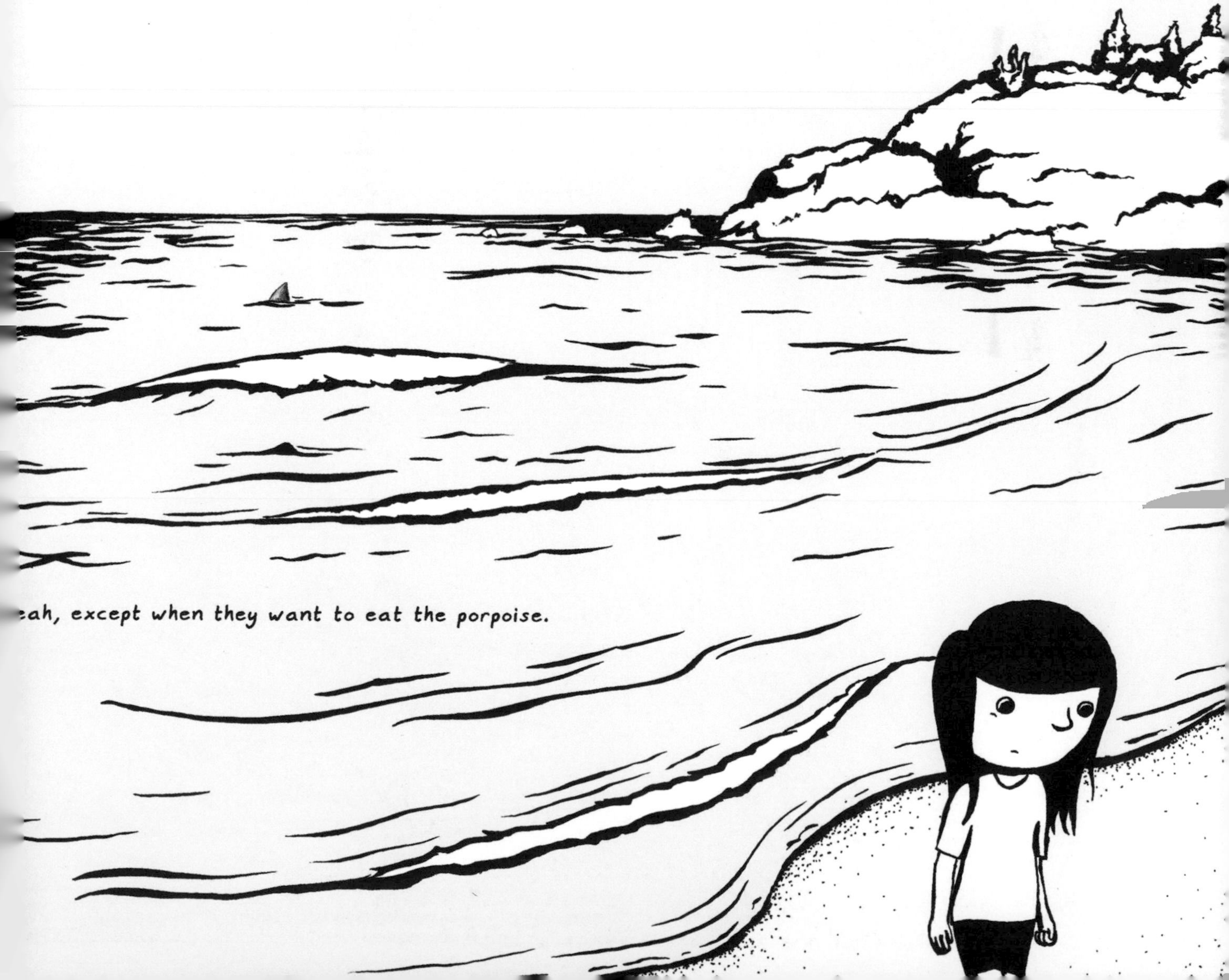
ah, except when they want to eat the porpoise.

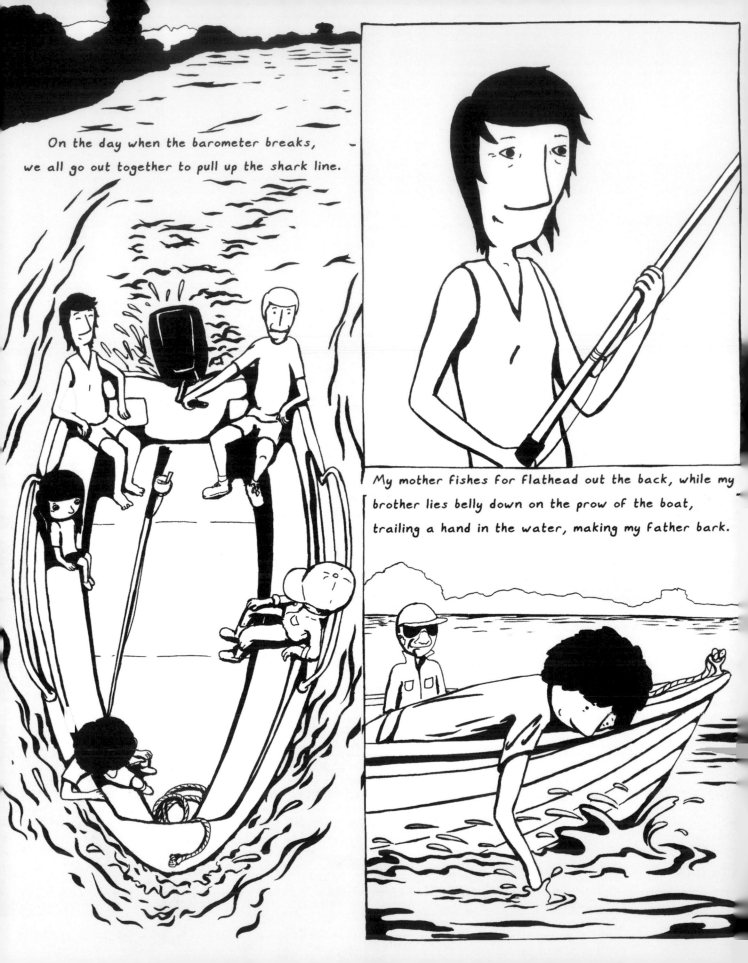

On the day when the barometer breaks,
we all go out together to pull up the shark line.

My mother fishes for flathead out the back, while my
brother lies belly down on the prow of the boat,
trailing a hand in the water, making my father bark.

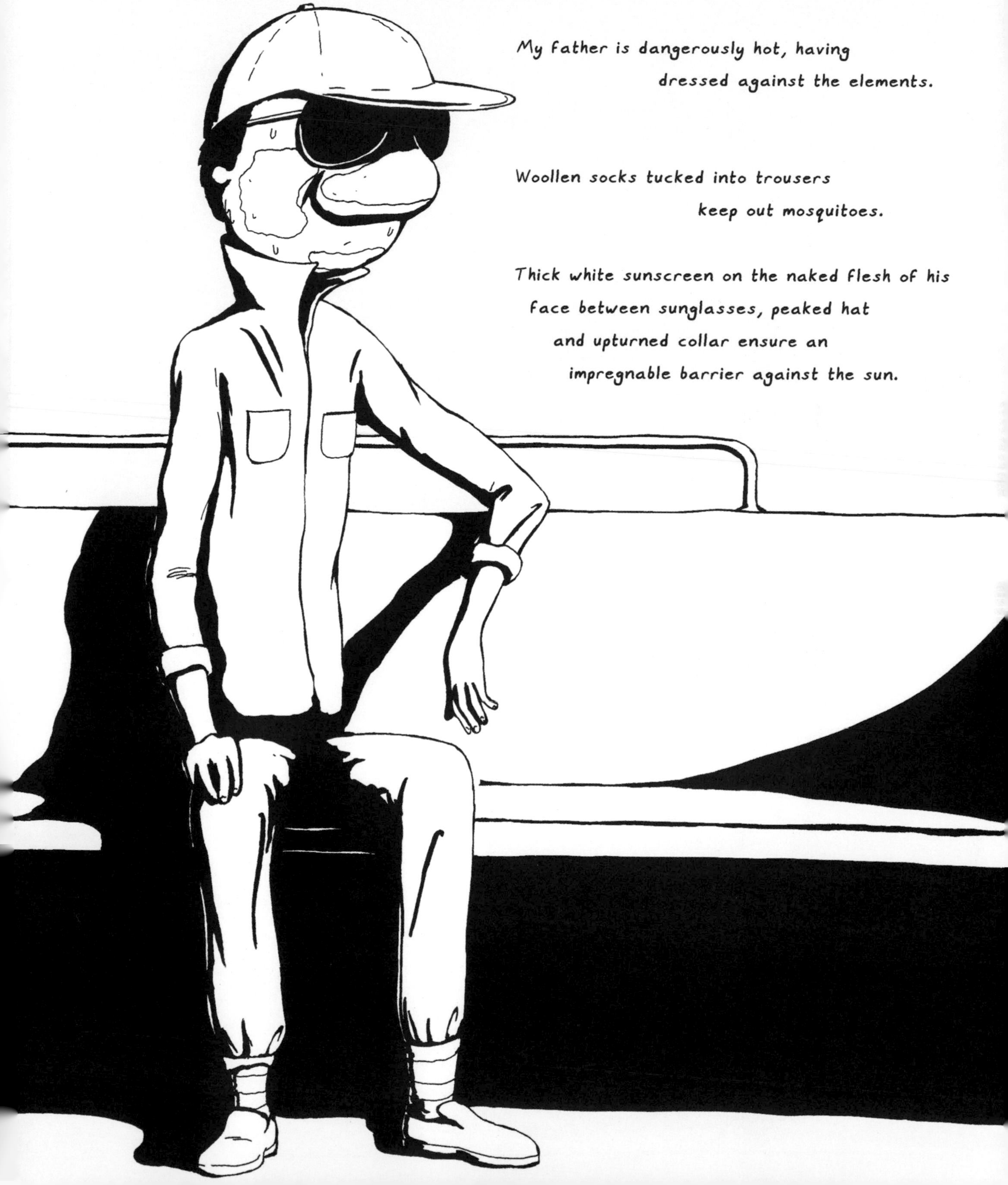
My father is dangerously hot, having dressed against the elements.
Woollen socks tucked into trousers keep out mosquitoes.
Thick white sunscreen on the naked flesh of his face between sunglasses, peaked hat and upturned collar ensure an impregnable barrier against the sun.

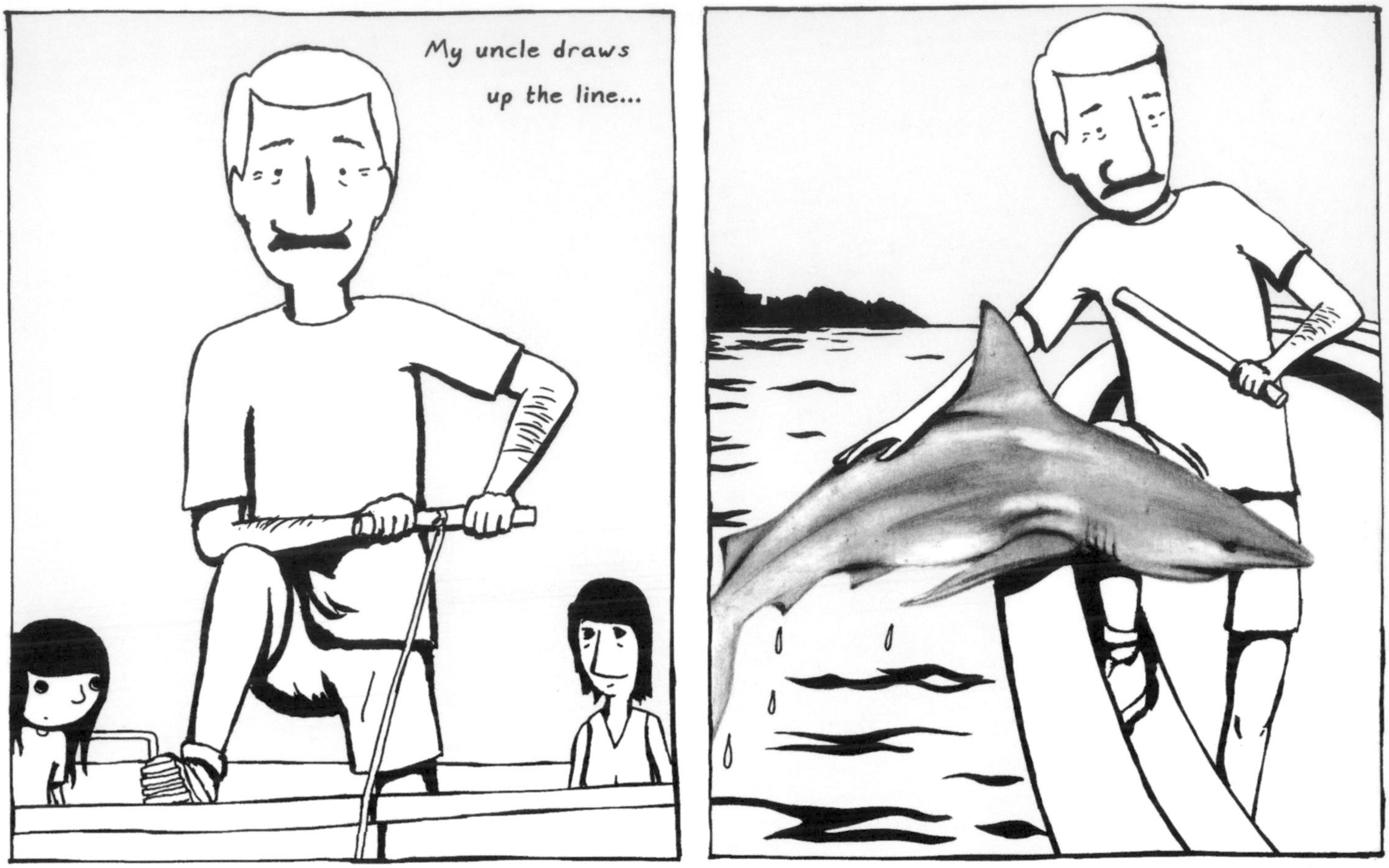
My uncle draws
up the line...

Smacking each four footer on the snout with a steel rod, pulling them into the boat, stunned but alive.

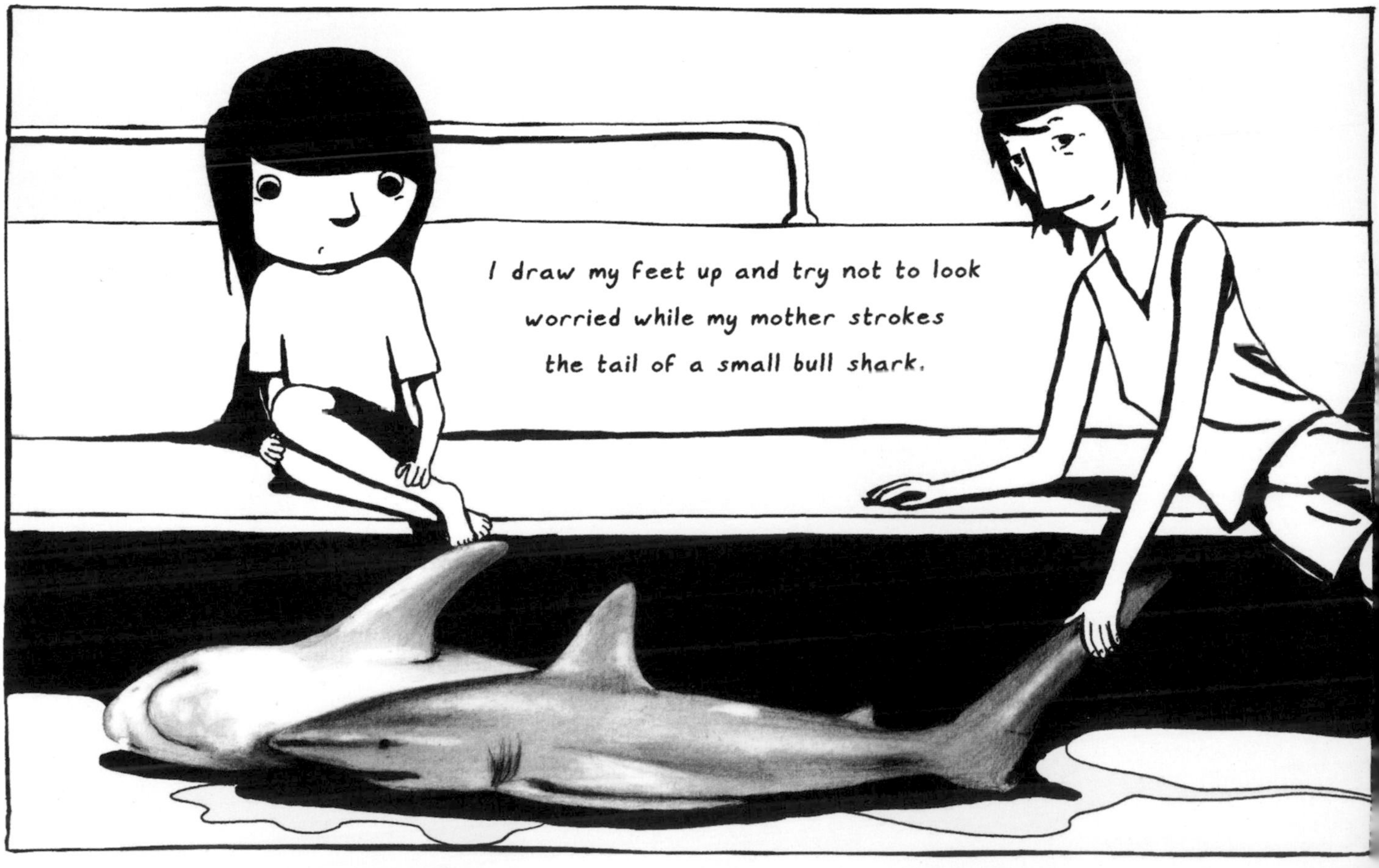
I draw my feet up and try not to look
worried while my mother strokes
the tail of a small bull shark.

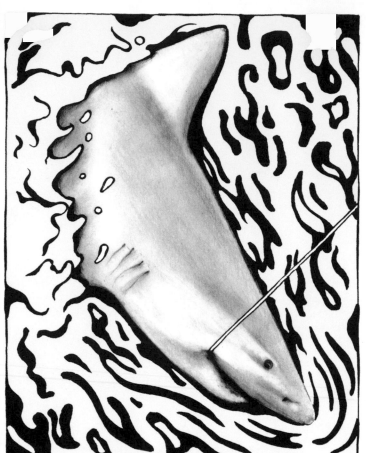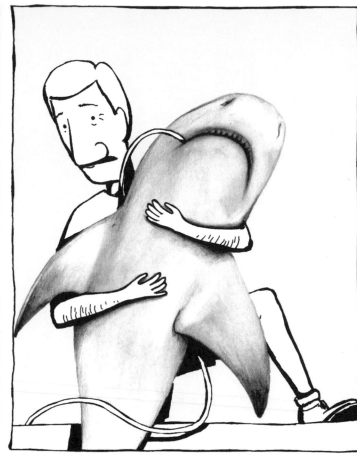

My uncle heaves up a live seven footer who shakes her head at him, more alive than the rest.

The tinny—sluggish, sharks inside and out—drags itself towards shore.

Looking over the side at the white belly, or the black eye as the shark twists against the motor, I can't help thinking...

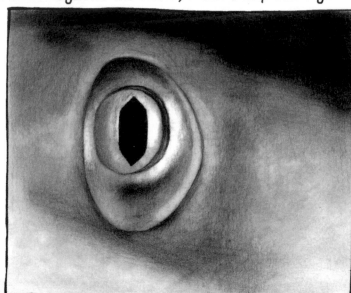

IF SHE JUST WENT UNDER THE BOAT SHE COULD TURN US OUT.

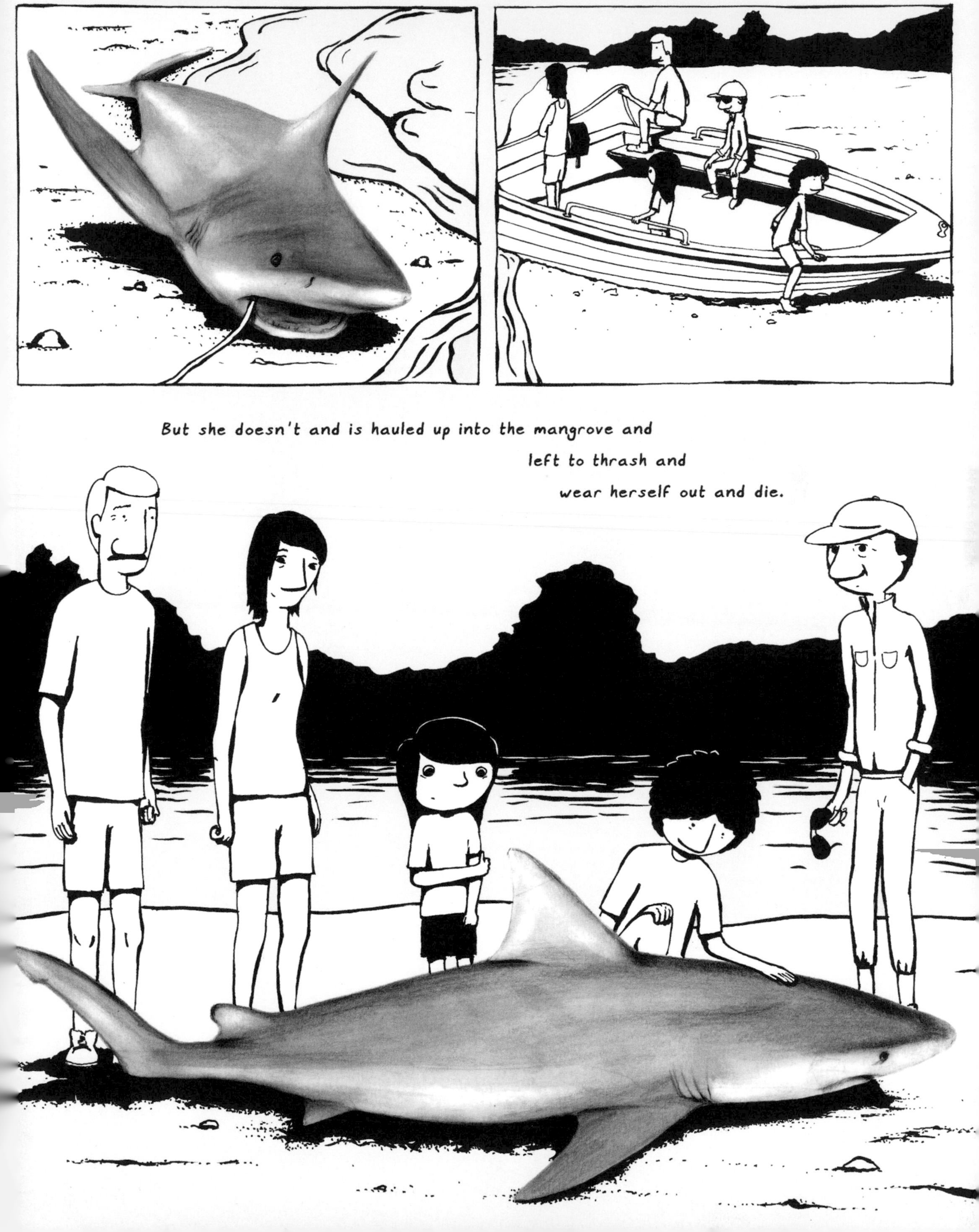
But she doesn't and is hauled up into the mangrove and
left to thrash and
wear herself out and die.

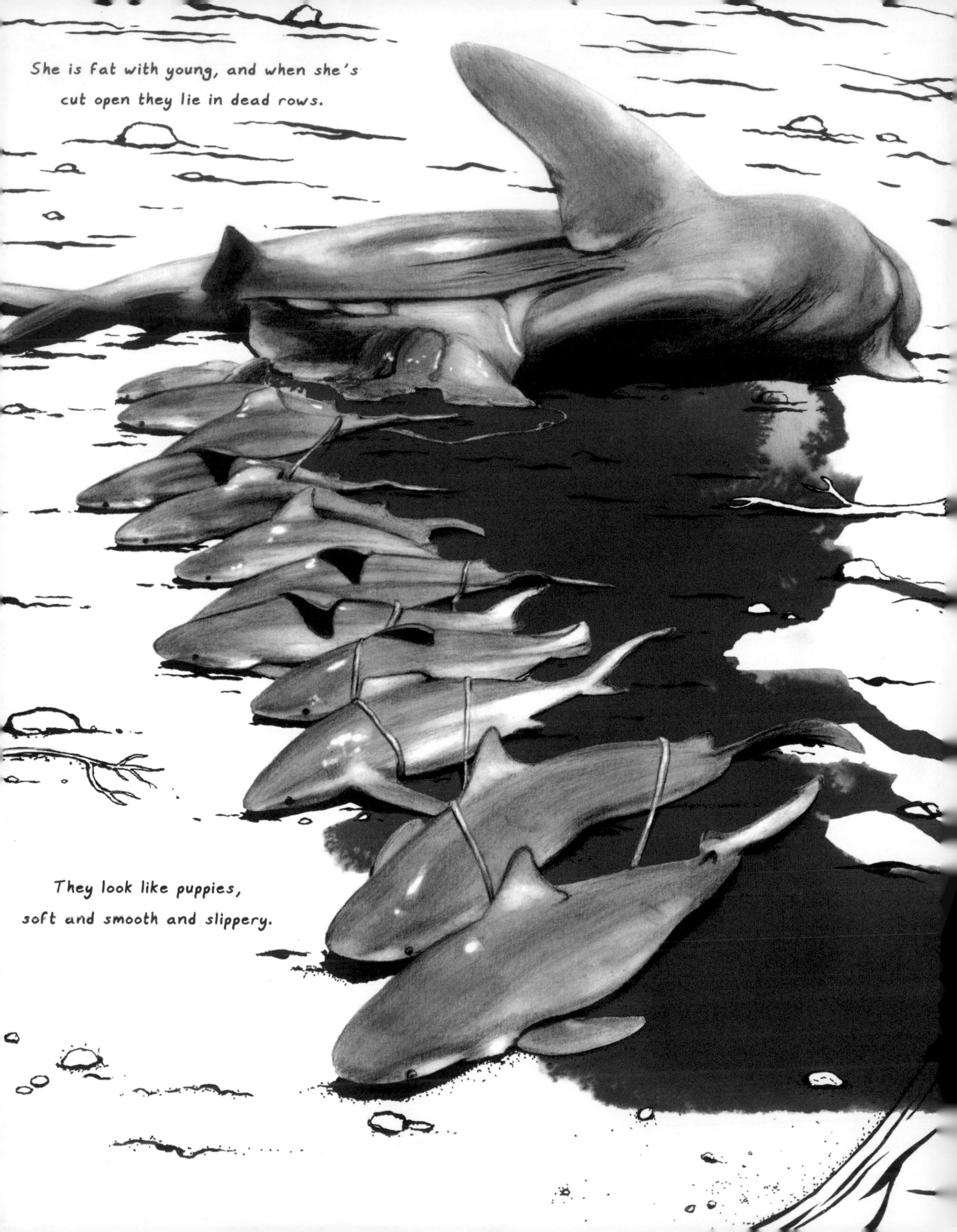
She is fat with young, and when she's cut open they lie in dead rows.
They look like puppies, soft and smooth and slippery.

I get one to hold and watch as my uncle cuts out the mother's mouth, then saws off her fins and rolls the trunk back into the river.

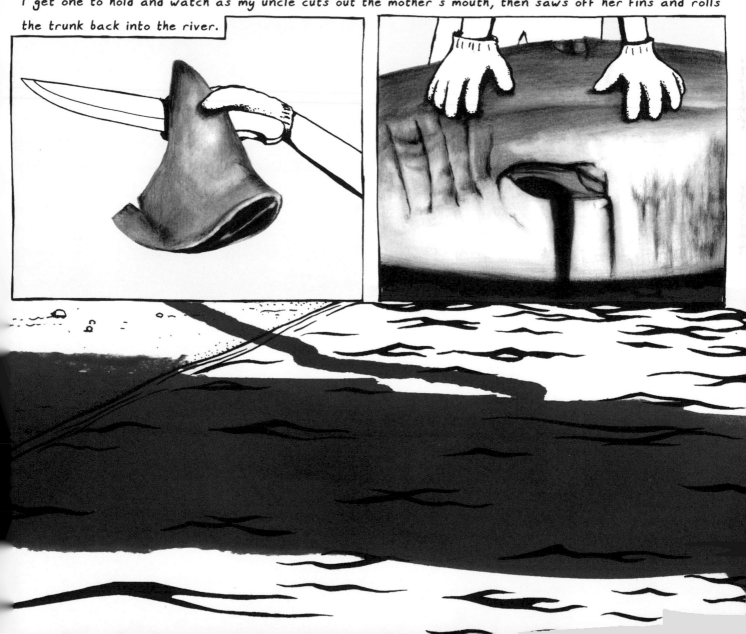

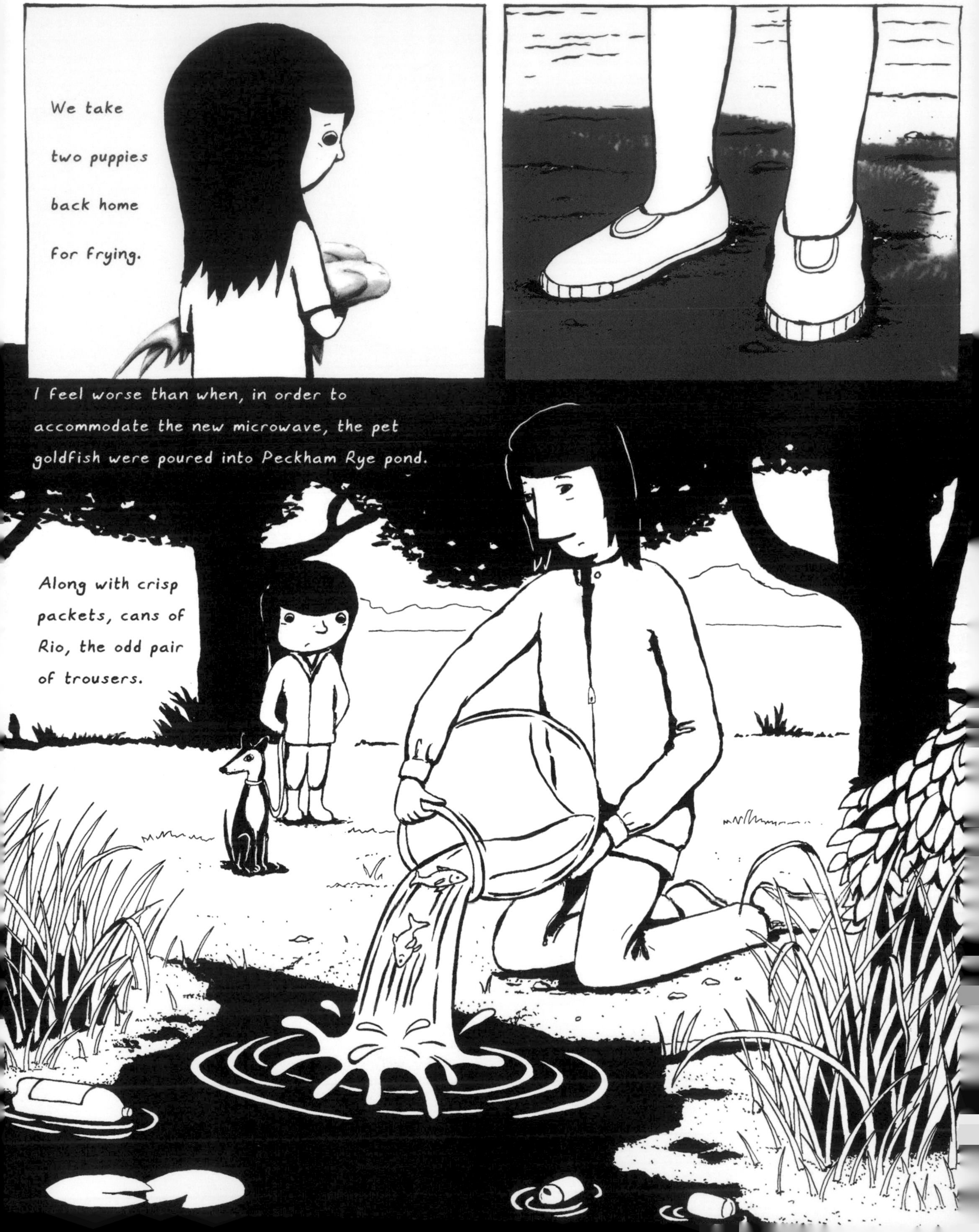
We take
two puppies
back home
for frying.
I feel worse than when, in order to accommodate the new microwave, the pet goldfish were poured into Peckham Rye pond.
Along with crisp packets, cans of Rio, the odd pair of trousers.

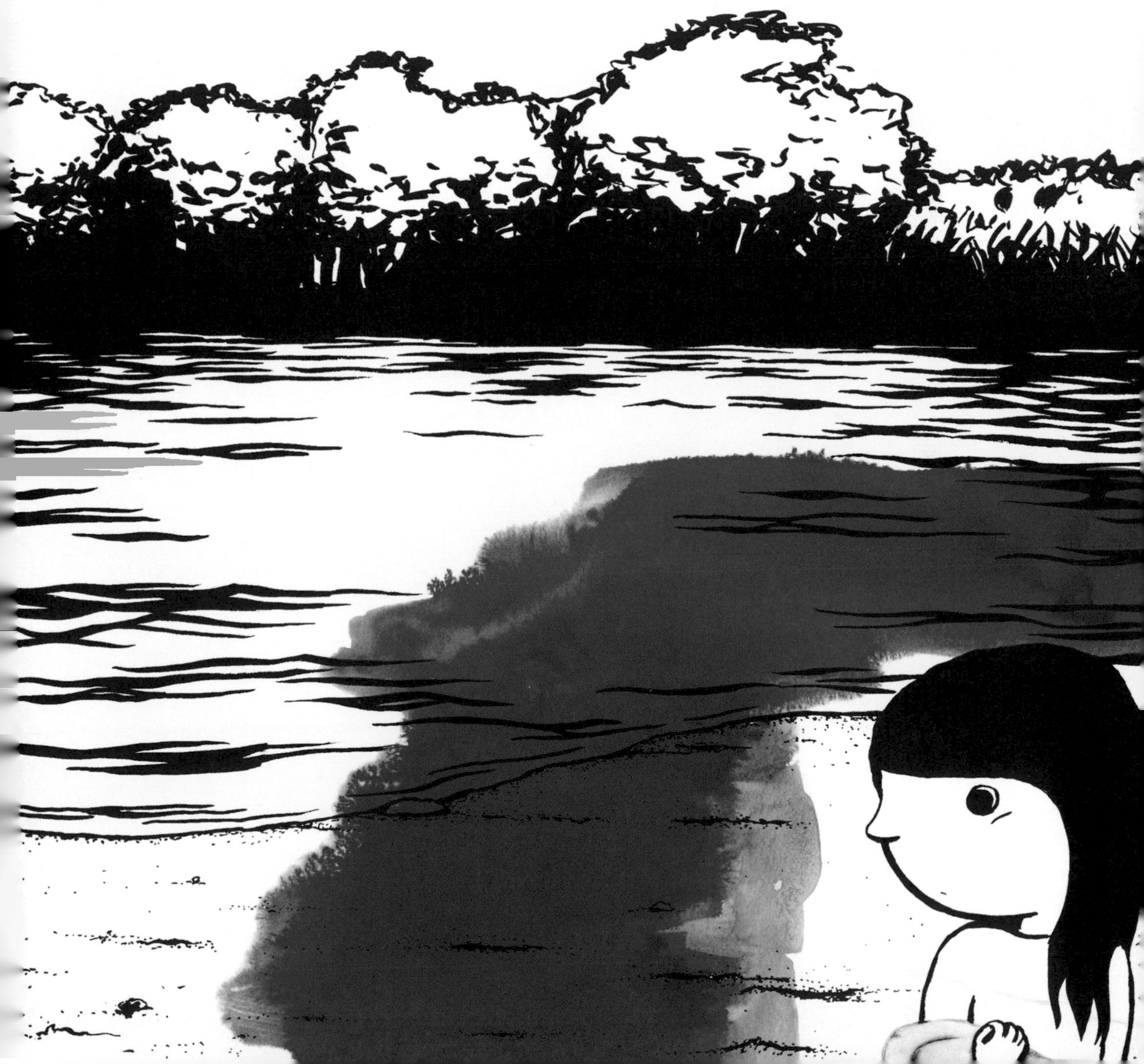

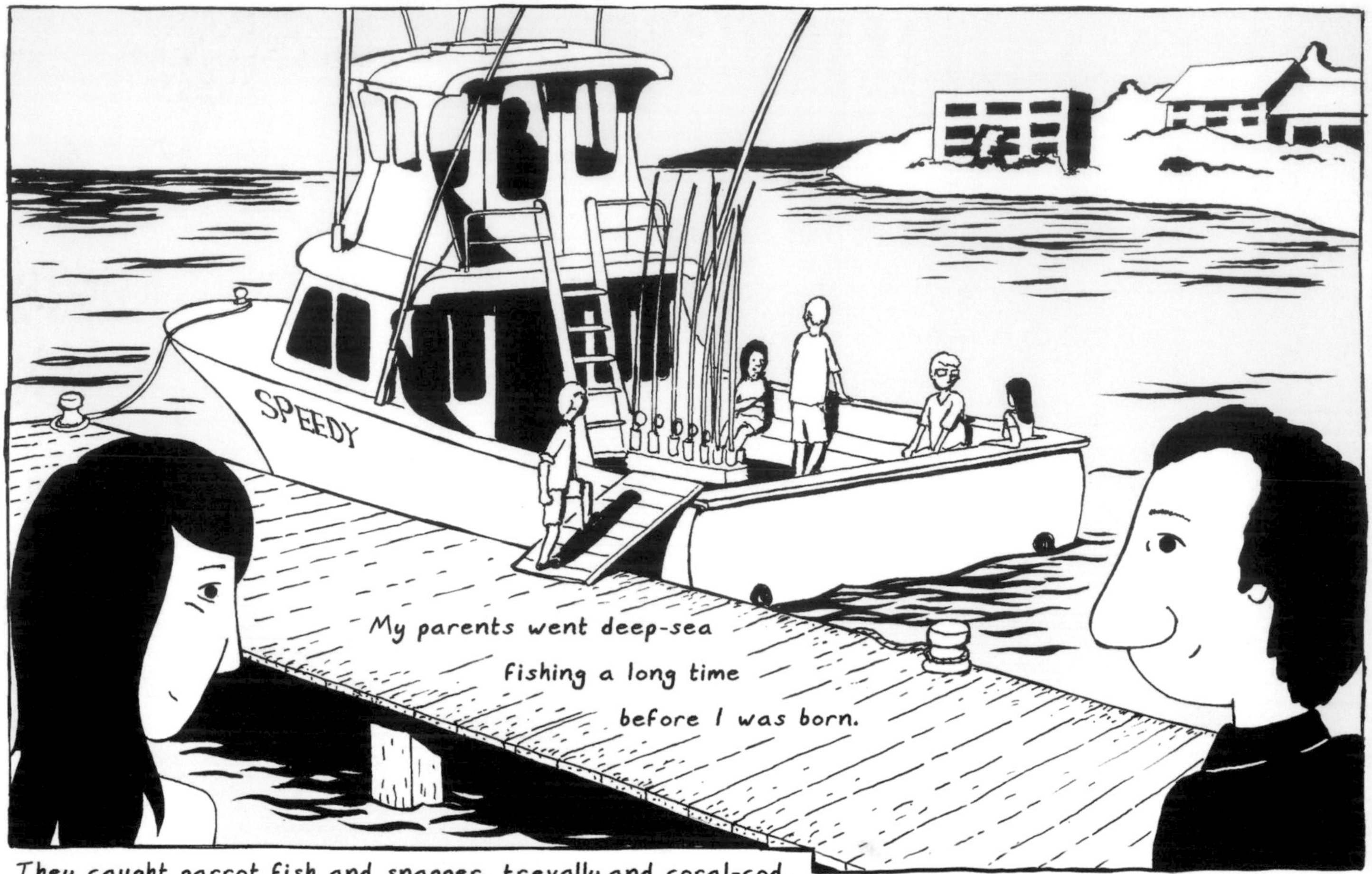
SPEEDY
My parents went deep-sea fishing a long time before I was born.

They caught parrot fish and snapper, trevally and coral-cod.

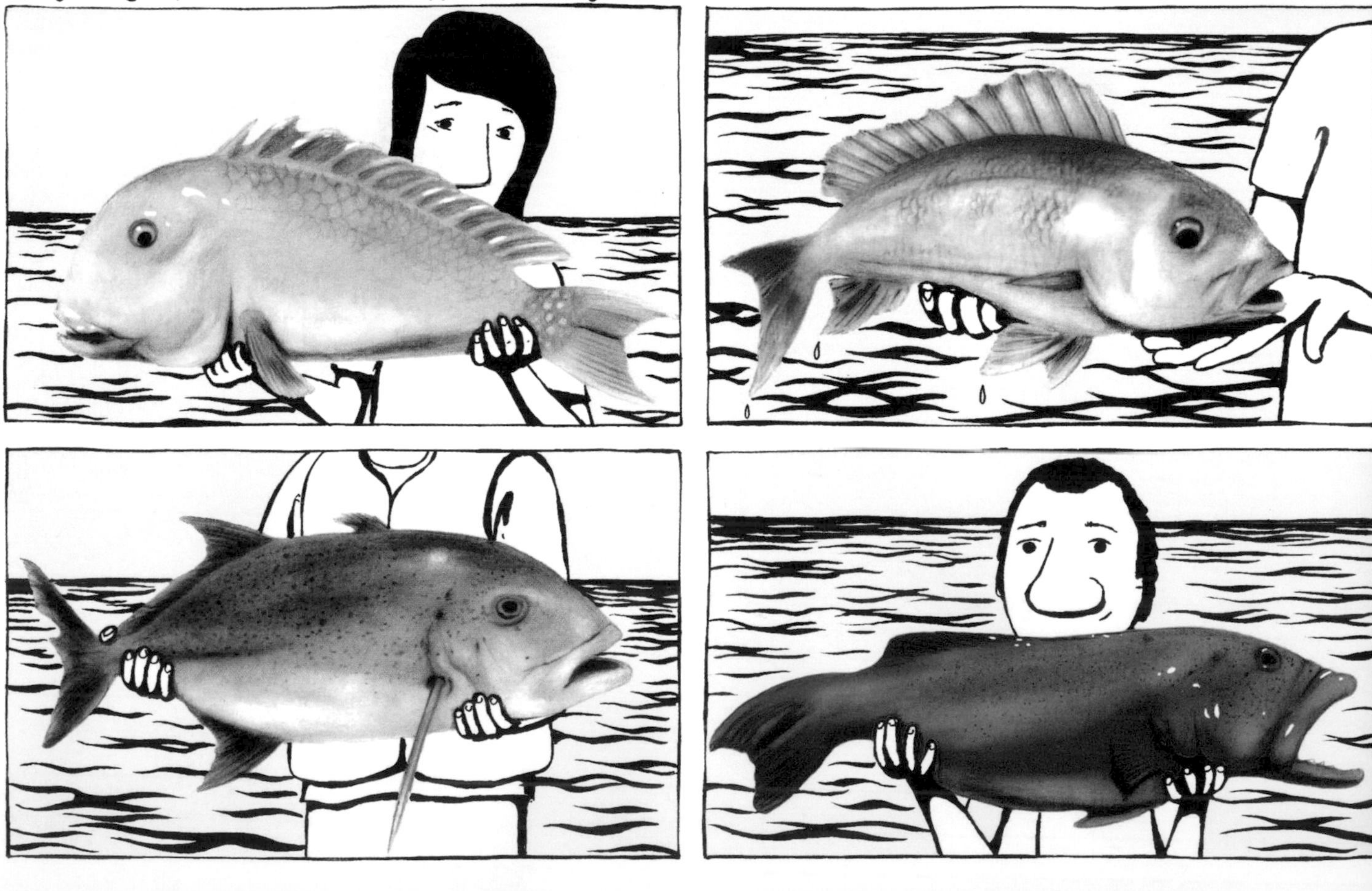

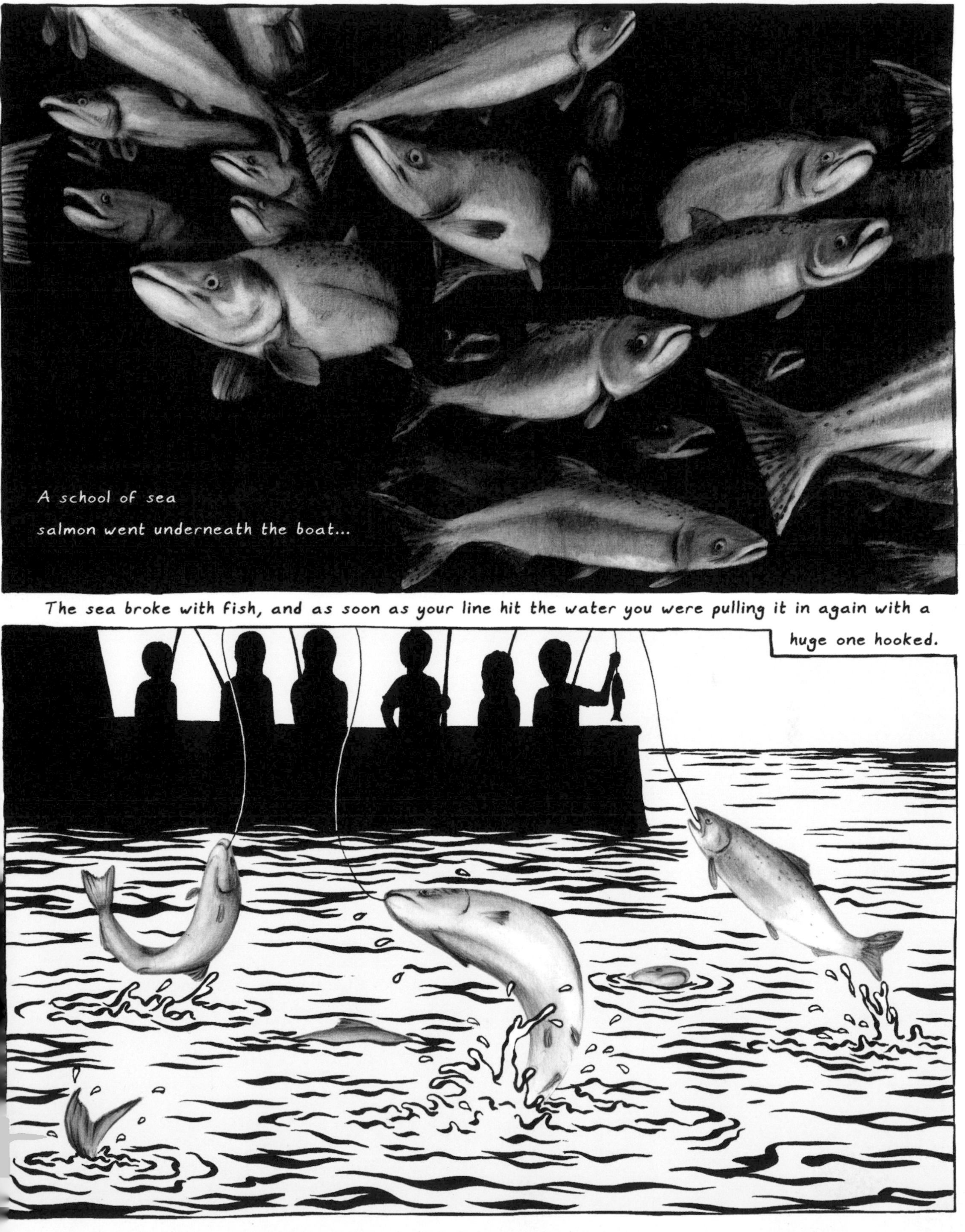
A school of sea salmon went underneath the boat...
The sea broke with fish, and as soon as your line hit the water you were pulling it in again with a huge one hooked.

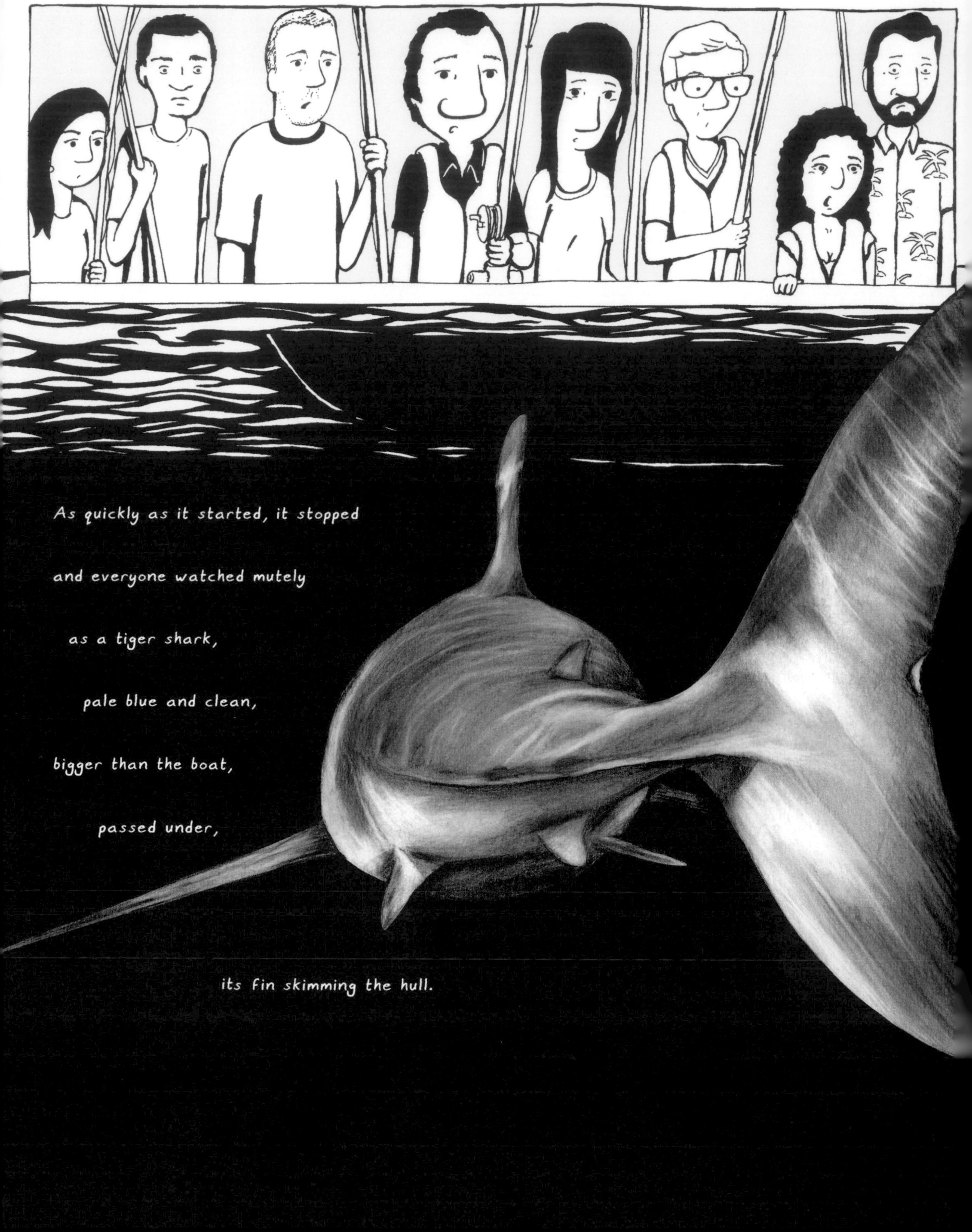
As quickly as it started, it stopped
and everyone watched mutely
as a tiger shark,
pale blue and clean,
bigger than the boat,
passed under,
its fin skimming the hull.

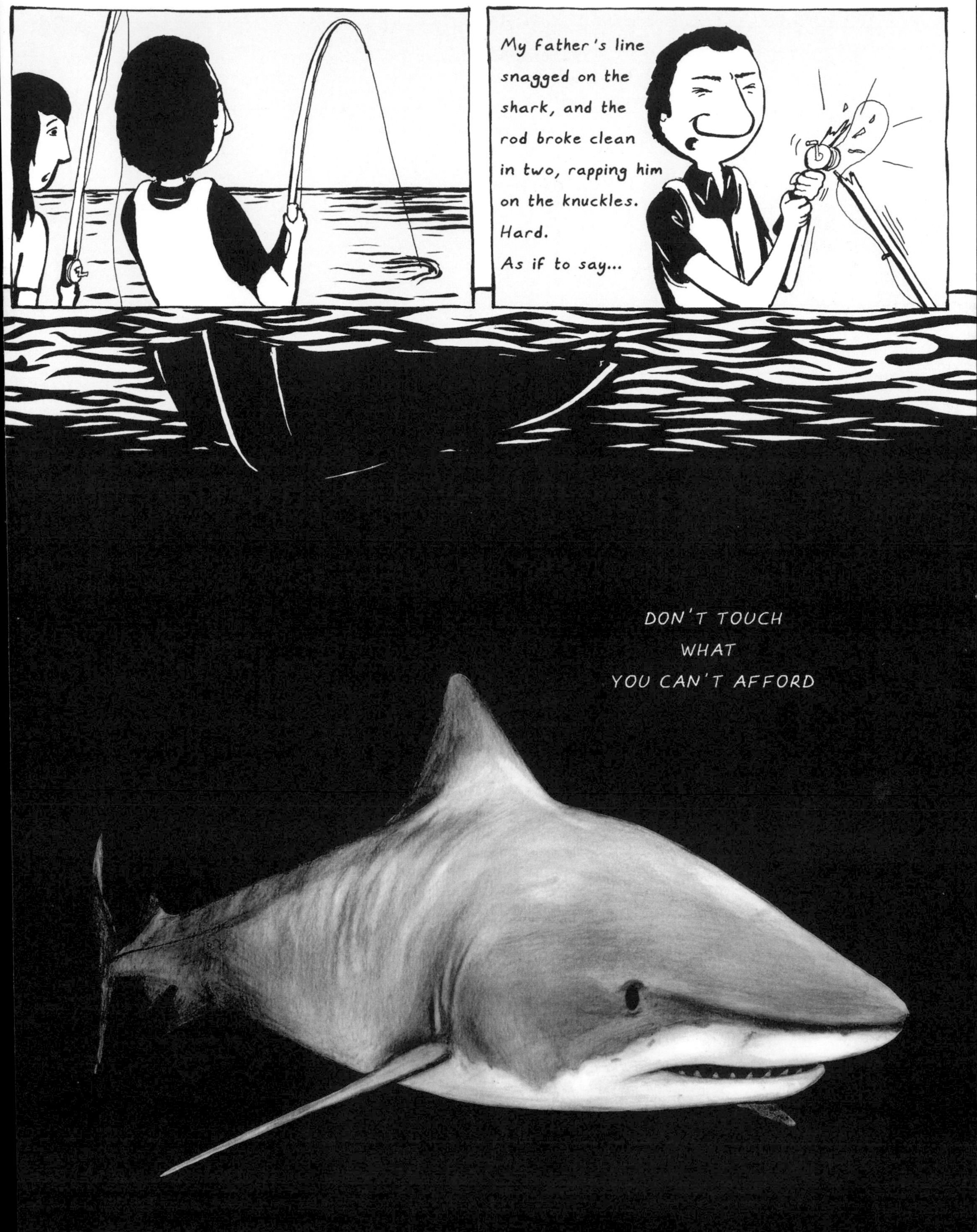
My father's line snagged on the shark, and the rod broke clean in two, rapping him on the knuckles.
Hard.
As if to say...
DON'T TOUCH WHAT YOU CAN'T AFFORD

When my week of no swimming is up, I'm unsure about the water again. The salt chews on my stings, but it's hot so I sit in the shallows watching my mother on her back, not far away.

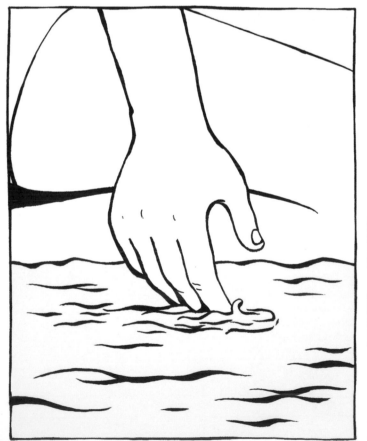

If I think the worst, then the worst is unlikely to happen.

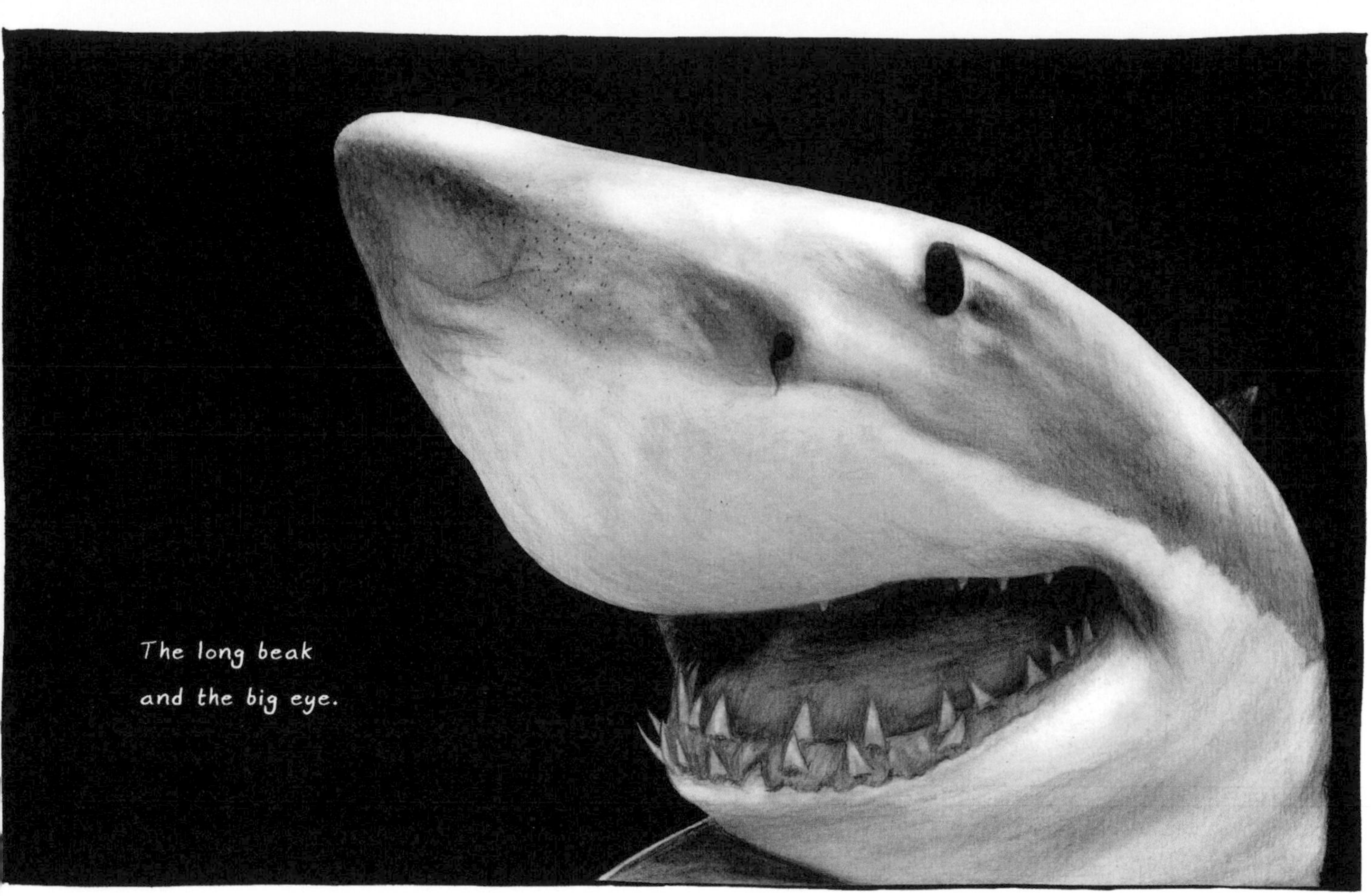
The long beak
and the big eye.

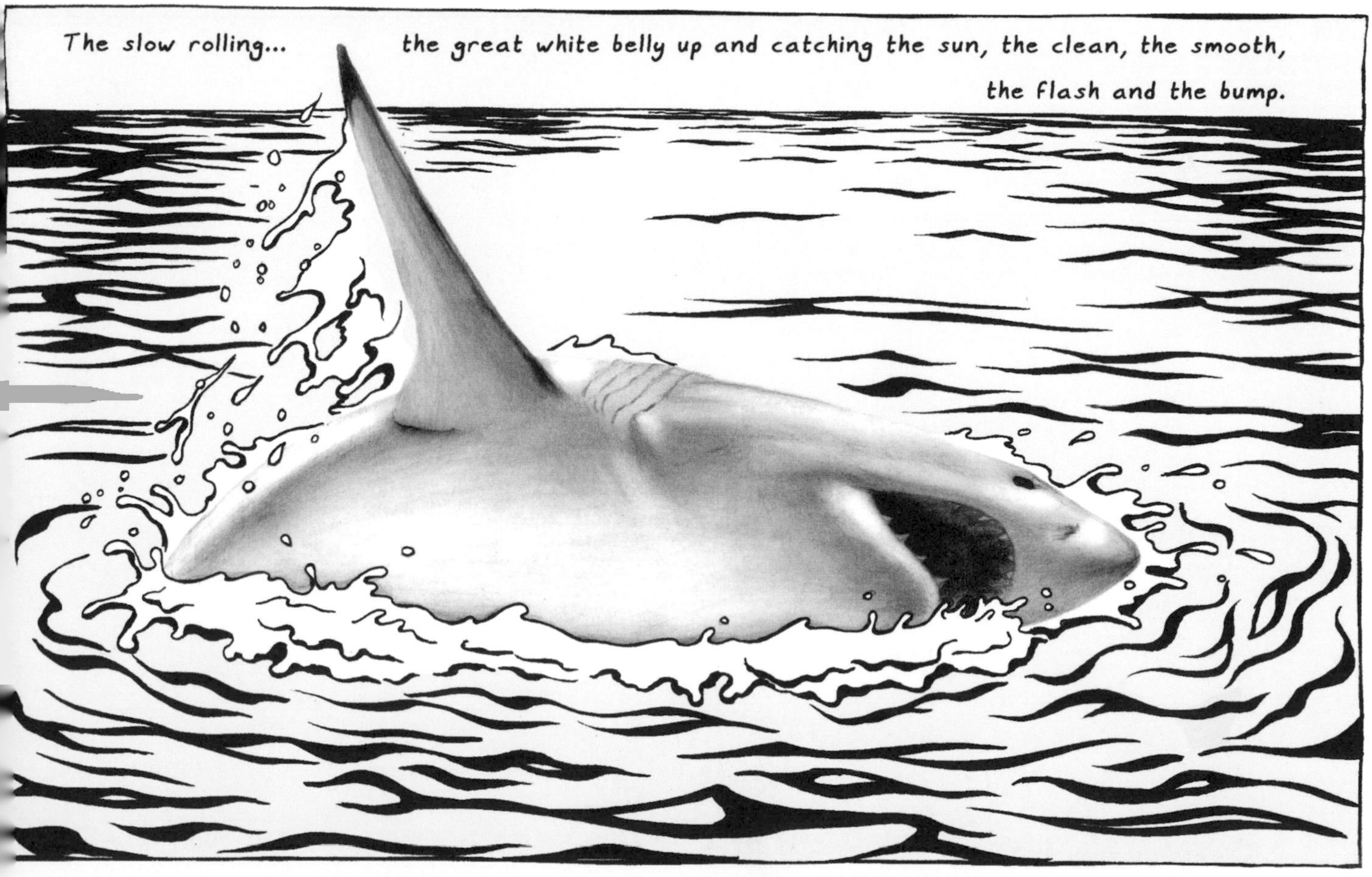
The slow rolling...
the great white belly up and catching the sun, the clean, the smooth,
the flash and the bump.

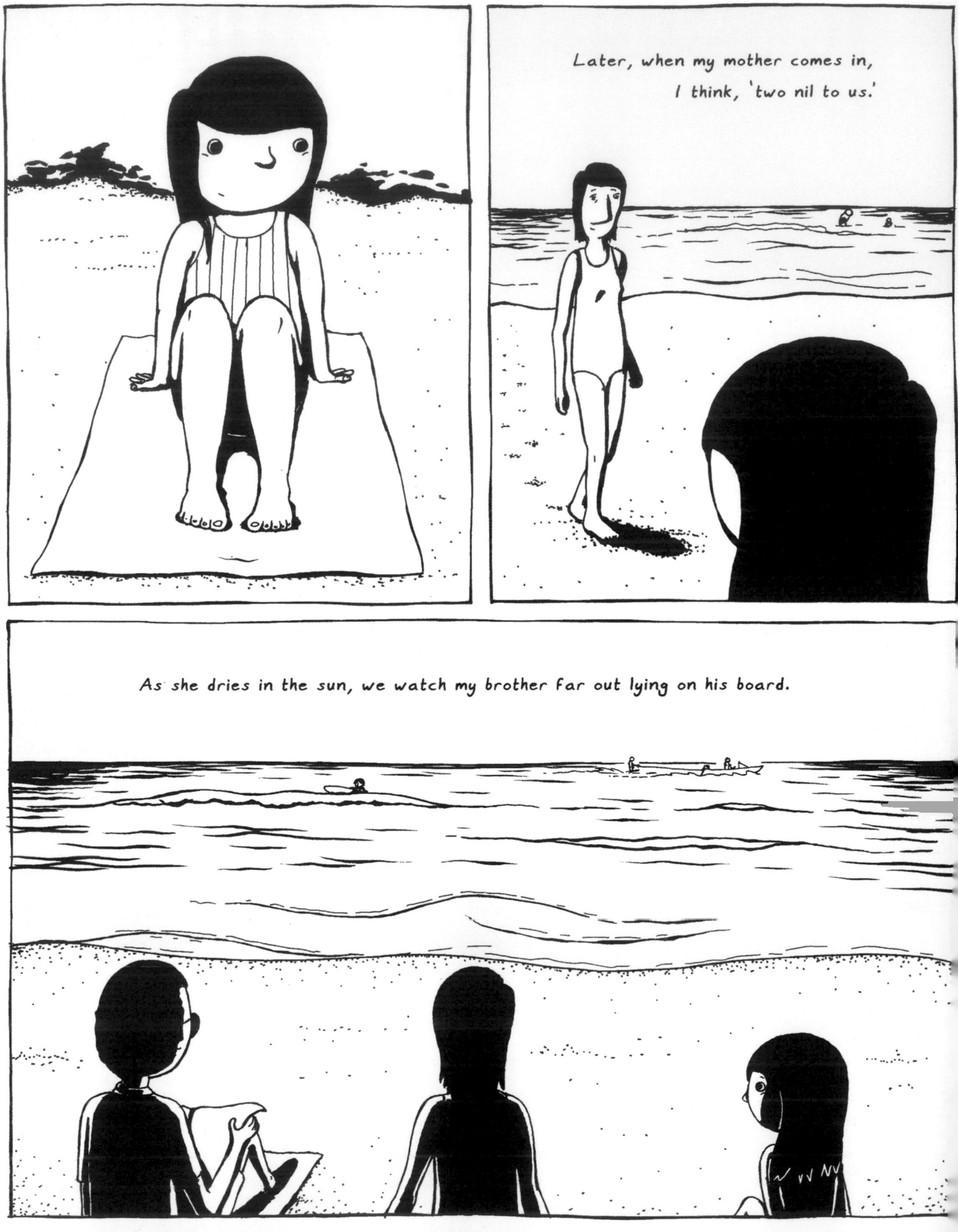
Later, when my mother comes in,
I think, 'two nil to us.'
As she dries in the sun, we watch my brother far out lying on his board.

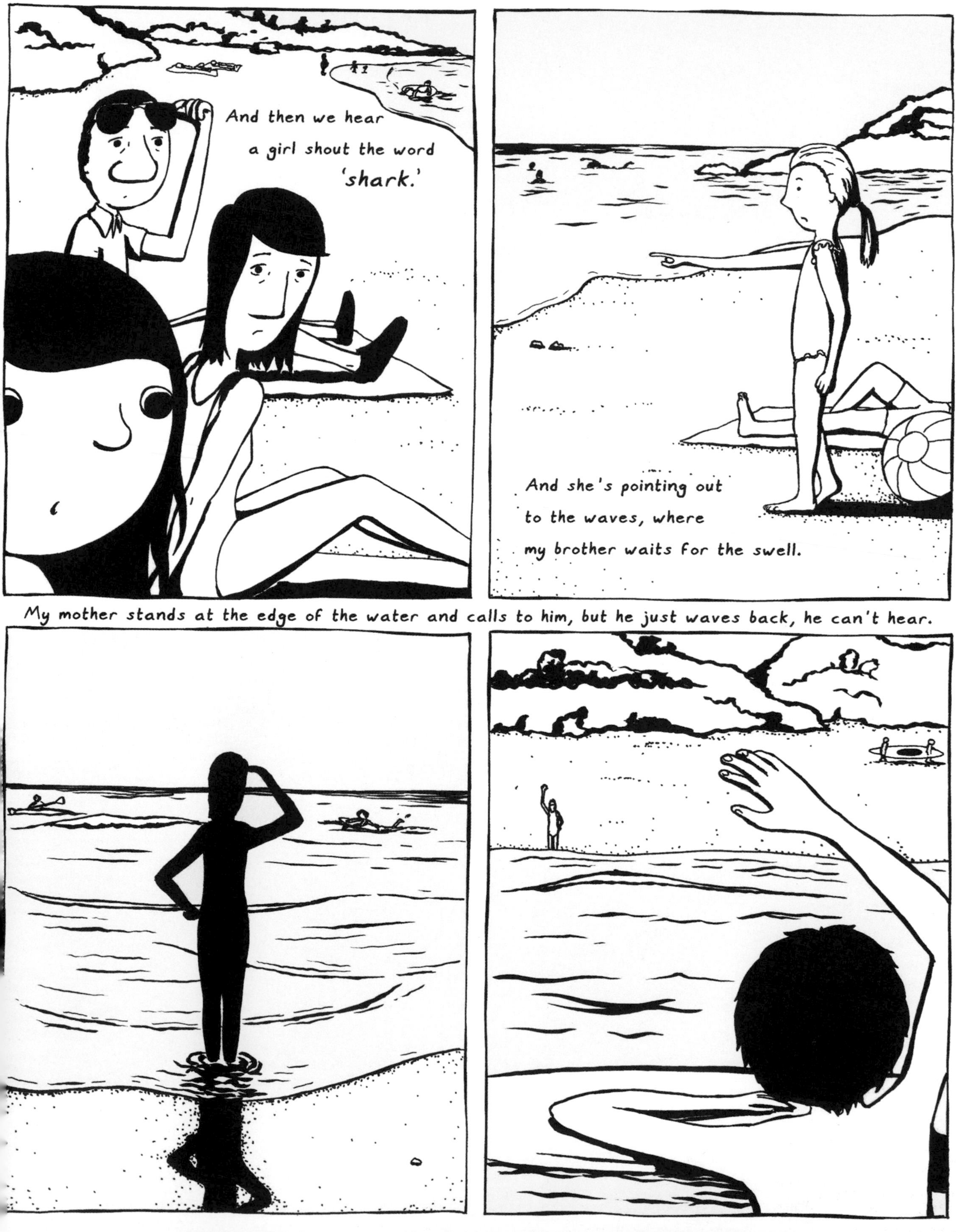
And then we hear
a girl shout the word
'shark.'
And she's pointing out
to the waves, where
my brother waits for the swell.
My mother stands at the edge of the water and calls to him, but he just waves back, he can't hear.

The worst can't happen –

a while pointer, breaching,

takes him down like a sea lion.

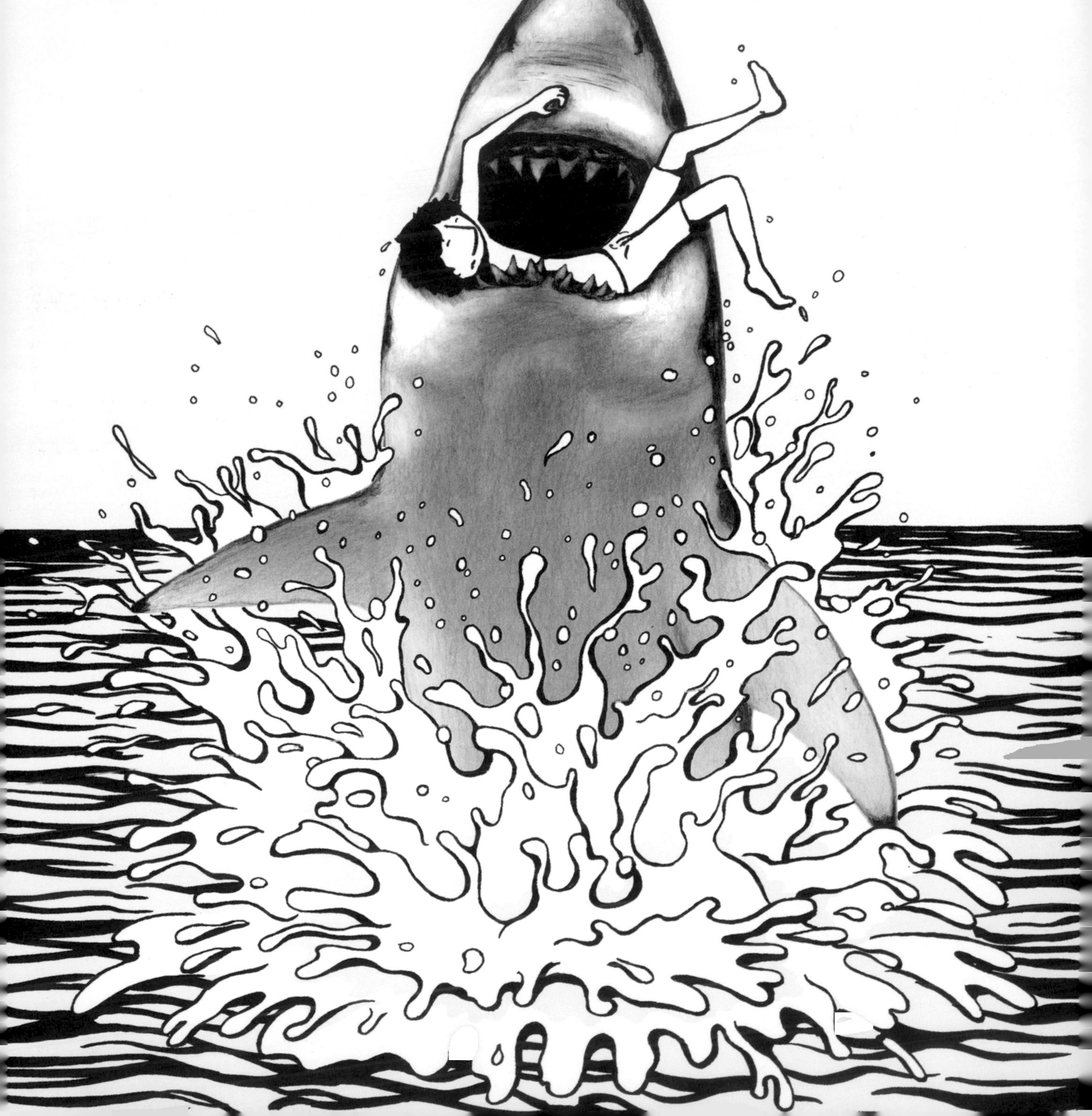

A red streak and a broken board, and nothing much else is left.

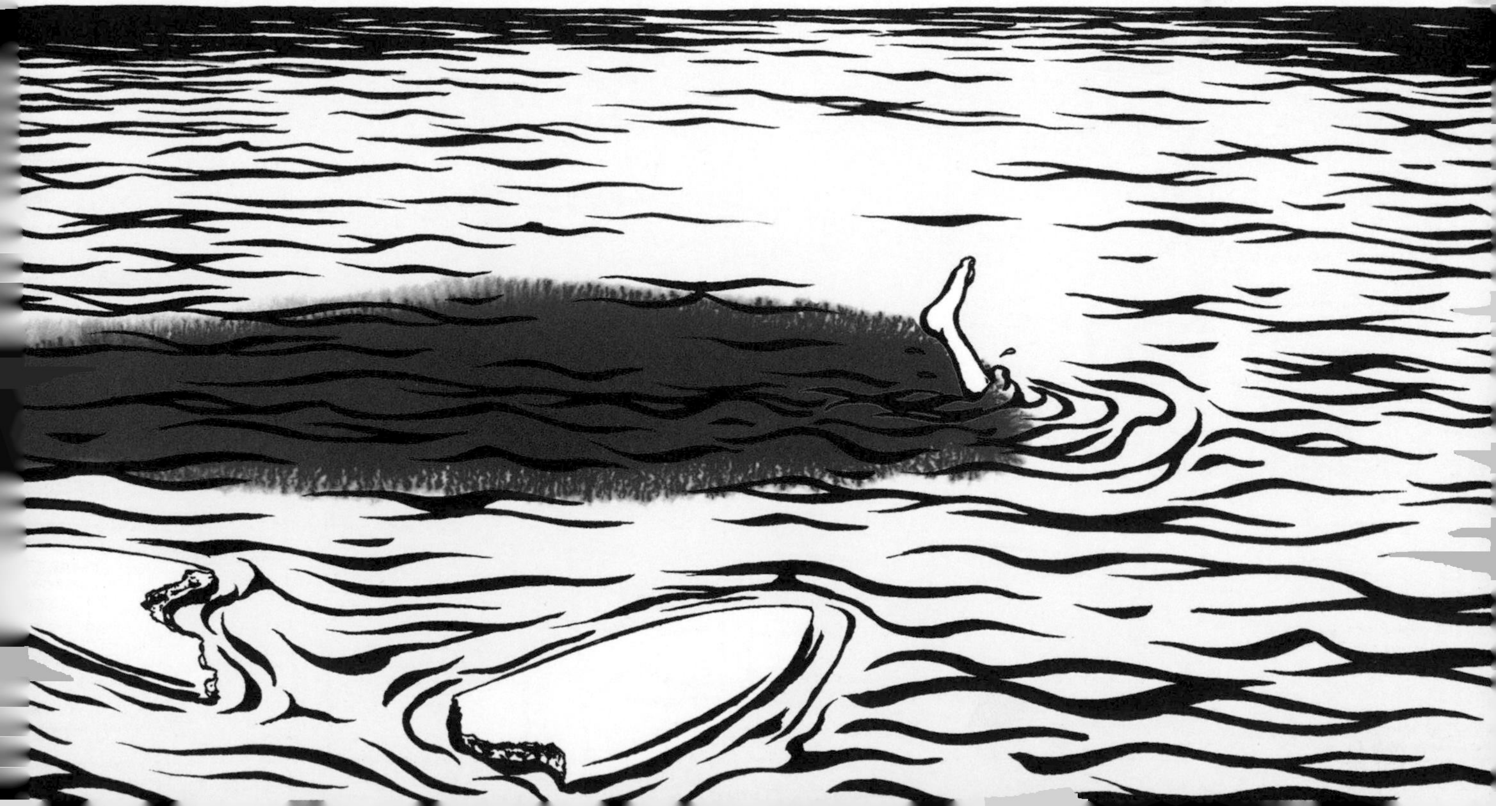

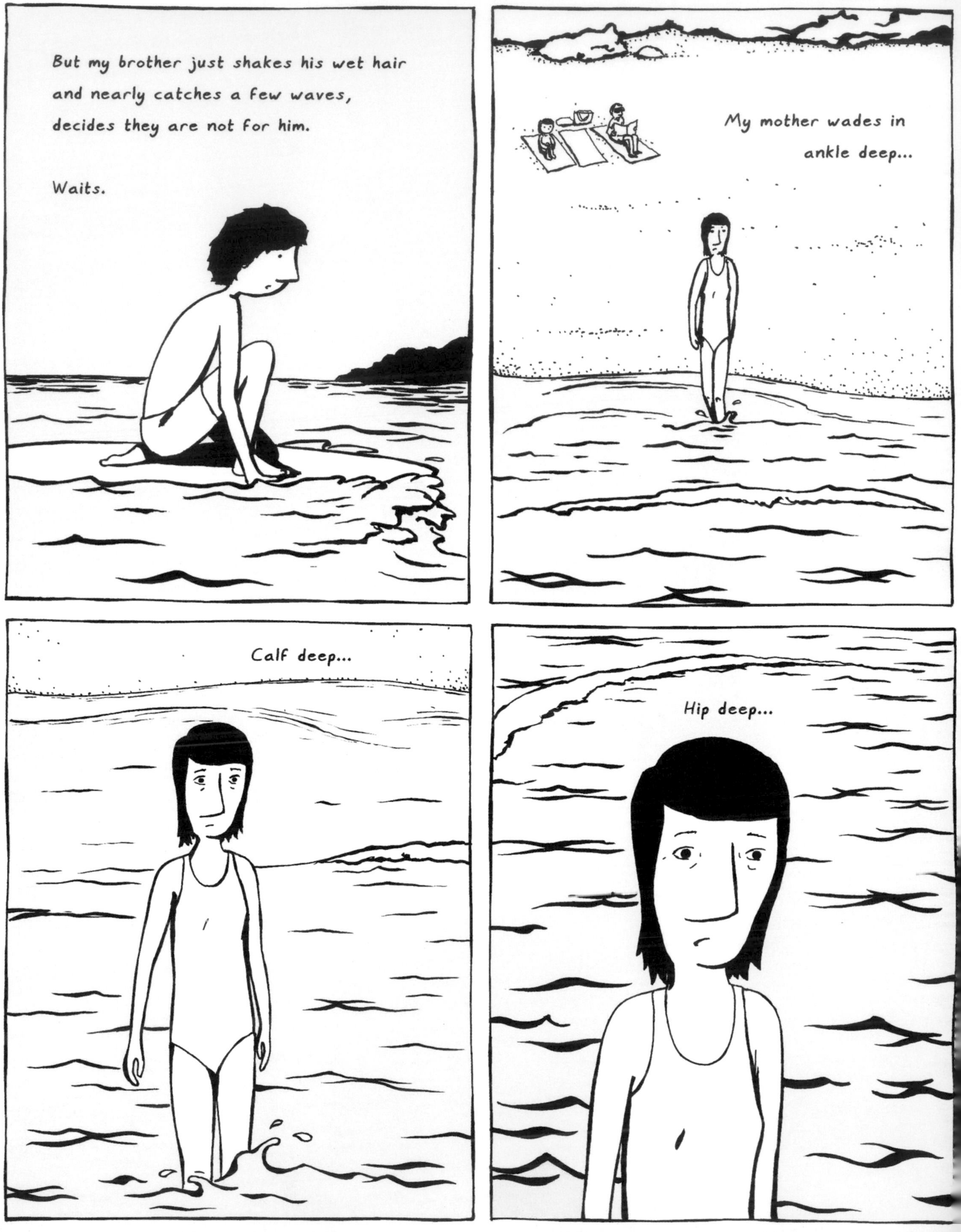
But my brother just shakes his wet hair and nearly catches a few waves, decides they are not for him.
Waits.
My mother wades in ankle deep...
Calf deep...
Hip deep...

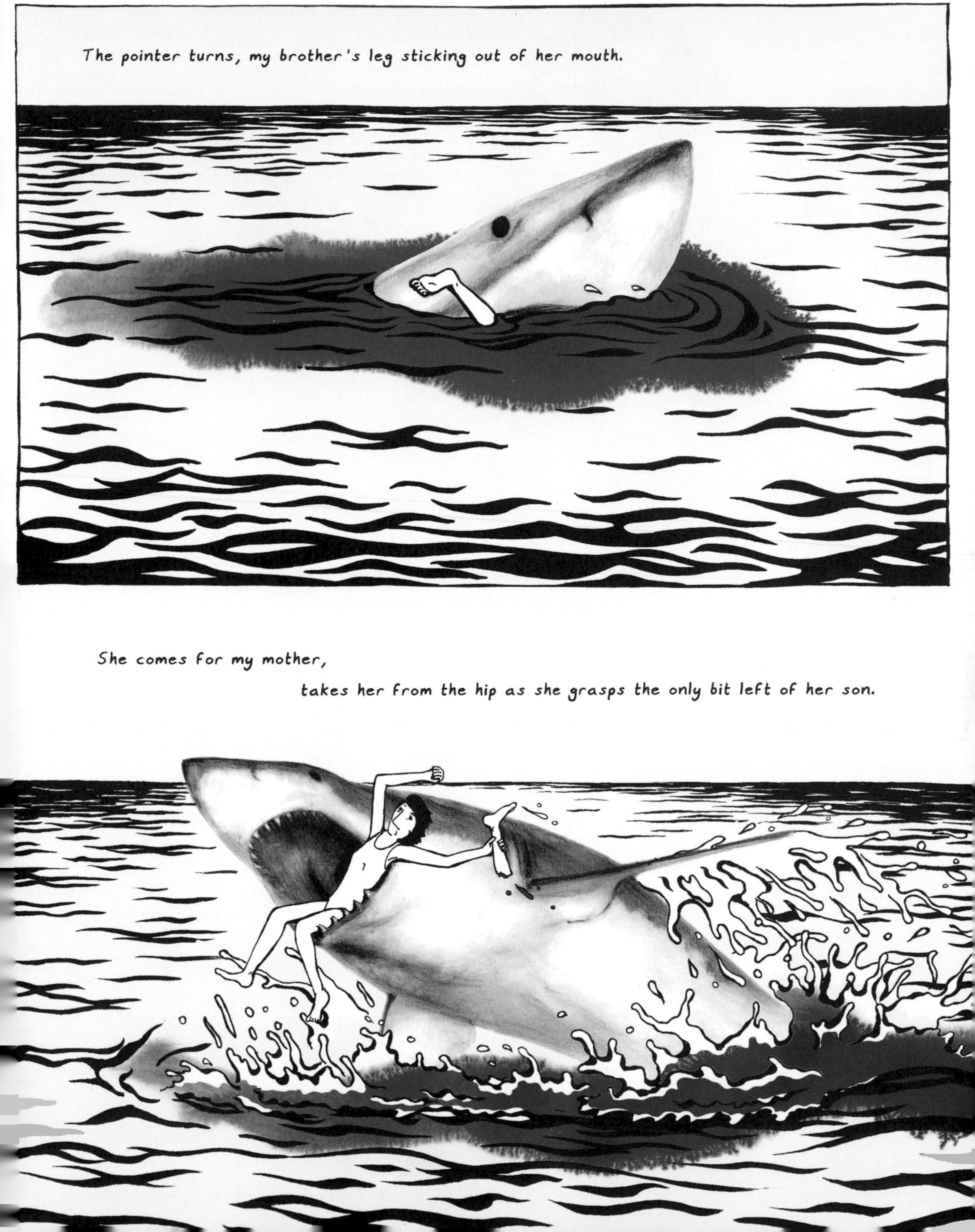
The pointer turns, my brother's leg sticking out of her mouth.
She comes for my mother,
takes her from the hip as she grasps the only bit left of her son.

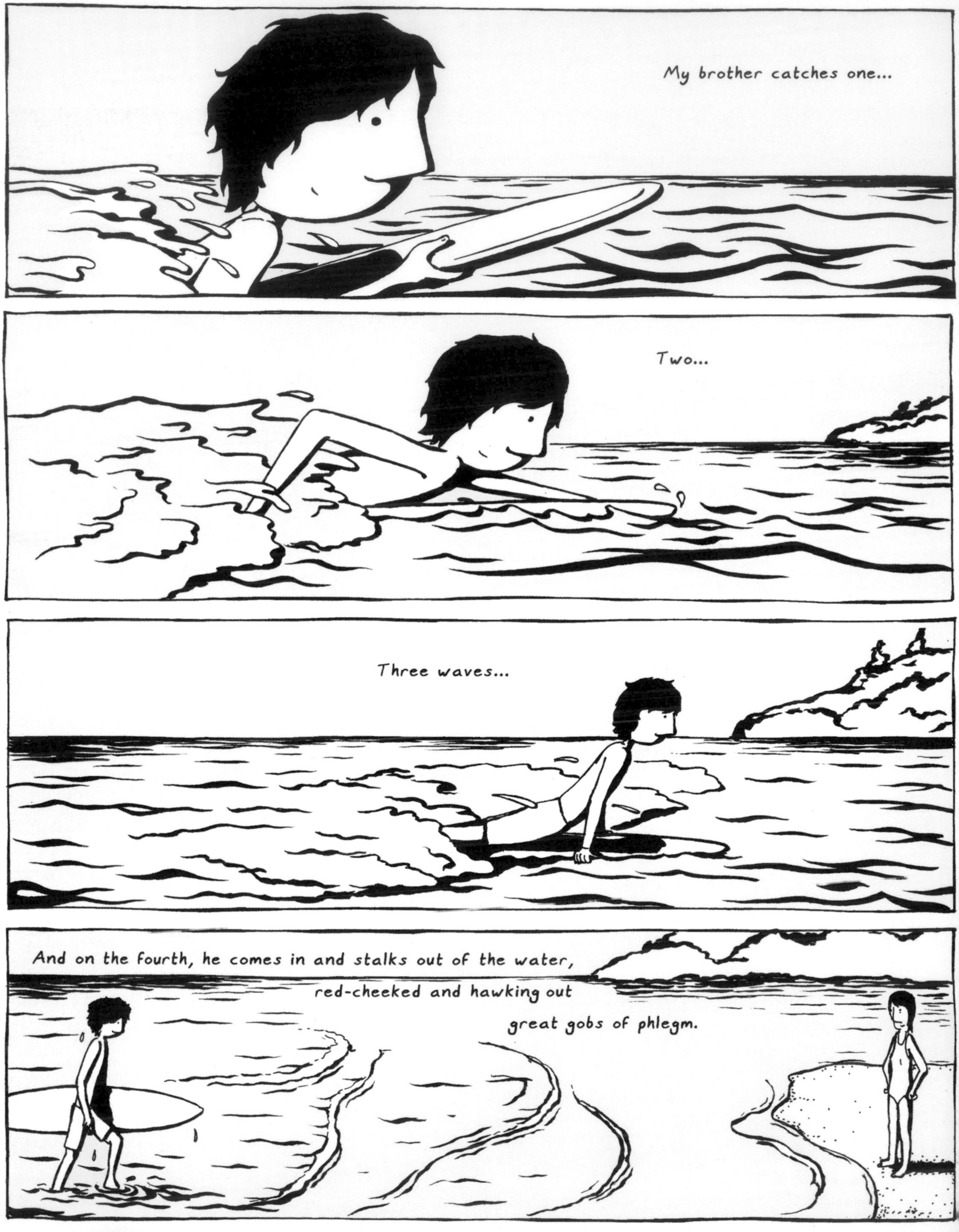
My brother catches one...
Two...
Three waves...
And on the fourth, he comes in and stalks out of the water,
red-cheeked and hawking out
great gobs of phlegm.

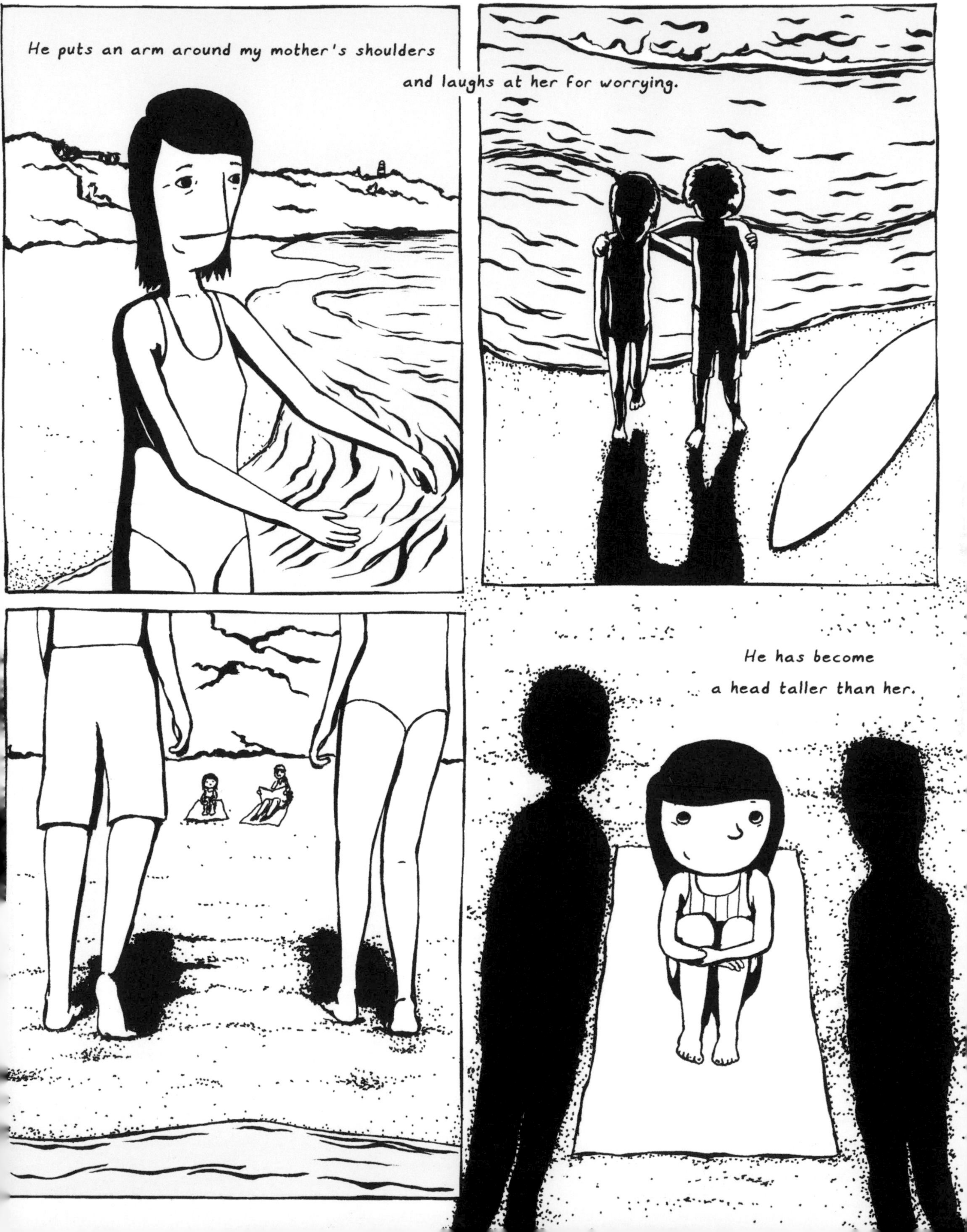
He puts an arm around my mother's shoulders
and laughs at her for worrying.
He has become
a head taller than her.

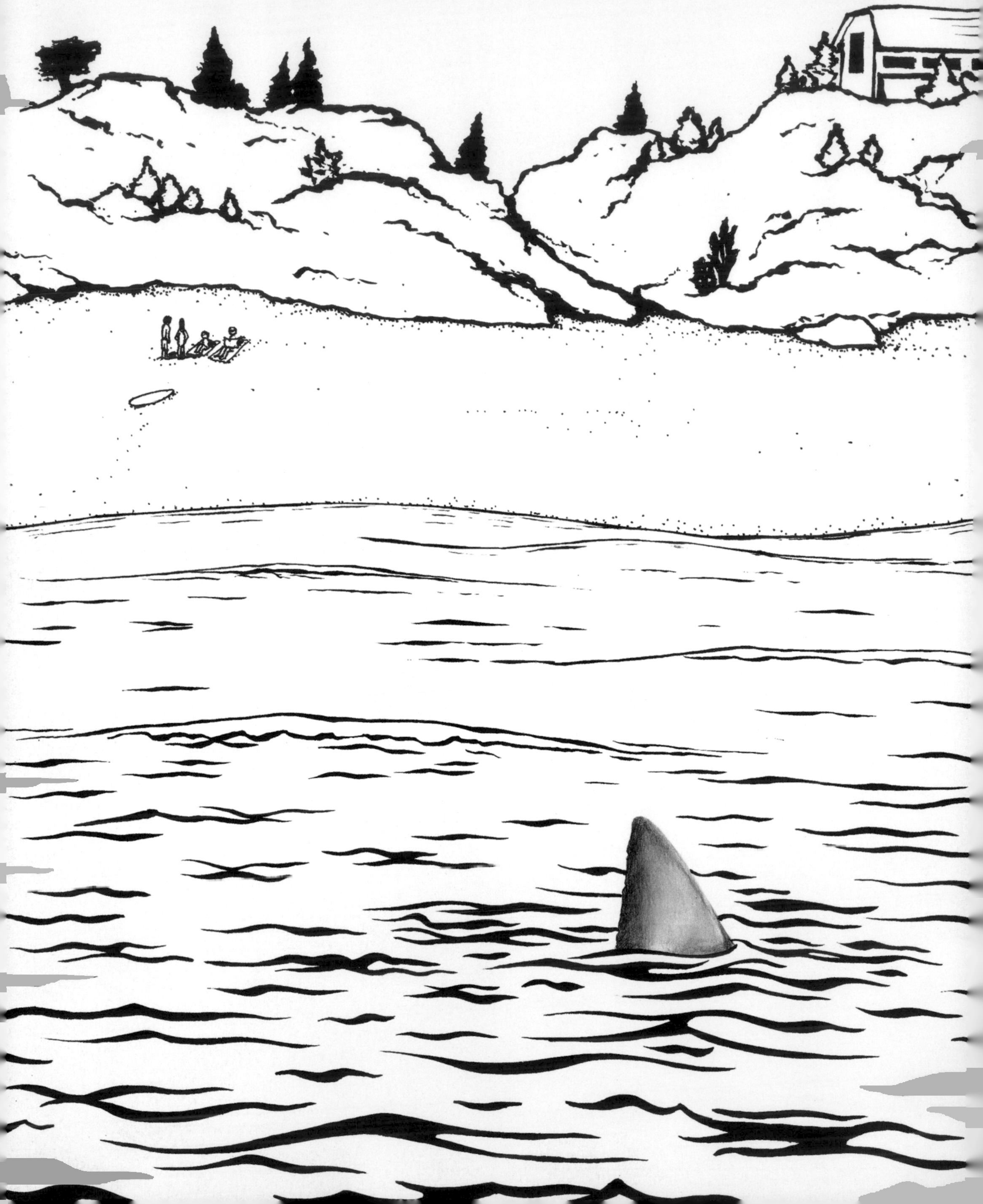

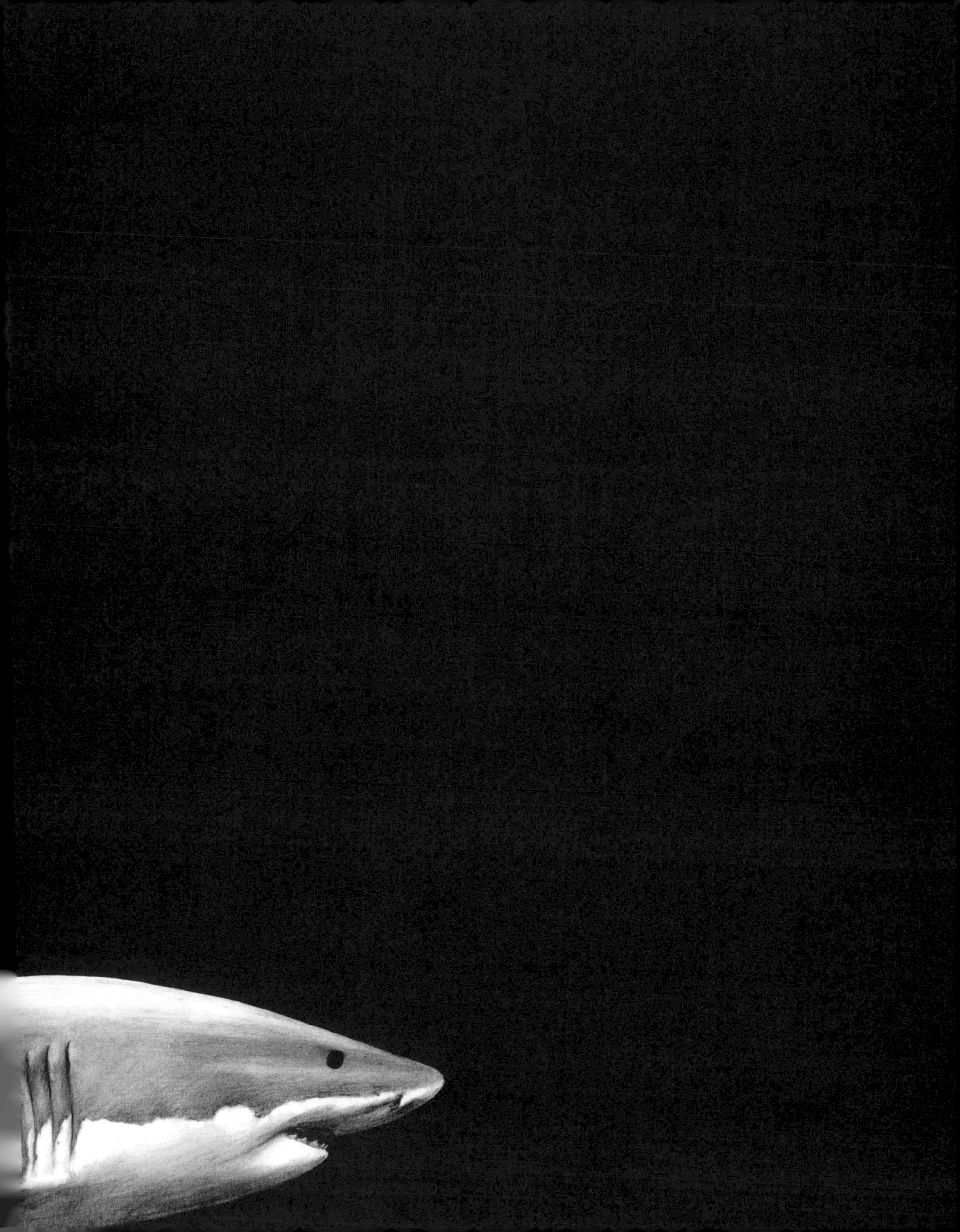

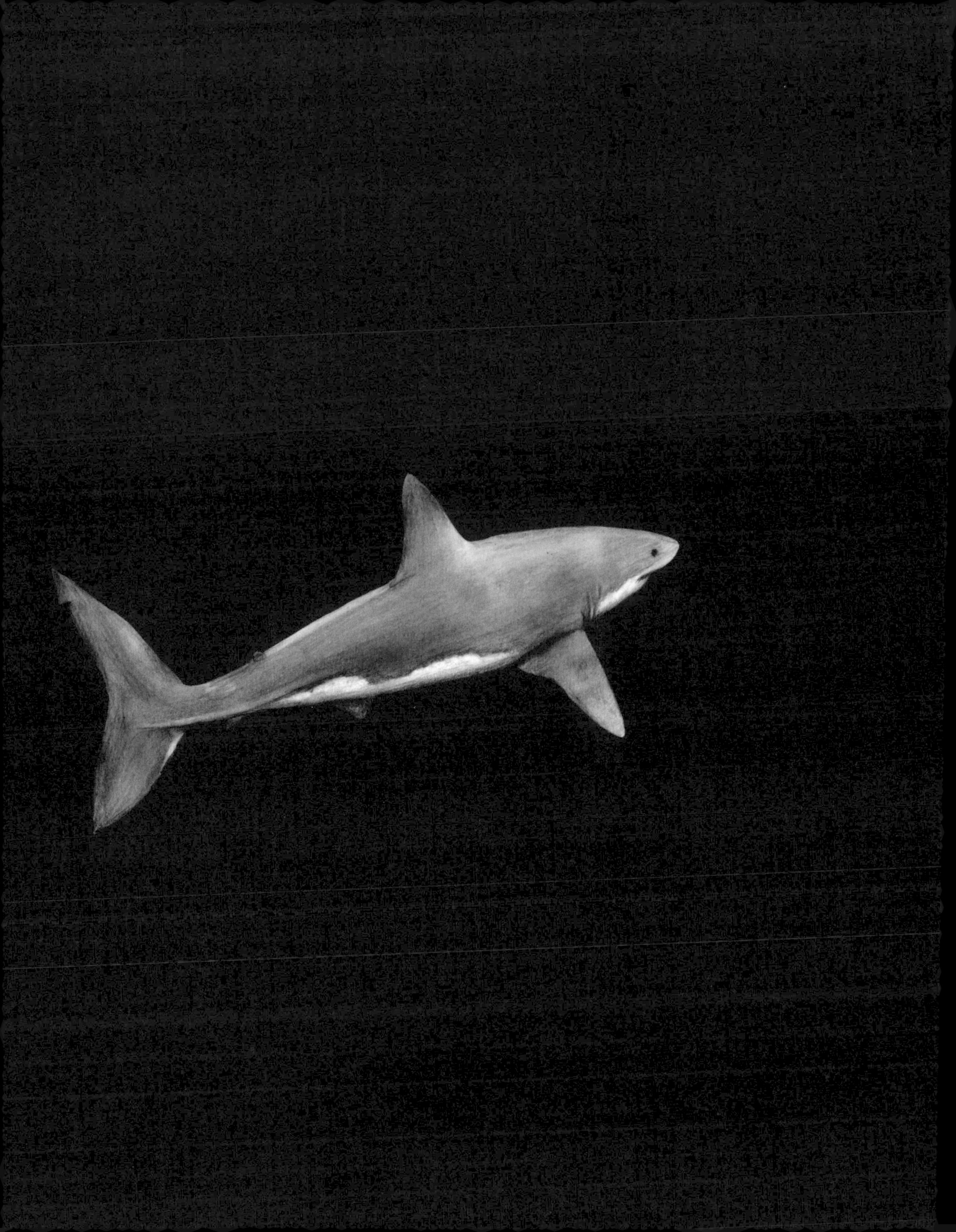

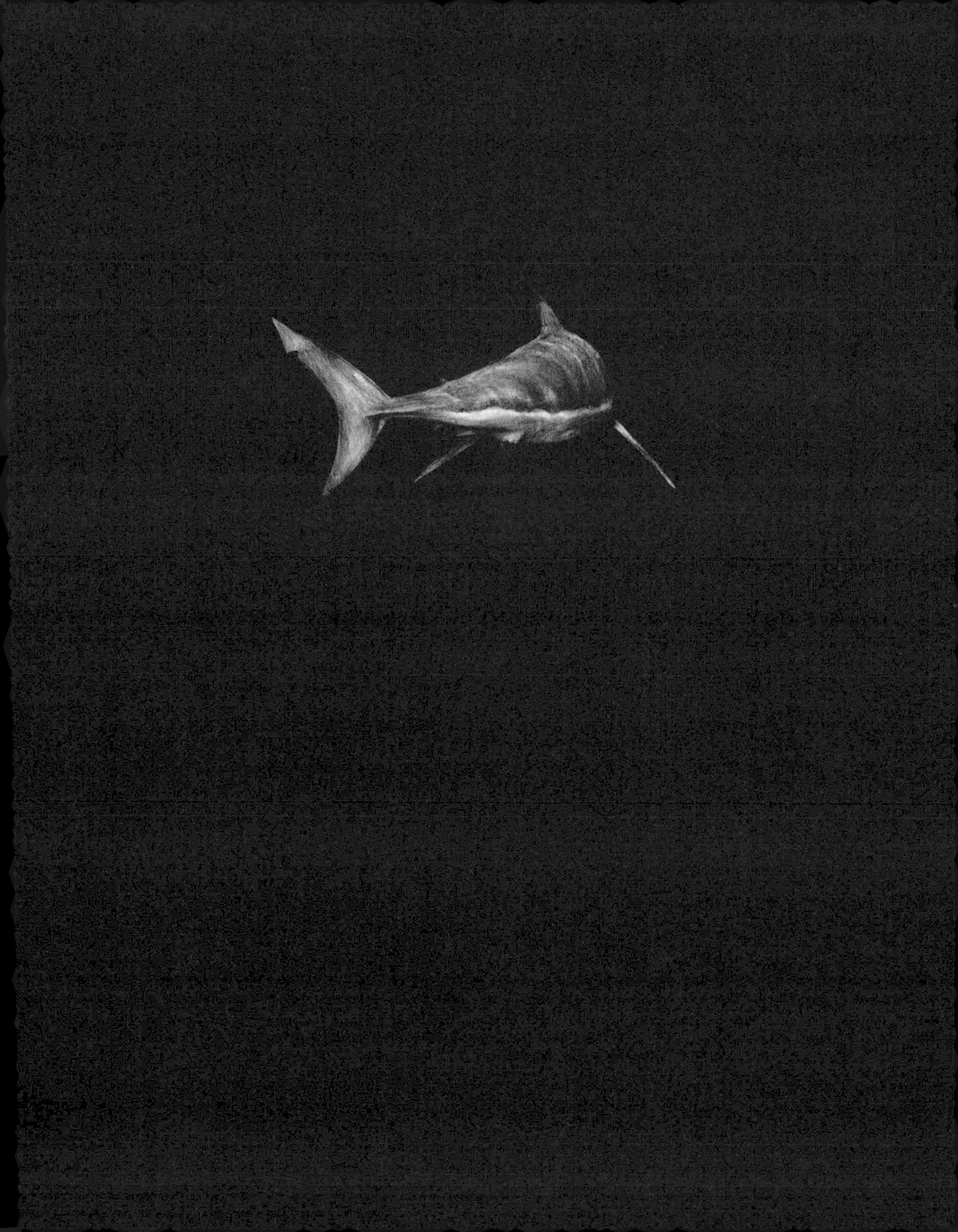

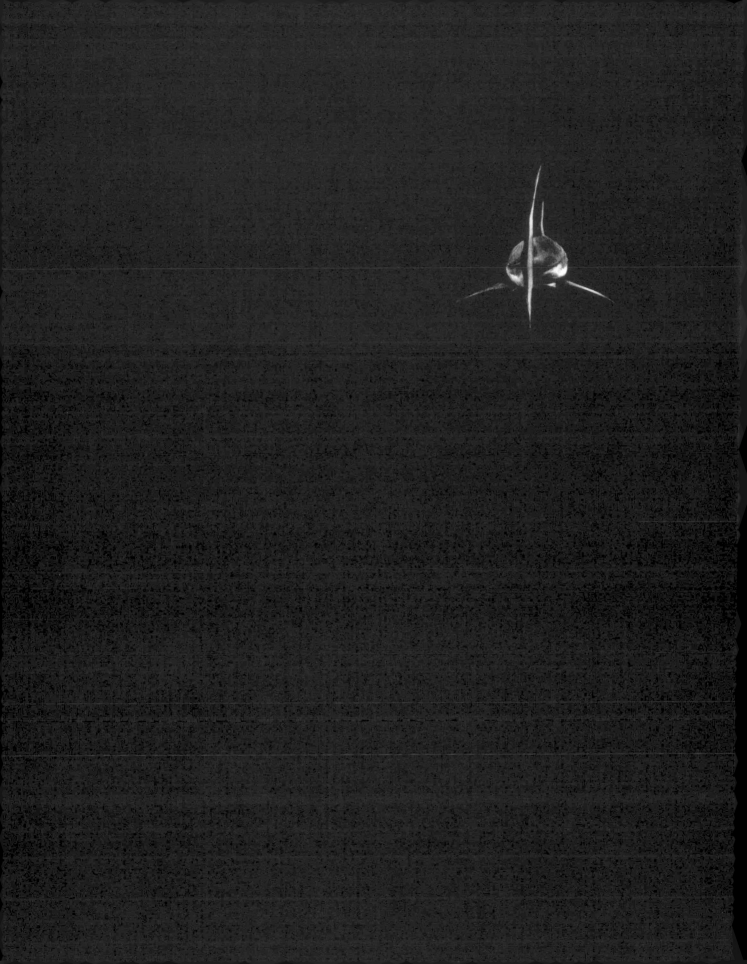

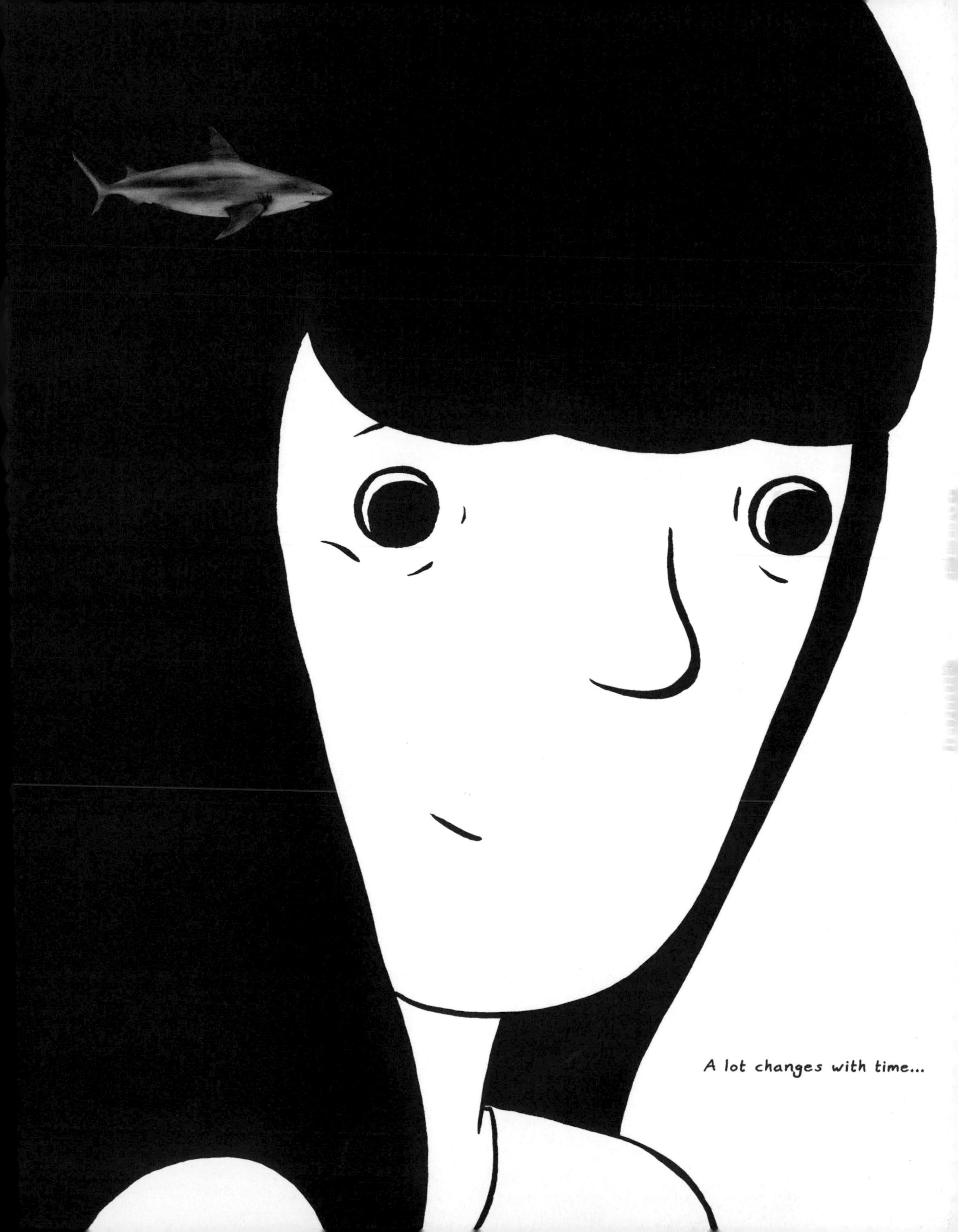
A lot changes with time...

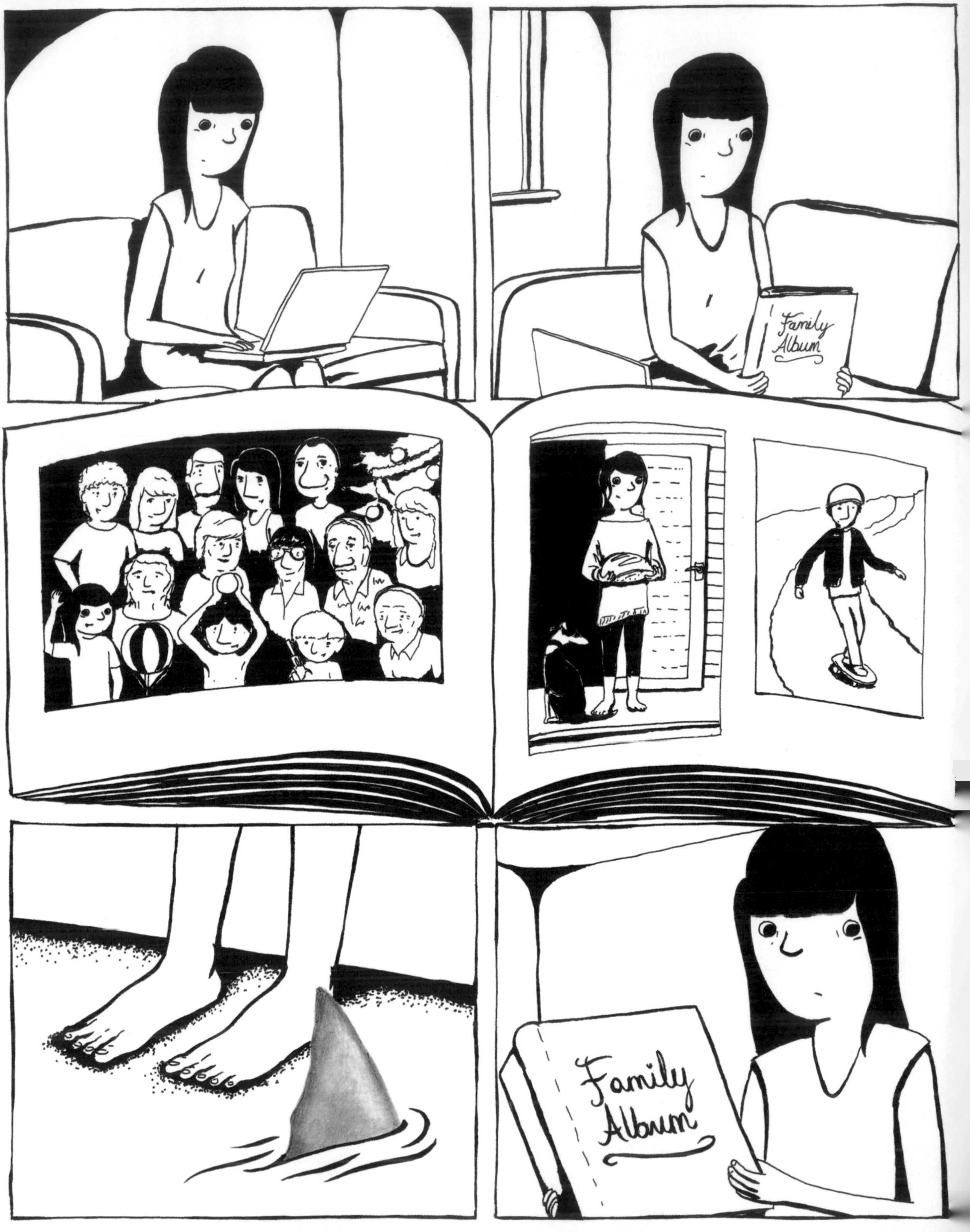
Family Album
Family Album

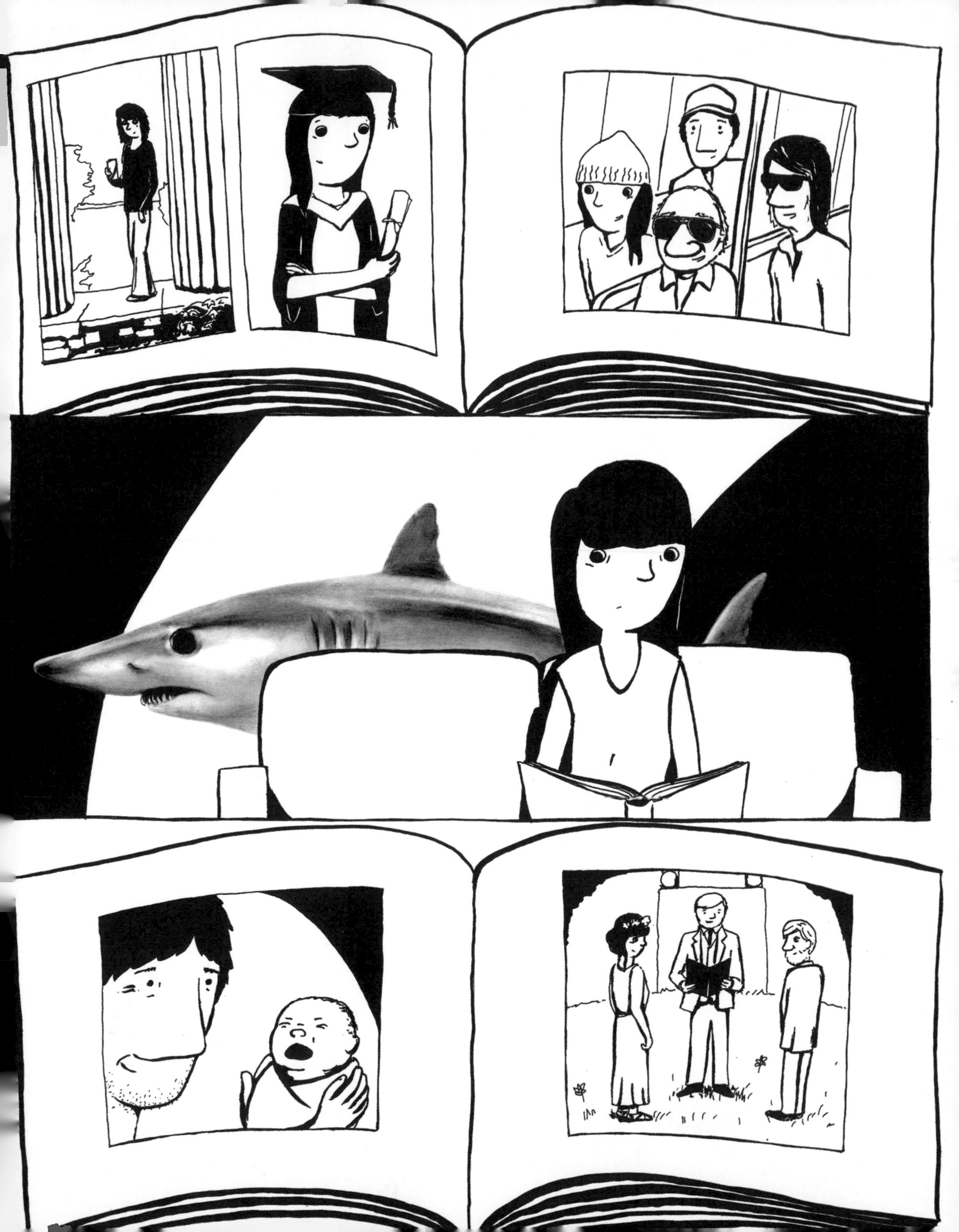

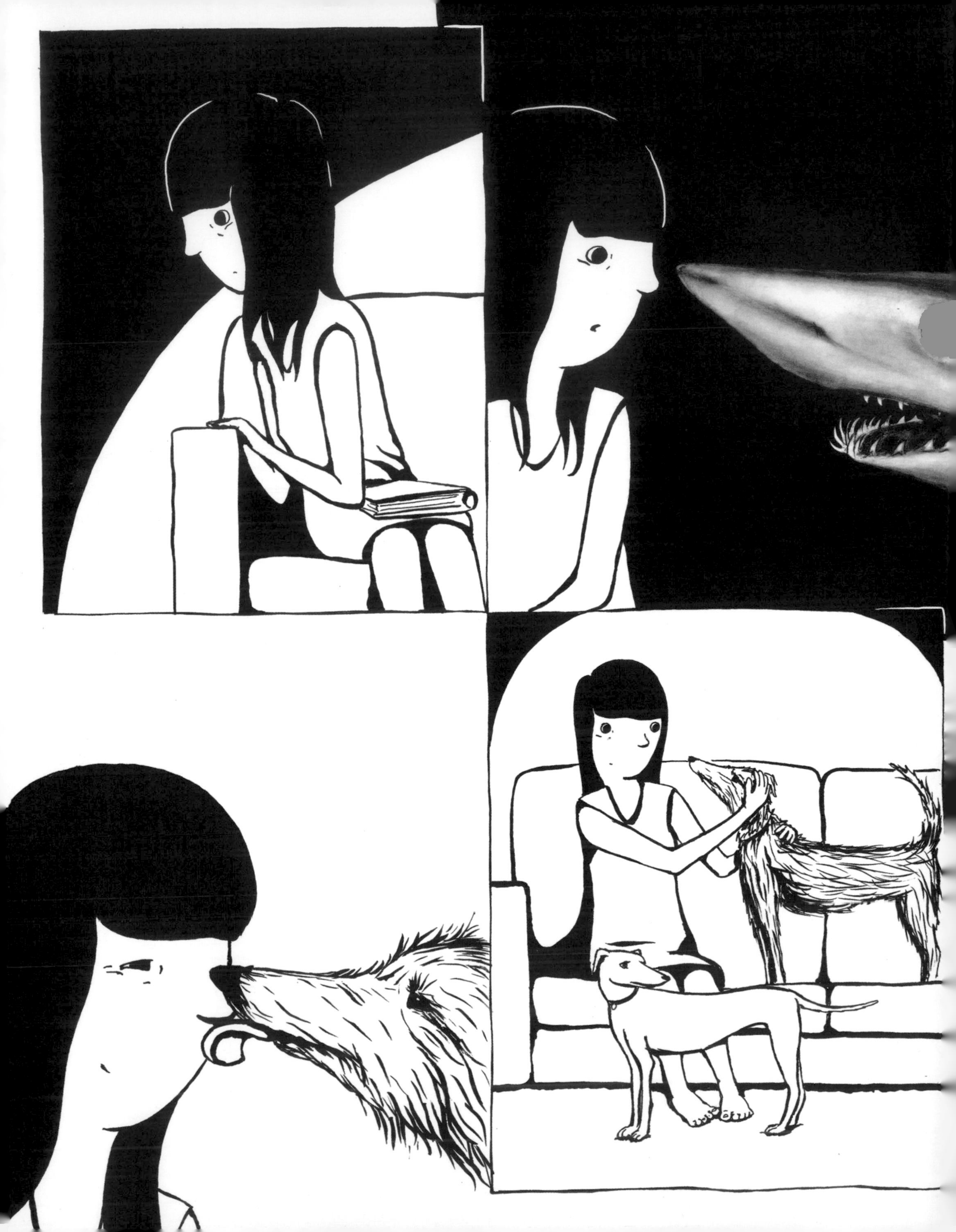

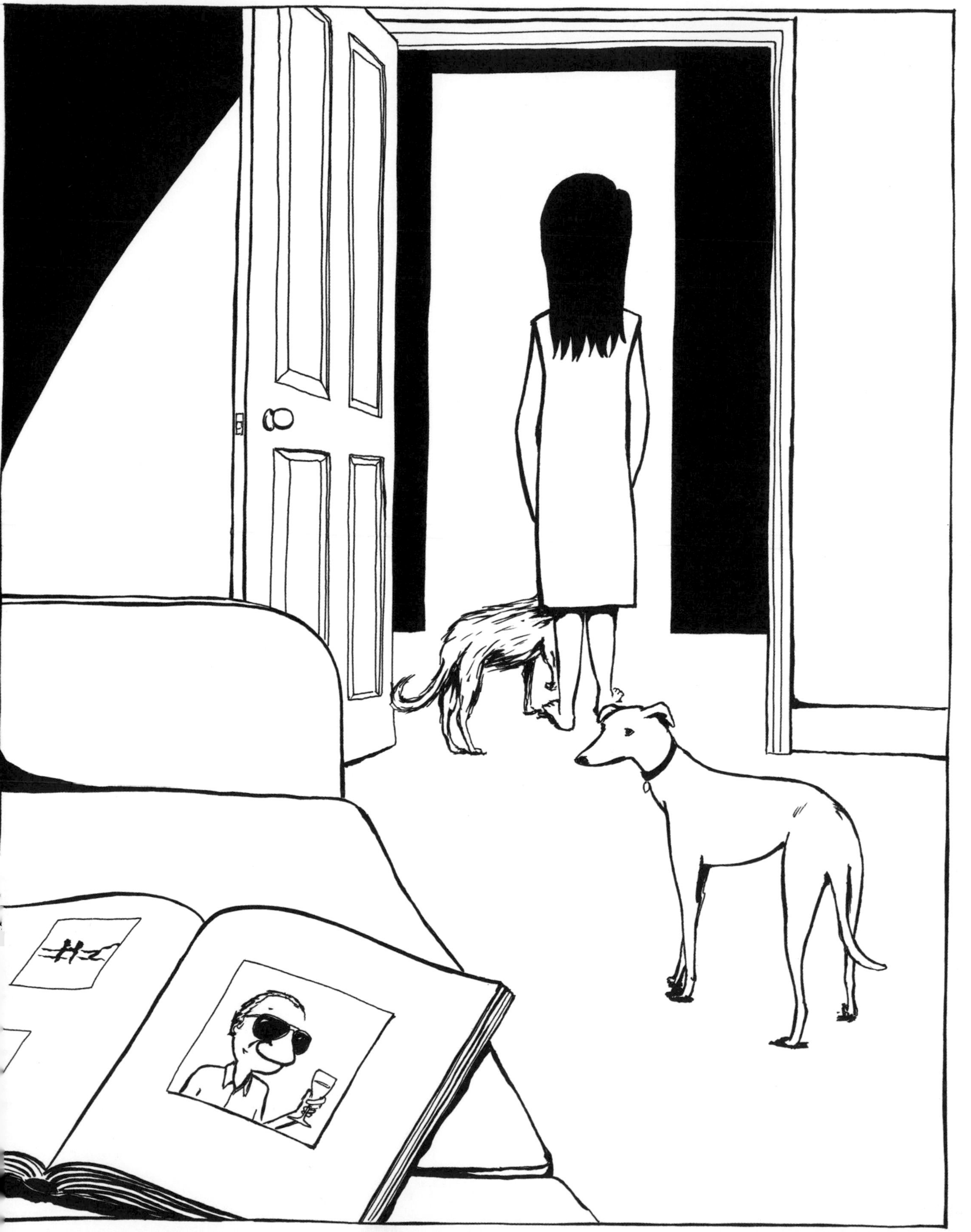

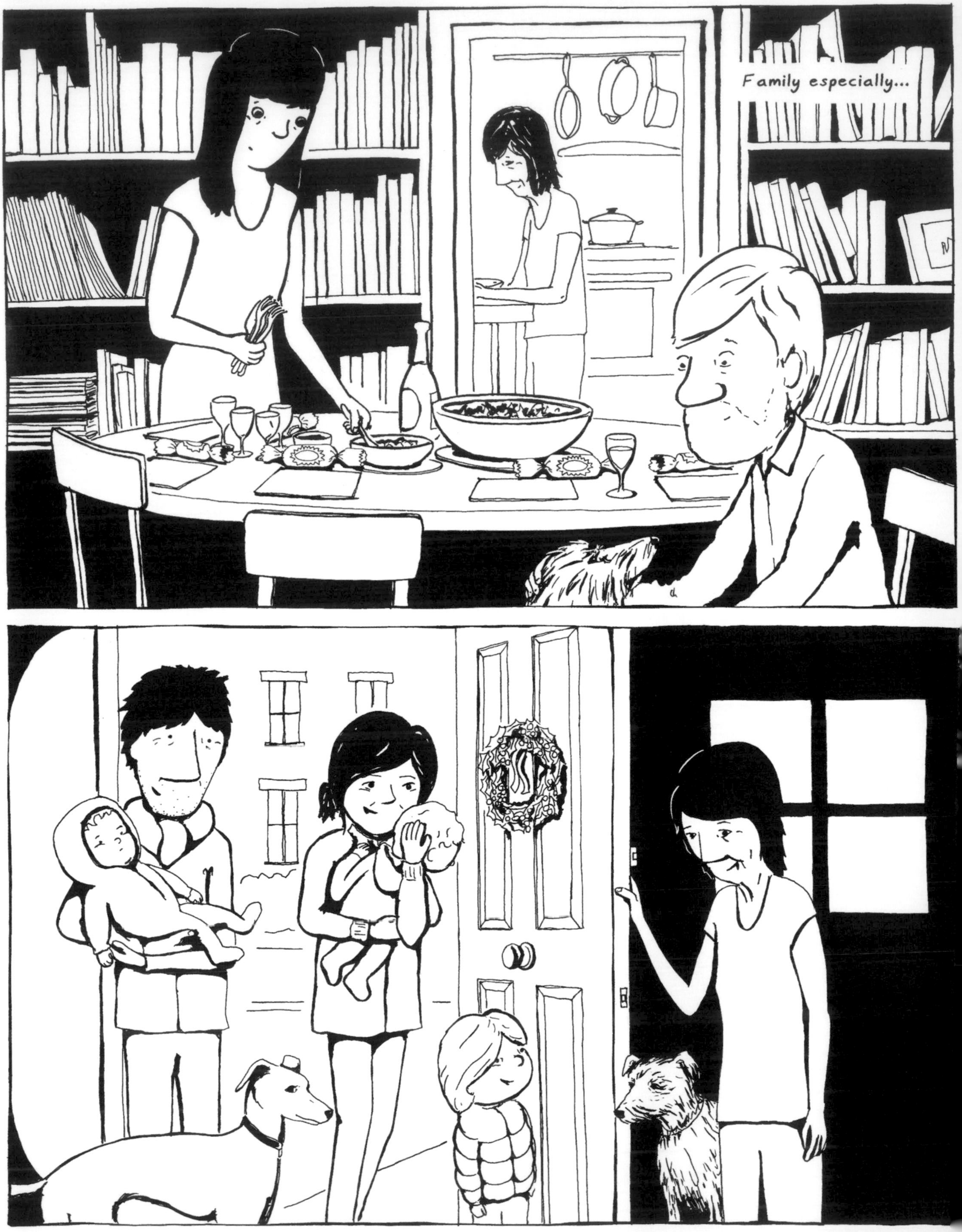
Family especially...

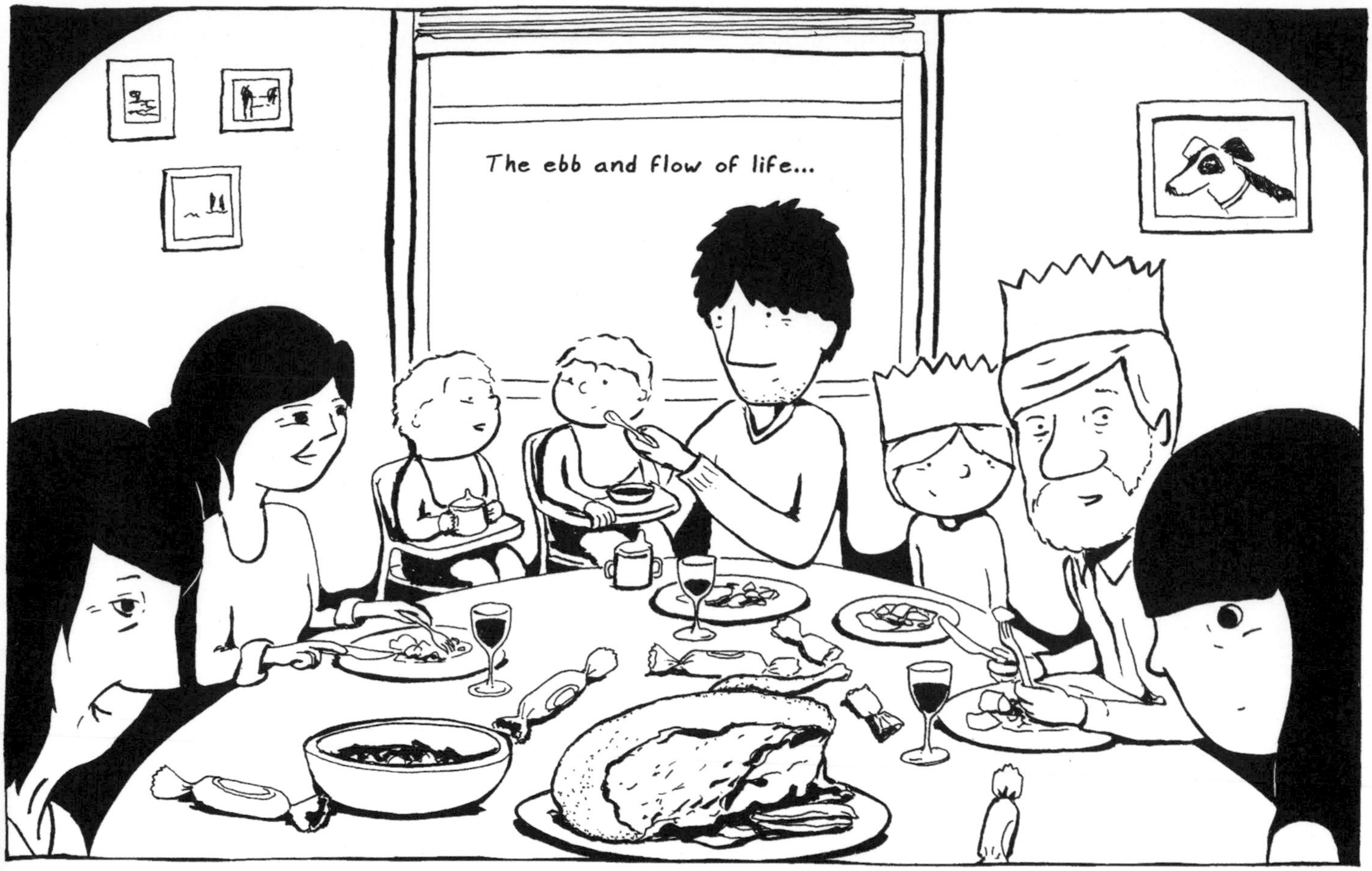
The ebb and flow of life...

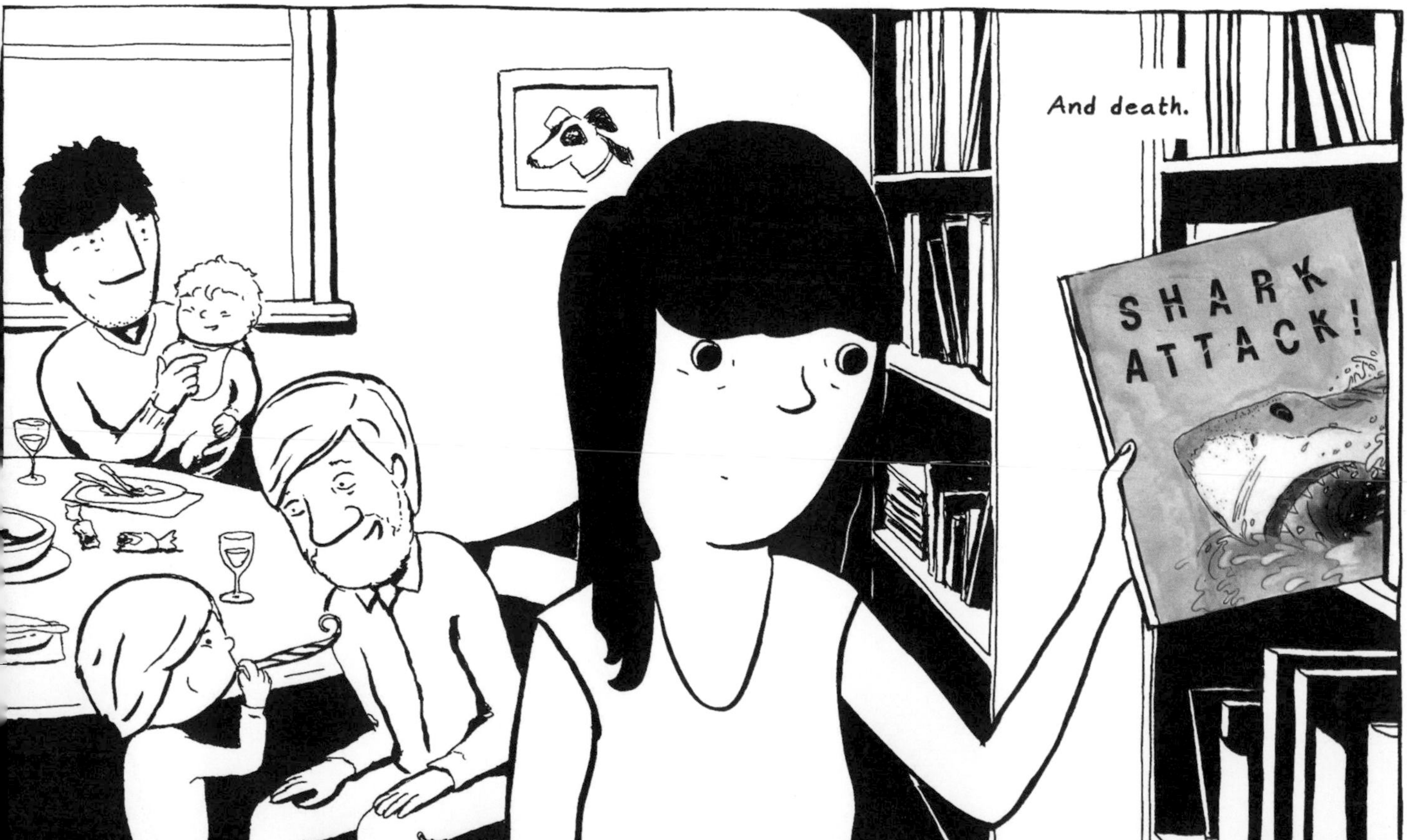
And death.
SHARK ATTACK!

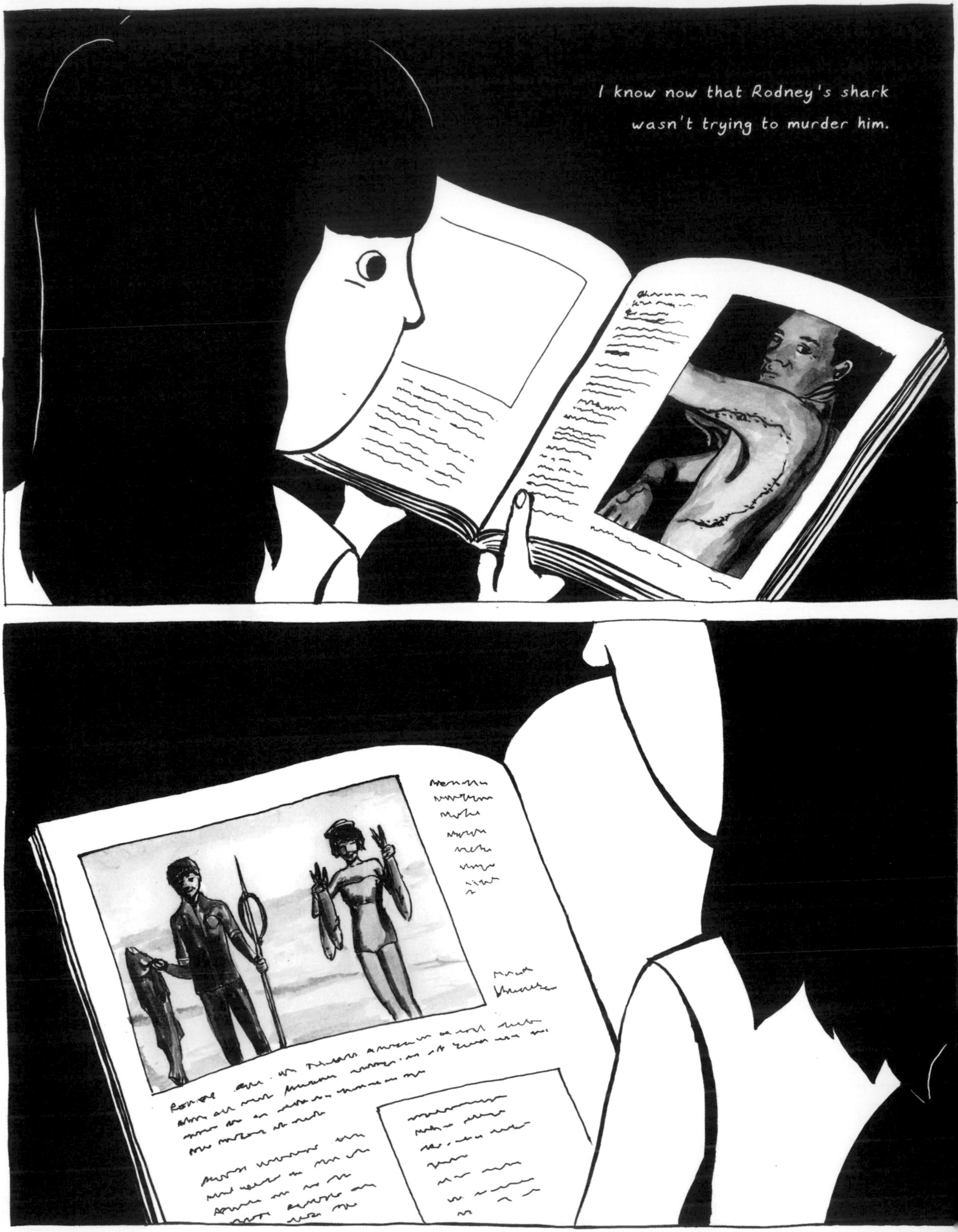
I know now that Rodney's shark wasn't trying to murder him.

Her thoughts were

only of the fish Fox

had tied to his

weight belt.

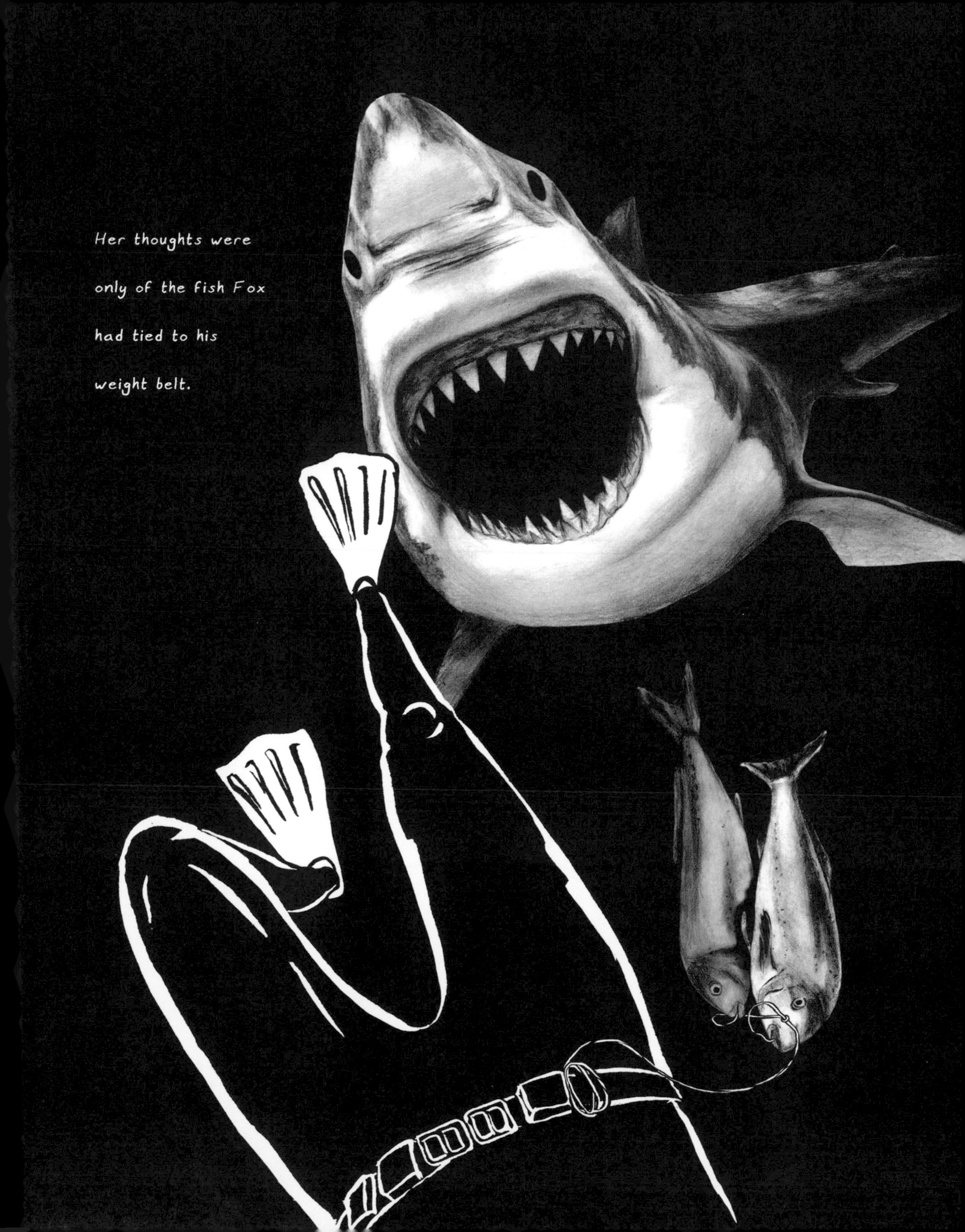

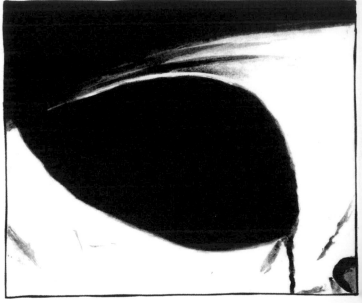

Benign, indifferent and essential, she passed through his life,
and left an open hole in her wake.

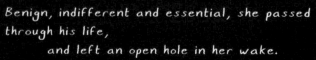

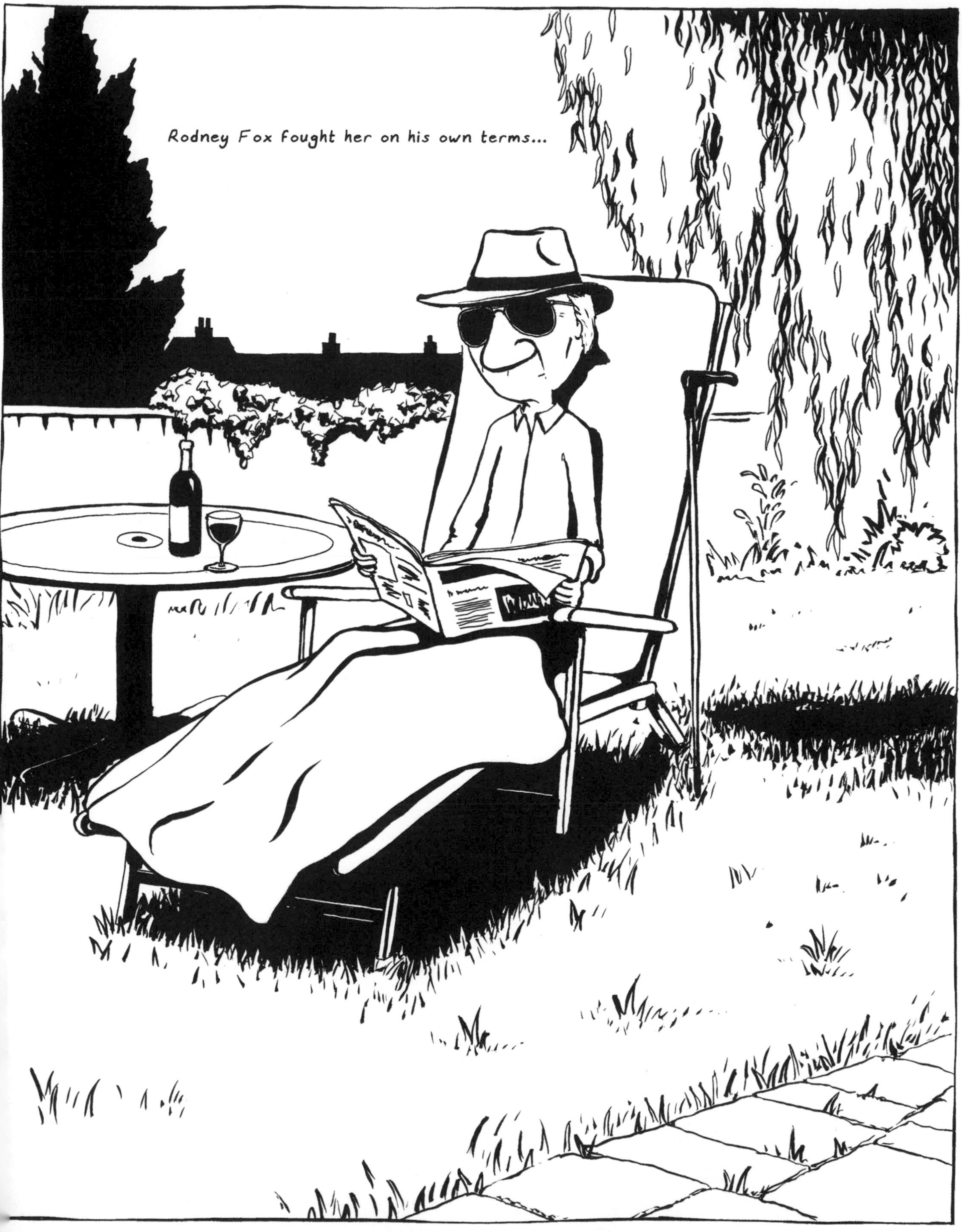
Rodney Fox fought her on his own terms...

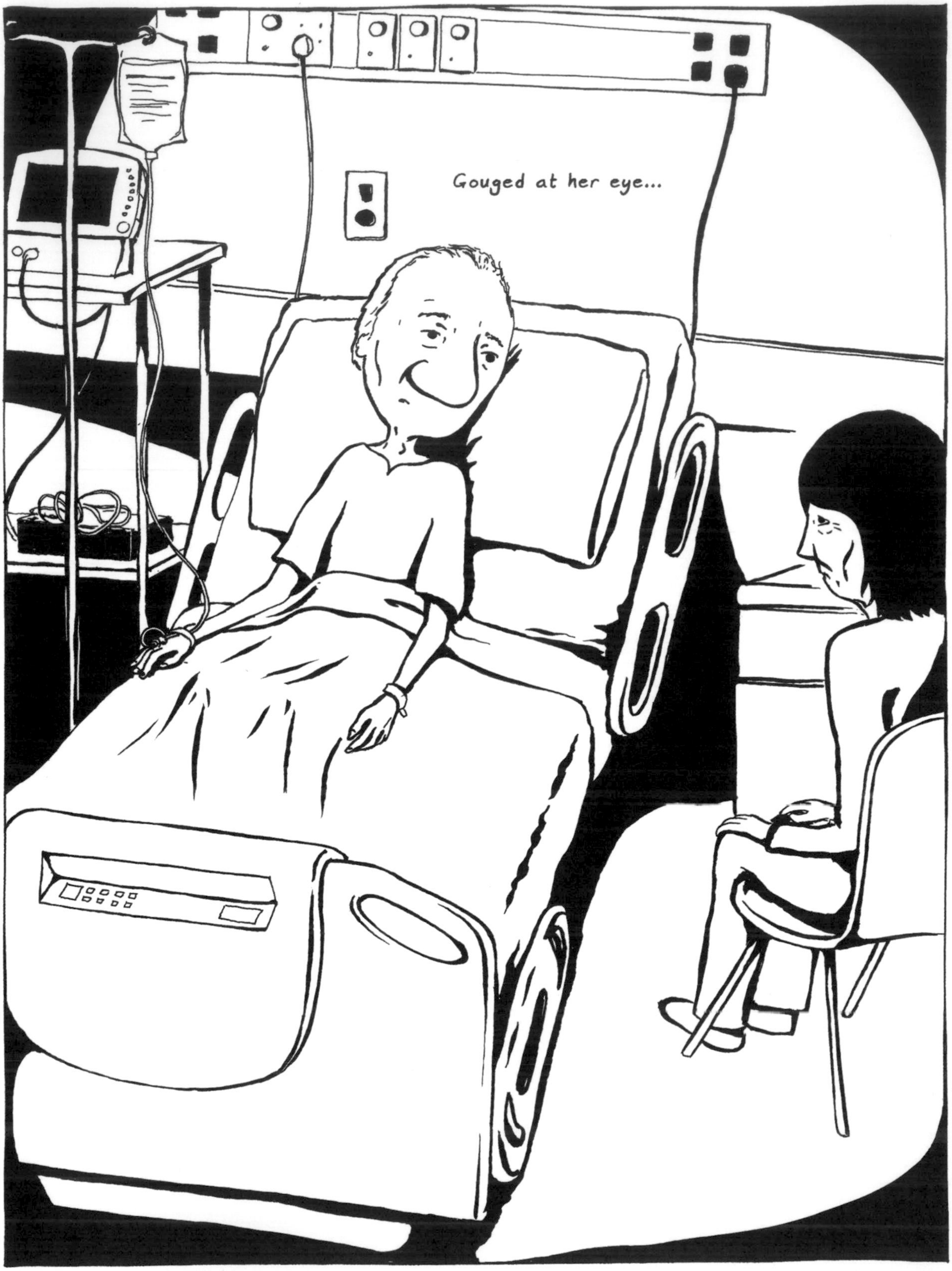
Gouged at her eye...

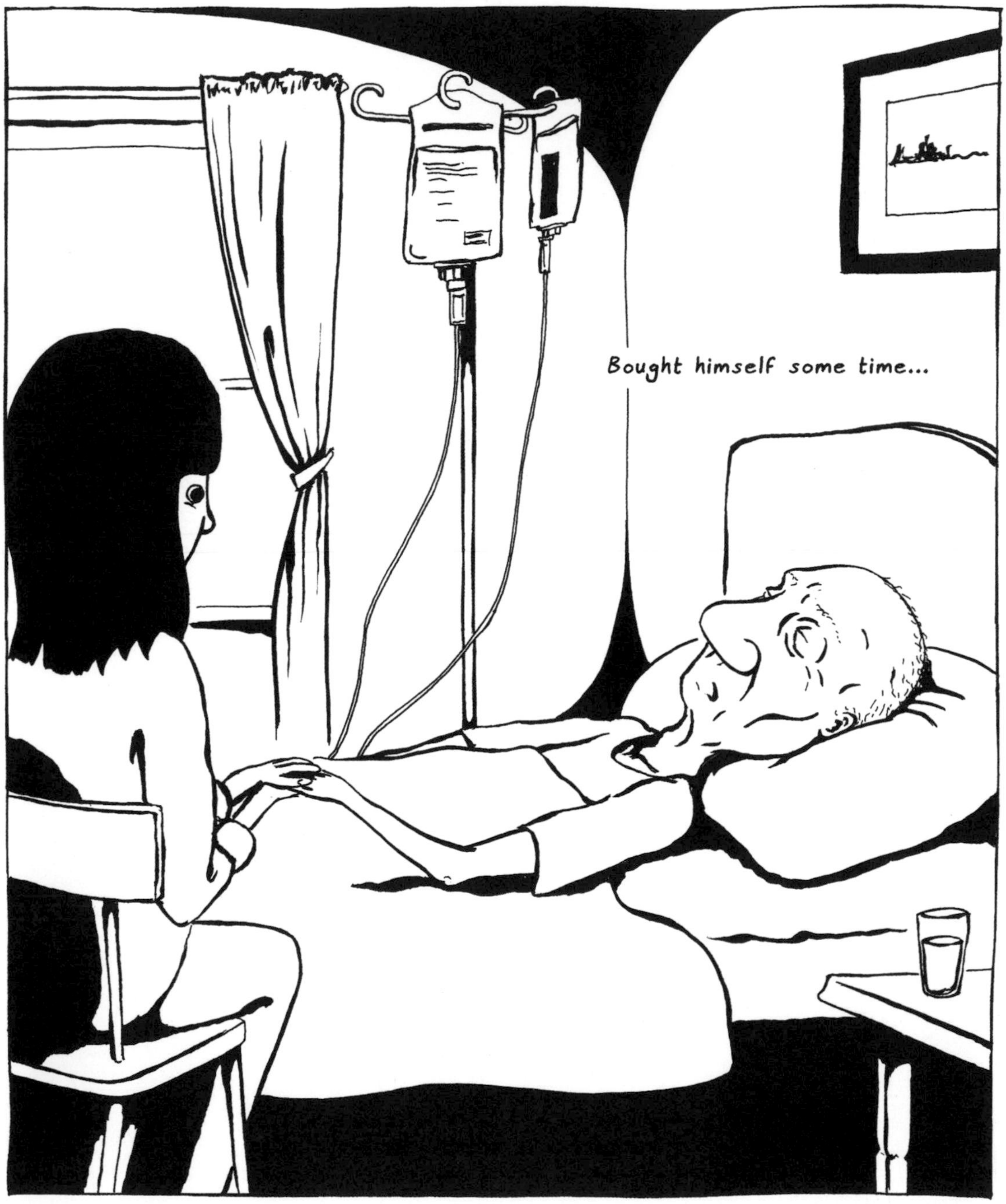
Bought himself some time...

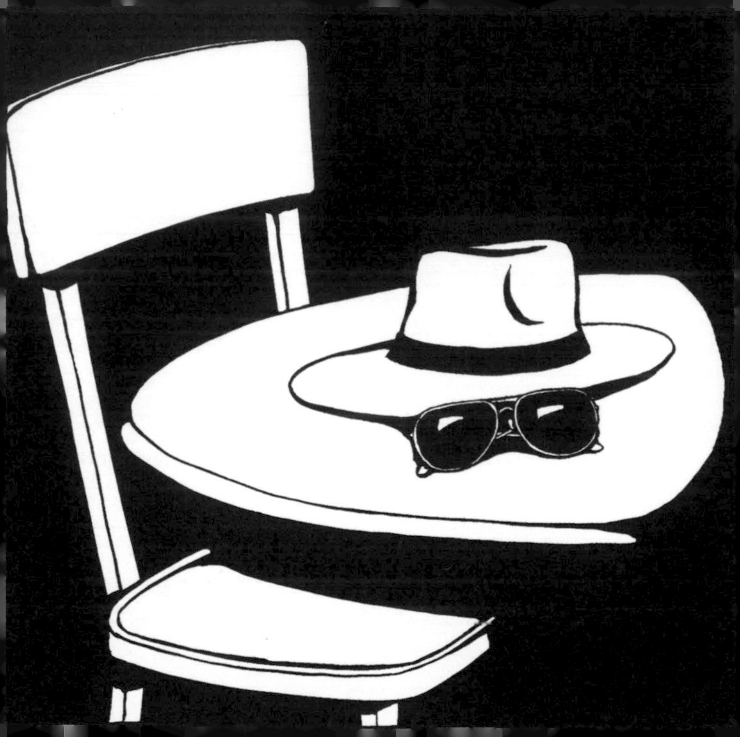

An inhalation of breath.

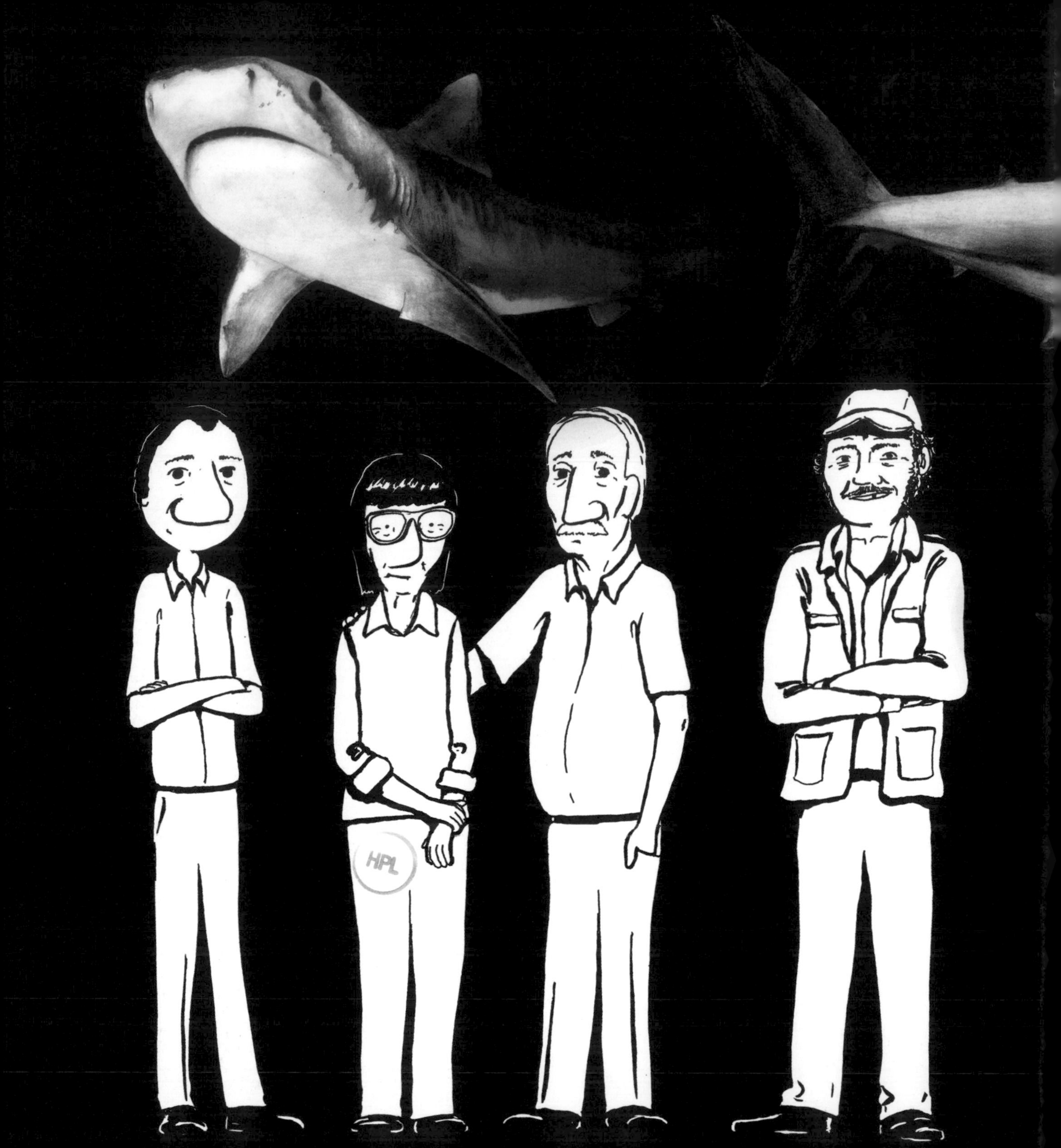
HPL

In memory of Andrew, Gladys, Phil,
Quint and Speedy.

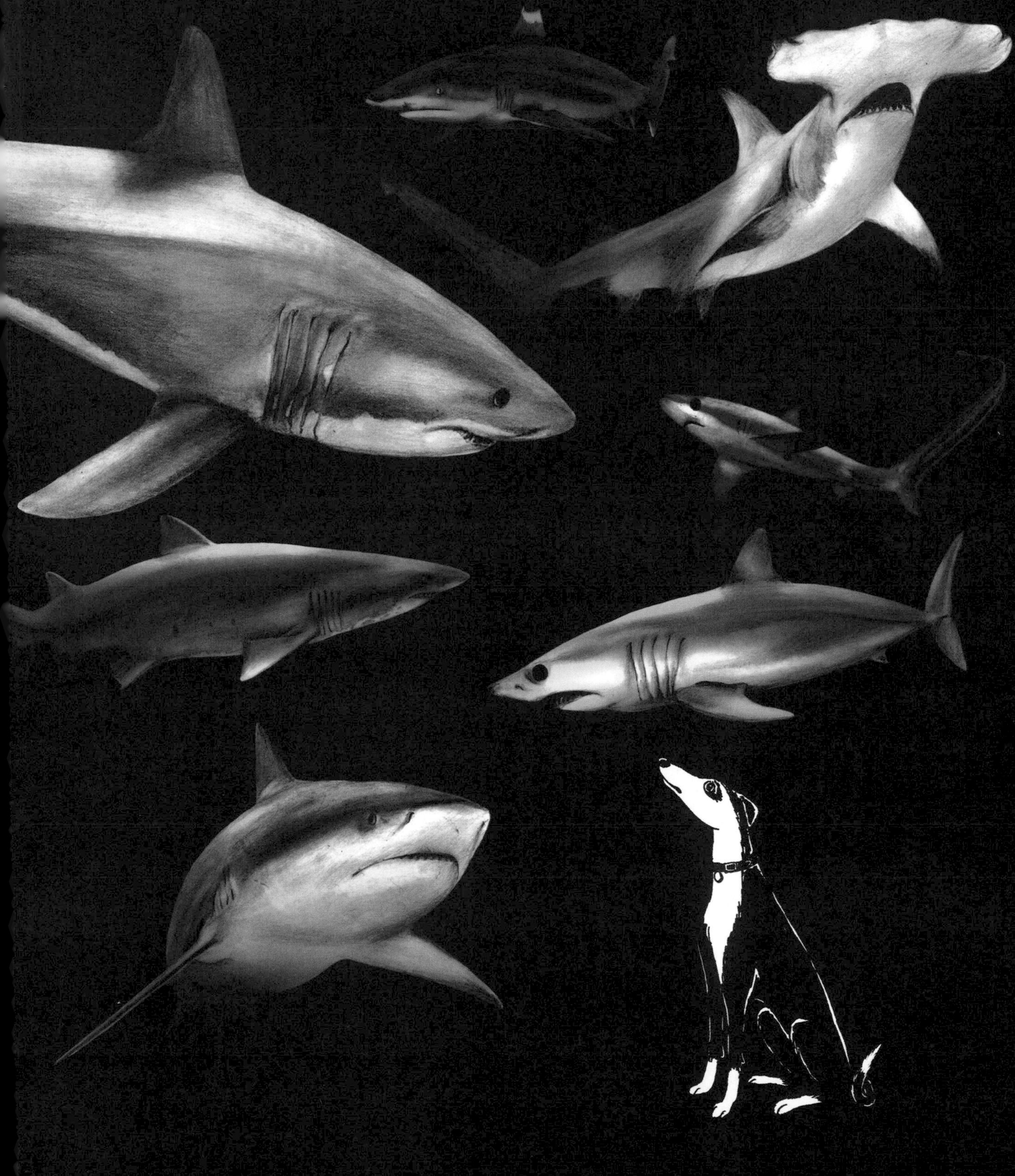

And in celebration of Rodney Fox
and the Shark Attack Survivors for Shark Conservation

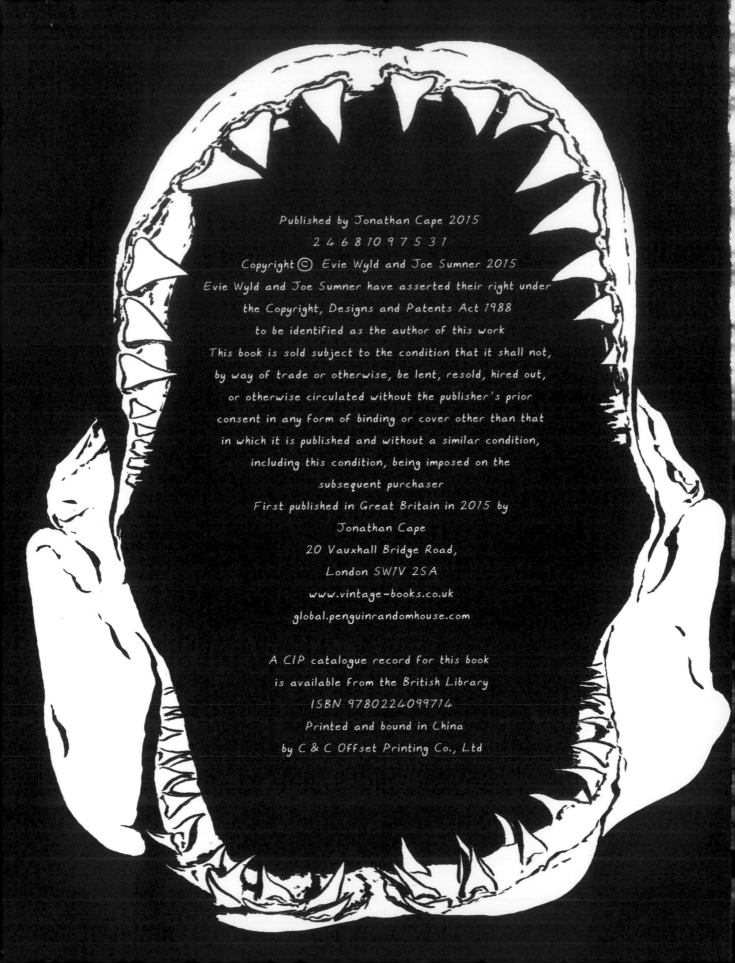

Published by Jonathan Cape 2015

2 4 6 8 10 9 7 5 3 1

First published in Great Britain in 2015 by
Jonathan Cape
20 Vauxhall Bridge Road,
London SW1V 2SA

www.vintage-books.co.uk

global.penguinrandomhouse.com

A CIP catalogue record for this book
is available from the British Library
ISBN 9780224099714

Printed and bound in China
by C & C Offset Printing Co., Ltd

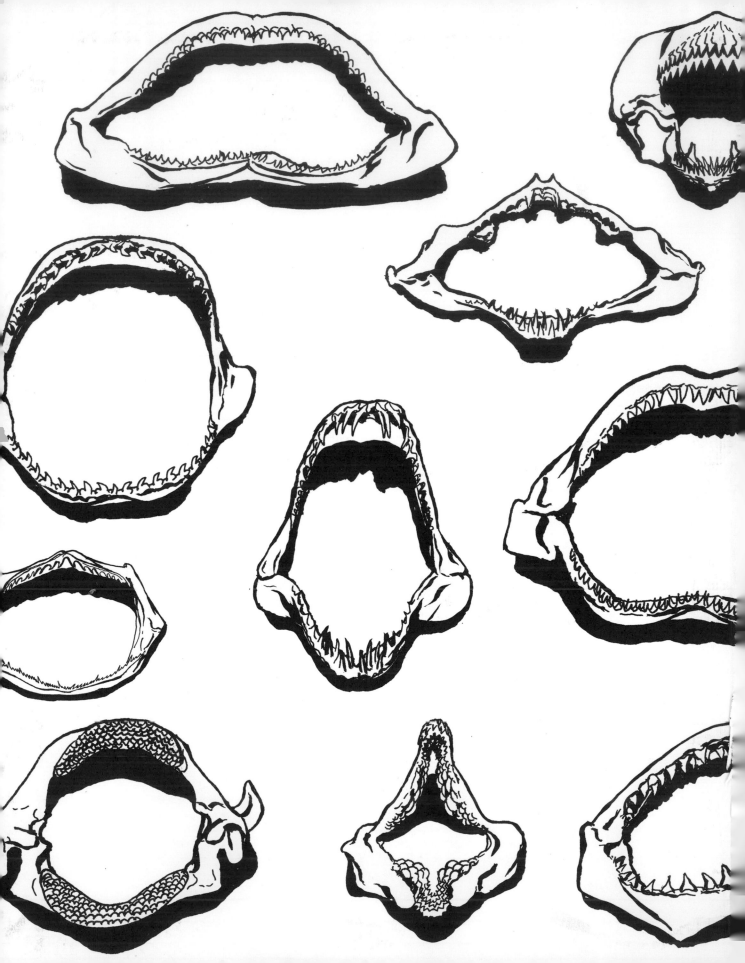